Willing Seduction

**Film Europa: German Cinema in an International Context**
*Series Editors:* **Hans-Michael Bock** (CineGraph Hamburg);
**Tim Bergfelder** (University of Southampton); **Sabine Hake**
(University of Texas, Austin)

German cinema is normally seen as a distinct form, but this new series emphasizes connections, influences, and exchanges of German cinema across national borders, as well as its links with other media and art forms. Individual titles present traditional historical research (archival work, industry studies) as well as new critical approaches in film and media studies (theories of the transnational), with a special emphasis on the continuities associated with popular traditions and local perspectives.

**The Concise Cinegraph: An Encyclopedia of German Cinema**
*General Editor*: Hans-Michael Bock
*Associate Editor*: Tim Bergfelder

**International Adventures: German Popular Cinema and European Co-Productions in the 1960s**
Tim Bergfelder

**Between Two Worlds: The Jewish Presence in German and Australian Film, 1910–1933**
S.S. Prawer

**Framing the Fifties: Cinema in a Divided Germany**
Edited by John Davidson and Sabine Hake

**A Foreign Affair: Billy Wilder's American Films**
Gerd Gemünden

**Destination London: German-speaking Emigrés and British Cinema, 1925–1950**
Edited by Tim Bergfelder and Christian Cargnelli

**Michael Haneke's Cinema: The Ethic of the Image**
Catherine Wheatley

**Willing Seduction:** *The Blue Angel*, **Marlene Dietrich, and Mass Culture**
Barbara Kosta

# WILLING SEDUCTION

*The Blue Angel*, Marlene Dietrich, and Mass Culture

Barbara Kosta

***Berghahn Books***
New York • Oxford

Published in 2009 by

**Berghahn Books**

www.berghahnbooks.com

©2009, 2012 Barbara Kosta
First paperback edition published in 2012

All rights reserved. Except for the quotation of short passages
for the purposes of criticism and review, no part of this book
may be reproduced in any form or by any means, electronic or
mechanical, including photocopying, recording, or any information
storage and retrieval system now known or to be invented,
without written permission of the publisher.

**Library of Congress Cataloging-in-Publication Data**
Kosta, Barbara.
  Willing seduction : The blue angel, Marlene Dietrich and mass culture / Barbara Kosta.
    p. cm. -- (Film Europa ; v. 8)
  Includes bibliographical references and index.
  ISBN 978-1-84545-572-9 (hbk.) -- ISBN 978-0-85745-619-9 (pbk.)
  1. Blaue Engel (Motion picture) 2. Dietrich, Marlene--Criticism and interpretation. 3. Motion pictures--Germany--History--20th century. 4. Culture in motion pictures. 5. Women in motion pictures. I. Title.
  PN1997.B6713K67 2009
  791.43'72--dc22
                                    2009006160

**British Library Cataloguing in Publication Data**

A catalogue record for this book is available from the British Library
Printed in the United States on acid-free paper.

ISBN: 978-0-85745-619-9 (paperback)   ISBN: 978-0-85745-620-5 (ebook)

To Mohsen and Maya

# Contents

List of Illustrations ... viii

Acknowledgments ... x

Introduction ... 1

  1  Mass Entertainment and "Serious" Culture ... 23

  2  Distraction, Deception, and Visuality ... 53

  3  Disillusionment and Esprit: Weimar's Modern Woman ... 85

  4  The Seductions of Sound ... 111

  5  The Actuality of *The Blue Angel*: Dietrich, Germany, and Mass Culture ... 141

Fade Out: The Credits ... 167

Bibliography ... 185

Index ... 191

# List of Illustrations

| | | |
|---|---|---|
| 0.1 | Marlene Dietrich and Josef von Sternberg, 1930. Source: *Deutsche Kinemathek—Marlene Dietrich Collection Berlin*. | xii |
| 0.2 | 1930 premier poster of *Der blaue Engel*. Source: *Deutsche Kinemathek*. | 2 |
| 0.3 | Advertisement in *Variety* for New York showing of *The Blue Angel* in 1930. | 3 |
| 1.1 | "I am an artist." Still from *Der blaue Engel*, 1930, directed by Josef von Sternberg. Source: *Deutsche Kinemathek*. | 42 |
| 2.1 | Dancing Eyes. Still from *Der blaue Engel*, 1930, directed by Josef von Sternberg. Source: *Friedrich-Wilhelm-Murnau-Stiftung*. | 57 |
| 2.2 | Still from *Der blaue Engel*, 1930, directed by Josef von Sternberg. Source: *Deutsche Kinemathek*. | 59 |
| 2.3 | "Falling in Love Again." Still from *Der blaue Engel*, 1930, directed by Josef von Sternberg. Source: *Deutsche Kinemathek*. | 66 |
| 2.4 | Rath holding Dietrich's Lenci African doll, which became her mascot and part of a larger collection of Lenci dolls. Still from *Der blaue Engel*, 1930, directed by Josef von Sternberg. Source: *Deutsche Kinemathek*. | 67 |
| 2.5 | "Ya see, you could have this every day." Still from *Der blaue Engel*, 1930, directed by Josef von Sternberg. Source: *Deutsche Kinemathek*. | 69 |
| 2.6 | Still from *Der blaue Engel*, 1930, directed by Josef von Sternberg. Source: *Deutsche Kinemathek*. | 71 |
| 2.7 | Otto Hunte's sketch of the entrance to The Blue Angel nightclub. Source: *Deutsches Filmmuseum*. | 72 |
| 3.1 | "Marlene Dietrich plays Gretchen," *Uhu* (October 1931). Source: *Ullstein Verlag*. | 90 |
| 3.2 | The calendar serves as a temporal referent. Still from *Der blaue Engel*, 1930, directed by Josef von Sternberg. Source: *Friedrich-Wilhelm-Murnau-Stiftung*. | 91 |

| | | |
|---|---|---|
| 3.3 | "You have allowed this woman to support you for five years." Still from *Der blaue Engel*, 1930, directed by Josef von Sternberg. Source: *Friedrich-Wilhelm-Murnau-Stiftung*. | 93 |
| 3.4 | Rath slipping deeper into forbidden realms. Still from *Der blaue Engel*, 1930, directed by Josef von Sternberg. Source: *Friedrich-Wilhelm-Murnau-Stiftung*. | 99 |
| 3.5 | Lola on stage even while she is packing up her belongings. Still from *Der blaue Engel*, 1930, directed by Josef von Sternberg. *Friedrich-Wilhelm-Murnau-Stiftung*. | 103 |
| 3.6 | "You want to marry me!" Still from *Der blaue Engel*, 1930, directed by Josef von Sternberg. *Friedrich-Wilhelm-Murnau-Stiftung*. | 104 |
| 4.1 | "Beware of Blonde Women." Still from *Der blaue Engel*, 1930, directed by Josef von Sternberg. Source: *Deutsche Kinemathek*. | 130 |
| 5.1 | Advertisement for *Spiegel Reporter*, March 2000. Source: *Spiegel Reporter*. | 143 |
| 5.2 | Advertisement for a Marlene Dietrich Exhibition in the department store KaDeWE, 2005. Source: Author's collection. | 145 |
| 5.3 | Still taken on the set of *The Blue Angel*; Marlene Dietrich with Emil Jannings and Josef von Sternberg. Source: *Deutsche Kinemathek*. | 146 |

# ACKNOWLEDGMENTS

As with any book that has been long in the making, the project is larger than its single author. It is the result of an extended dialog with friends, colleagues and students over the years and in many different settings. Also, many institutions provided support in various ways. My thanks to the Department of German Studies and College of Humanities at University of Arizona for providing financial support. Without the help of the Fulbright Scholar Program whose generous support made possible my research stay in Berlin, the book may not have been written. While I was in Berlin, the stars were in alignment. I discovered by chance that I was living around the corner from Heinrich Mann's house and down the street from where Marlene Dietrich used to live.

So many friends, colleagues and students have contributed to this book both directly and indirectly that it is impossible to thank them all by name. My thanks go to my graduate students at the University of Arizona who participated in my Marlene Dietrich seminar. I am especially indebted to Caryl Flinn, Beverly Haviland, Helga Kraft, Elke Liebs, Hermann Rebel, and Thomas Kovach for reading earlier parts of the manuscript and offering their valuable feedback and advice. I would like to thank Steven Martinson for our lengthy discussions on the *Bildungsbürgertum* and to Hermann Rebel who provided the inspiration for the title and lively conversations on the history of the Weimar Republic. I am grateful to Mary Beth Haralovich, Sabine Hake, Anton Kaes, Richard McCormick and Inge Stephan, who supported my project and who provided comments on research proposals and presentations that enriched the manuscript.

My special thanks to Silke Ronneburg and Werner Sudendorf at the Marlene Dietrich Collection in Berlin and the Deutsche Kinemathek. The wealth of material on Marlene Dietrich, which they curate, not to mention the inventory Dietrich left behind made for easier access to Dietrich's Berlin phase. Moreover, the newsletter and exhibits, that they organize, create a community among Dietrich fans and allows us to indulge in the details of her stardom. I also want to express my appreciation to Robert Münkel at the Friedrich-Wilhelm-Murnau-Stiftung who supplied high quality images from *The Blue Angel* and to the staff at the Deutsches Filmmuseum.

I especially thank my family and friends who were there behind the scenes. I owe my gratitude to my parents Konstantin and Barbara Kosta, to Lilian Crato, Susan Mallet, Eric Britten and Eileen Foley. I especially thank Mohsen Haddad-Kaveh for his humor and loving patience, and our daughter Maya who always will remember our pilgrimage to Dietrich's grave.

I would like to extend my thanks to Marion Berghahn, Sabine Hake, Tim Bergfelder and Mark Stanton for their support of my project and to Berghahn's anonymous readers whose perceptive comments improved the manuscript.

My friend, Janis Falco, reminded me that my fascination with Dietrich and *The Blue Angel* began while I was an undergraduate. Thanks to Marlene, it continues even after this project.

**Figure 0.1** Marlene Dietrich and Josef von Sternberg, 1930. Source: *Deutsche Kinemathek—Marlene Dietrich Collection Berlin.*

# Introduction

> History tells us that the artist is judged rarely by a jury composed of his equals; more often judgment is given by a self-appointed jury of unqualified arbiters of "taste."
> **Josef von Sternberg,** *Fun in a Chinese Laundry*

> Dietrich: In the German language: the name for a key that opens all locks. Not a magic key. A very real object, necessitating great skill in the making.
> **Marlene Dietrich,** *Marlene Dietrich's ABC*

Josef von Sternberg's 1930 film *The Blue Angel* (*Der blaue Engel*) is one of the best-known films to emerge from the Weimar Republic (1919–33)—a landmark in German film history, internationally acclaimed.[1] A significant milestone as one of Germany's first major sound films, it is famous for launching Marlene Dietrich into Hollywood stardom and for initiating the mythic pairing of the Austrian-born American director von Sternberg with the star performer, Dietrich. Kept alive by the image of Dietrich and her iconization, *The Blue Angel* must be counted among the films that have acquired a value that goes beyond the film itself. It has become Dietrich's signature film, despite her protest to director/ actor Maximilian Schell that "I've had my fill of the Blue Angel" ("*der blaue Engel* hängt mir zum Hals heraus"), and despite its initial billing as an Emil Jannings film.[2] Indeed, *The Blue Angel* has lived on in the popular imagination, and as her biographer, Donald Spoto, suggests, *The Blue Angel* not only became synonymous with Dietrich, it shaped her persona.[3]

Originally, the film's foremost association was not with Marlene Dietrich. The first posters of *The Blue Angel* featured Emil Jannings, as Professor Rath, more prominently in name, if not in image, than Dietrich, the cabaret performer, Lola Lola (see Figure 0.2), yielding his figure narrative authority, if only tenuously.

In 1929, Jannings's prominence seemed natural given his long-standing national and international reputation for such starring roles as the demoted doorman in Friedrich Murnau's *The Last Laugh* (1924) and Mephistopheles in *Faust* (1926), a trapeze artist in Ewald André Dupont's (1925)

**Figure 0.2** 1930 premier poster of *Der blaue Engel*. Source: *Deutsche Kinemathek*.

**Figure 0.3** Advertisement in *Variety* for New York showing of *The Blue Angel* in 1930.

*Varieté* (1925), and an exiled Russian officer in von Sternberg's 1928 Hollywood production *The Last Command*, for which Jannings won the first Oscar for best actor. In contrast to Jannings's achievements, Dietrich's many previous engagements had been minor. Among her first major roles were those in *Ich küsse Ihre Hand, Madam* (1929, I Kiss Your Hand, Madam) and *Die Frau, nach der man sich sehnt* (1929, the woman for whom everyone longs); while well received, these films had short-lived success soon to be overshadowed by *The Blue Angel* performance. Shortly after its premier Dietrich received top billing, with Lola drawing moviegoers like "moths to a flame" in much the same way as she drew Rath into her world of popular entertainment.

Compared to other German films of the 1920s and early 1930s, *The Blue Angel* inhabits a singular place in German film history, both in terms of its production history and its national attribution. Made at a time in which films were identified as national products (even if boundaries remained somewhat fluid), von Sternberg's "German" film was an uncommon hybrid. While Berlin had become a gathering point for talents from across Europe, and German studios even regularly sent its own to learn abroad, it was rare for an established Hollywood director to make a film in Berlin. It was more common for Ufa (Universum Film AG), Germany's largest studio company resembling a major Hollywood studio, to import American actors such as Louise Brooks, who came from Hollywood to perform in G.W. Pabst's 1929 films *Pandora's Box* and *Diary of a Lost Girl*, or Betty Amann, star of Joe May's 1929 film *Asphalt*. In the case of *The Blue Angel*, it was von Sternberg (who went to the United States from Austria in 1908 at the age of fourteen) who returned to Europe in 1929 with American technological know-how to make one of Germany's first sound films.

*The Blue Angel* thus was a product of two competing film industry giants with a history of collaborating and talent sharing, or of plundering each other's resources (the latter indicative more of Hollywood's relationship with German film studios). In fact, Dietrich became another one of Hollywood's coups, in a fairly long list of German film talent recruited during the 1920s—including directors Ernst Lubitsch and Friedrich Murnau—once von Sternberg advised Paramount quickly to offer Dietrich a contract after finishing *The Blue Angel*. Despite Hollywood's success in landing its European star, Paramount continued to compete with the European market while creating Dietrich to fit its own image. In a move to stall and even thwart the success of the German film abroad, in order to secure Dietrich's reputation as an American star and deliver a less risqué Lola, Paramount postponed the release of the American version of *The Blue Angel* until after the release of von Sternberg's *Morocco*, hoping that *The Blue Angel* would be outdated and consequently less attractive to American audiences by the time it hit American theaters. *The Blue Angel* opened at the Rialto Theater in New York on December 5, 1930. Figure 0.3 shows an image of the advertisement, whose cut-and-paste quality speaks to the "under advertisement" of the film. Contrary to expectations, the film enjoyed success in its smaller venue. *Variety* reported that it "was slipped into this house for emergency purposes" to save the theater and brought in an astonishing $24,000 over one weekend, adding, "it looks as though Marlene Dietrich has made a decided impression."[4]

Given *The Blue Angel*'s unique position as a German film, it is understandable that American film studies has directed only cursory attention to this Weimar classic, except to acknowledge the film as the starting point for Marlene Dietrich's stardom and to explore the infamous pairing of von Sternberg and Dietrich, and to discuss von Sternberg's oeuvre. Then again, looking back on the cultural significance of *The Blue Angel*, its near-canonical status, and the permanence of Dietrich's *Blue Angel* image, it is surprising how little critical analysis the film has inspired especially in Germany. Except for publications that chronicle production, or the plethora of Dietrich biographies and documentaries, the film has hardly received the attention it deserves. Paradoxically, *The Blue Angel* is so present in film history that it seems to have affected its under-theorization. Therefore, *Willing Seduction* sets out to address *The Blue Angel* within the larger cultural context of the Weimar Republic as a German film. It returns the film to the tumultuous days of the Weimar Republic, and looks at the lasting effect of the film, as it is embodied in Marlene Dietrich. The film lives on through her image, as her revival in Germany today suggests.

Surveying scholarship in either film studies or German studies reveals a trajectory of criticism that is closely aligned with disciplinary trends. One finds that early attention focused primarily on the relationship between *The Blue Angel* and Heinrich Mann's 1905 novel, *Professor Unrat*, on which the film is loosely based. These studies of *The Blue Angel* treat the film as literary adaptation. More significantly, they use the opportunity to lay the foundation for film studies as a new academic field. Indeed, critical focus on film adaptations of literature dominated 1960s and 1970s film scholarship – a time when film studies was establishing itself as a legitimate discipline. In an effort to gain legitimacy, film scholars defended the integrity of film and argued for its autonomy as art; they challenged a persistent belief that films were inferior renditions of their literary counterparts or products of mass culture (that is, kitsch) that could never achieve the quality of great literature. Walking this fine line in judgment of literature's translation into another medium, Richard Firda in 1972 persuasively argued for the successful adaptation of *The Blue Angel*, but maintained that it was an exception: "The marriage between a film and its adopted novel is nevertheless a complex one: creative, aesthetic and social factors are relevant topics in any meaningful discussion of the filmed novel. Josef von Sternberg's film ... survives to this day as an exception to the rule that good books should be left alone, that intellectually, the film will never match the novel."[5] Remaining within the German literary context (literature remaining the privileged reference point), Firda identifies Frank Wedekind's 1904 play *Pandora's Box* and its femme fatale, Lulu, as the antecedent of Lola Lola and an image weighing heavily on von Sternberg's decision to cast Dietrich.[6] Given the trajectory from Lulu to Lola, it is interesting to note that Wedekind's play was published one year before Mann's novel and that in the year of Mann's publication, Wedekind was being tried for "purveying obscene materials."[7] By the 1930s, sexual mores had changed so much that representations of Lulu-like figures became commonplace.

With the advent of the women's movement in the 1970s, feminist film scholars turned their attention to questions regarding the representation of gender and the sexualized female body, to gendered power relations, spectatorship and (more specifically regarding *The Blue Angel*) to the construction of Dietrich/Lola as spectacle. This research primarily theorized the gaze; that is, the exchange of looks in cinema, predominantly thought to be male, and Dietrich as femme fatale, fetish, also as cross-dresser and destabilizer of gendered norms. Even here, film scholarship focused more on Dietrich's Hollywood films with von Sternberg (*Morocco, Shanghai Express, Blonde Venus, Dishonored*) than on *The Blue Angel*. For instance, Gaylyn Studlar's significant 1988 study of Dietrich's performance (*In the Realm of Pleasure: Von Sternberg, Dietrich, and the Masochistic Aesthetic*) conspicuously excludes *The Blue Angel* from her very extensive discussion of von Sternberg/Dietrich Paramount productions. This omission may reflect boundaries traditionally defining national cinema studies, boundaries that film studies increasingly traversed as questions of transnationalism and migration became more pressing in a globalized economy. Work on *The Blue Angel* by prominent film and literary scholars Judith Mayne (1989) and Elizabeth Bronfen (1999) continues in the vein of feminist film studies, as does the work of Gertrud Koch (1986) and Patrice Petro (2002)—to be discussed in later chapters.

Also important, of course, are Siegfried Kracauer's critiques of *The Blue Angel*. In 1930, Kracauer criticized the film as a vacuous ornament concealing the social reality of the Weimar Republic. In 1947, he endowed Lola with a power that Weimar's vocabulary hardly would have given her, turning the alluring and powerful Lola into "fascism's ultimate icon" and thus transforming the sexually promiscuous modern woman into a Nazi dame and the zany but uncertain days of the Weimar Republic into a prelude to the Third Reich.[8] Rath, suggestively an image of wounded manhood, is read as fertile ground for Nazism. Andrea Slane (2001) takes Kracauer as her point of departure and charges postwar readings of Lola with harboring a contemporary fascination with fascism, with fascism embodied in the dangerously sexualized female. Even more, as Slane perceptively writes, "a socially conservative mechanism sees her *ambiguity itself* as a sign of fascism," which invariably carried into Dietrich's casting in post-World War II Hollywood films. She shows how Dietrich later became an effective symbol for democracy and concludes that Dietrich's image is so evasive that she "does not easily conform to any one particular rhetorical function."[9]

In 2002, the British Film Institute (BFI) included in its series a publication on *The Blue Angel*. Its author, S.S. Prawer, eloquently focuses on the film's production history and music. In Germany, this publication was preceded by Luise Dirscherl and Gunther Nickel's *Der blaue Engel: Die Drehbuchentwürfe* (2000), a valuable resource that presents various film scripts or treatments of the film and a chronicle of the film's making from Werner Sudendorf. In the same year, German filmmaker Helma Sanders-Brahms, known chiefly for her film *Germany, Pale Mother* (1980), published her own poetic vision of Dietrich's enchanted relationship with von Sternberg, the man who allegedly discovered and made her, in *Marlene and Jo: Recherche einer Leidenschaft* (2000). Many of these publications appeared after Dietrich's death and reflect renewed interest in Dietrich and, by extension, renewed interest in *The Blue Angel*.[10] Most recently, *The Dietrich Icon* (2007), edited by Gerd Gemünden and Mary Desjardins, presents a multifaceted study of Dietrich's work, image, and life.

As can be seen from the various approaches to the film outlined above, interest in the *Blue Angel* has changed over time. The multiple approaches and interpretations, as with any interpretations, "depend in part upon the subjectivity of the various readers," as Janet Staiger perceptively notes, "but also significantly upon the context of the experience of encountering the text."[11] My own encounter, or, more accurately, my own reading of the film is influenced by my work on the new woman of the Weimar Republic and German cinema of the 1920s, and an approach to film analysis indebted variously to feminism, new historicism, and cultural studies. It is my intention to expand on previous studies by bringing *The Blue Angel* back to its historical stage so as to view the cinematic text and its subtexts within contemporaneous debates and discourses of the Weimar Republic, emphasizing especially the culture wars that characterized it, and to offer a rich context for reading a very complex, multivalent film. To develop these various levels of meaning, I place *The Blue Angel* into the larger framework of the prevalent attitudes toward mass culture and high art. These, I find, are integral to the film's thematic and narrative structure at the twilight of the Weimar Republic (1919–33), as well as to the ways in which gender and concepts of culture are debated at the time. At stake in this film are definitions of culture and cultural hegemony.

The deep divide between high and mass culture during the Weimar Republic expressed itself in the clash between traditional culture (*Kultur*), which stood for an intact community, the individual, rootedness, and stability, and civilization (*Zivilization*) or modernity, perceived as the Americanization of Germany, which stood for urban development, transience, anonymity, and fragmentation. The complexity of these cultural antagonisms during the Weimar Republic that arguably persisted in Germany throughout the postwar period was intensified by Germany's precarious status as a fledgling democracy struggling to define itself, while beset by the traumatic experiences of World War I, by years of economic and political instability, by social upheaval and vast social and technological changes. Given the profound historical connection between art and nation that had been established before Germany became a nation in 1871, the cultural arena served as a major battleground in the formation of a new national identity and a new democratic republic. This transition was all the more difficult because of the crisis of national identity, which resulted as much from losing the war as from the admission of guilt as stipulated in the Versailles Treaty, and the large reparations Germany owed despite hopes of a lenient armistice. As a result of all these factors, divergent definitions of culture became magnified and more dramatically polarized during this period. While cultural conservatives struggled to preserve culture, as they knew it during the nineteenth century, cultural liberals looked to modernity to transform society. Leftist avant-garde movements such as Dadaism radically assaulted both bourgeois values and traditional notions of art. At the same time, technological developments ushered in forms of mass-cultural productions calling for new sensibilities and new kinds of audiences.

Since film stood at the apex of mass culture, with more than two million people going to the movies in Germany by the mid-1920s, it became an easy target for differing views toward social and cultural developments. Peter Jelavich affirms: "To be sure, the cultural terrain was contested throughout the 1920s, and much of the battle was focused on the two media that most directly experienced legal or de facto censorship:

film, the only privately owned medium that was subjected to preemptive censorship in the Weimar era, and radio, a state monopoly governed by political oversight boards."[12] Viewpoints on cinema diverged as much as did political affiliations and loyalties since notions of art (that is, "high or serious culture") were inextricably bound to configurations of class and national identity. In the eyes of cultural conservatives, for example, German national identity was perceived as perilously close to ruin because of mass culture's trivialization and standardization of culture (an argument that the Frankfurt School later promoted). Mass culture was seen as effecting the Americanization of Germany to the detriment of traditional notions of cultural cohesion. Americanism, largely a symptom of displaced discontent, was frequently synonymous with shallow liberalism, with unwanted social changes, and with fears of cultural degeneracy as evidenced by the plethora of sensational films, by the popularity of jazz, the dramatic transformation of both the private and the public sphere, the destabilization of gender roles, and especially the appearance of the modern women. In reaction to the chaos and uncertainty of the interwar years, cultural conservatives sought either to preserve past values and control venues of cultural production or to nestle themselves in the sanctuaries of cultural traditions. Cultural liberals, in contrast, generally celebrated film and mass culture for its potential to democratize Germany, to rescue it from institutional and cultural inertia and to advocate for a progressive politic. For example, taking up the cause of ennobling cinema as early as 1924, by advocating for an intellectual engagement with cinema's aesthetic properties, Béla Balász powerfully sketches the battle filmmakers fought: "Like the disenfranchised and despised mob before a grand manor house, film stands before your aesthetic parliament and demands entry into sacred halls of theory."[13] The left saw in mass culture a potential for leveling the social playing field by wresting the arts from the hands of the intellectual elite and appealing to broad audiences. Initially, film challenged traditional notions of art scrupulously tended by the educated middle class. As Anton Kaes observes: "In the Americanism of the 1920s, film became synonymous with the aesthetic opposition against both the educated and moneyed middle class."[14] *The Blue Angel* thus presents a productive starting point for understanding the extreme tensions over definitions of culture that persisted throughout the interwar years. With the right wing beginning to gain strength in 1929, the battle inferred in distinctions between mass or popular culture and serious or high culture took on an additional meaning and intensity. I deliberately use the term "mass culture" (*Massenkultur*) as it was used in the 1920s, to mean culture that is industrially produced to serve large populations, instead of deferring to today's use of popular culture.[15]

\* \* \*

To better understand the cultural conflicts played out in *The Blue Angel*, and to grasp the unique situation in Germany fueling the cultural debates during the Weimar Republic to unprecedented extremes, one needs to understand the development of the *Bildungsbürger* (the educated middle class), whose impact on German self-awareness and identity cannot be underestimated. Furthermore, it is essential to understand the close partnership of culture, class, and national identity that developed in Germany, and how German high culture produced a value system and national consciousness, and even carved national boundaries where none had existed before 1871. Given Germany's unique appellation of the "Land of Poets and Philosophers," Benedict Anderson's notion of the "imagined nation" takes on a new dimension in the context of Germany's belated nationhood—with culture serving as a significant unifying agent and German writers and intellectuals positioned as key players in the projection of nation (a project that filmmakers later assumed). Culture stood against political fragmentation and regional differences, and served to establish the common ground of German self-awareness. Thus, German national identity was intricately identified with both high culture and local traditions. In fact, as Georg Bollenbeck writes, "the German esteem for high culture was one of the unique characteristics of a civilization that prided itself on its intellectual reputation."[16] Despite the proliferation of art forms and visual media in the early part of the twentieth century that powerfully challenged concepts of education, high art, and middle-class identities, the profound relationship between Germany's cultural heritage and concept of itself as a nation continued to influence the cultural subconscious throughout the Weimar Republic.

When Heinrich Mann wrote his novel *Professor Unrat* in 1905, clearly targeting the ruling elite and educational system of Wilhelminian Germany, he hardly anticipated the transformation of his literary endeavor into a filmic landmark, much less his original title being replaced by a film title, or his novel becoming one of mass culture's most successful exemplars. At the time of the novel's publication, film, a technological wonder, was still in its infancy (with most films ranging from three to fifteen minutes in length). Moreover, the call was still out for authors to participate in the new medium. Hanns Heinz Ewers provocatively wonders in 1909: "Where are the writers and painters who work for the movies?"[17] In 1905, Berlin had sixteen standing movie theaters; by 1907 the city had 139. Films such as *Meissner Porzellan* (1906), directed by Hans Porten, cinematography by Carl Froelich, and, starring in her first film role, Henny Porten, a darling of early cinema, was typical of early film's capability in length (77 minutes) and quality. This one, a "Tonbild" (sound picture) with a gramophone for sound, a technique pioneered by the producer Oskar Messter, featured Porten as a singing porcelain figure and actors lip-syncing. At the time, Marlene Dietrich was just five years old. Later on, she would become a big Porten fan, serenading the silent film star on two occasions and more often sending her cards and flowers. Emil Jannings was twenty-two and was just beginning his stage career.

In Heinrich Mann's biting critique of bourgeois society, Raat, a member of the petit bourgeoisie, prowls through the town in search of the singer Rosa Fröhlich, hoping to intercept his student Lohmann, his nemesis, whose very existence reflects Raat's inadequacies. After marrying Rosa and leaving his job, Raat establishes a gambling casino, with Rosa as alluring entertainer, and exacts his revenge on the town by corrupting and exposing its upstanding citizenry, many of whom used to be his students. Lohmann returns after a few years, and unexpectedly effects both Raat's and Rosa's incarceration, thereby freeing the town of the means for moral corruption. Curiously, the emphasis in Mann's novel is on Raat's Oedipal relationship with his students, a topic that takes on various forms in expressionist plays featuring the father–son relationship.

Even though the new medium, with its altering effect on modern sensibilities, influenced neither the thematic nor narrative structure of Mann's novel explicitly, the novel's dramatic trajectory alludes to cultural and social changes that were brewing in the culture at large.[18] The Expressionist movement that began just as the novel was being published resonates in Mann's portrayal of Professor Rath and his demise (in the novel, Rath is spelled Raat). Challenging bourgeois notions of culture and suspicious of technological developments, militarism, and the emergent metropolis, the new generation of Expressionists criticized Wilhelminian authoritarian practices and expressed their discontent in performances of patricide, and their delivery of a "new man." A critique of the school system and patriarchal authority actually sets the novel in motion: "Since his name was Raat, everyone at the school called him Unrat <garbage>."[19] The reader learns shortly thereafter that this appellation was not limited to students but that colleagues, and townspeople as well, commonly referred to the teacher as "Unrat." If *nomen est omen*, then the slippage from Raat (counsel) to Unrat (refuse, rubbish, trash, or filth) signifies a transition to something no longer useful or valued in the current economy or to something that has outlasted its effectiveness. Trash also belongs to the category of the abject, the undesirable. In Mann's novel, Raat is plagued with this name for twenty years, personifying the rigid, authoritarian structure that first tooled and legitimized him. Moreover, his representation suggests that the system in which he functioned was never really suited to humanistic goals—much less fostered them.

Allegedly, neither the theme of the corrupt bourgeoisie, nor of the vindictive tyrannical teacher, attracted von Sternberg when he agreed to adapt the novel to film, but rather the theme of the fallen patriarch at the hands of the sexualized female. Perhaps it was the chance to cast the femme fatale in the spirit of many of her fictional predecessors, the most powerful of which he saw in the erotic paintings of Félicien Rops, whose female figures are sexually charged, or often diseased figures of death, or in Franz Wedekind's *Lulu*, the mythic eternal feminine that drains men of life energy—a figure that Maria Tatar describes as "harbor<ing> a threat that is not always transparent or predictable <but> linked with discourses on sexuality, urbanization, technology, and modernity."[20] The change in title from *Professor Unrat* to *The Blue Angel* indeed suggests a shift in focus from Raat's battle with the town to the erotic space of the cabaret as a "counterworld" to the classroom and the spectacle of the elusive, sexualized female. In his introduction to the English translation of the novel and screenplay, von Sternberg describes the retooling of the novel, which met with Heinrich Mann's approval: "Rosa Fröhlich would be Lola Lola, deprive her of her child, give the pupils intriguing photographs of her, make her heartless and immoral, invent details that are not in the book, and best of all change the role of the teacher to show the downfall of an enamored man à la Human Bondage."[21]

Thus, on the surface, *The Blue Angel* depicts the demise of a reserved middle-aged prep school teacher, who strays from his socially sanctioned path, surrenders to his desires, and hazards falling in love with the sultry cabaret singer, Lola Lola. Yet, the narrative reaches beyond this conventional (and banal) dramatic trajectory of succumbing to sexual desire or the perilous sexual awakening of a middle-aged man. It reveals and conceals simultaneously the larger issue of competing spheres of culture and, with it, notions of identity, which may be less transparent at first glance. That is to say, the relationship between Lola Lola and Rath is as complicated as the relationship between literature (the word, to which traditional culture ascribed a great importance) and film (the image), as well as between concepts of high art and mass culture. It is as knotty as the competing concepts of culture (and with it, Germanness) that beleaguered the Weimar Republic. More generally and much less transparent, their relationship speaks to the hunger for moving images that triggered a crisis in the arts and catalyzed new cultural formations during the 1920s that called for new forms of cultural literacy, effecting a highly differentiated palette of criticism—one that recognized the power of visual culture and feared the leveling potential of class distinctions.

As mass media, cinema in Germany struggled for legitimacy and finally, during the 1920s, gained more respectability as filmmaking techniques and technologies became more sophisticated. The years between 1909 and 1914 witnessed a shift from a cinema of attractions to a narrative cinema based on classical narrative structures familiar to middle-class consumers. This ambition to upgrade film began soon after its invention, with the German film industry's early endeavors to "gentrify" the medium and to purge cinema of its vaudevillian roots, aligning it more closely with the expectations of the educated middle class. Of course, as Adolf Behne sardonically points out in 1926, there were still those highbrows who eyed film with suspicion: "Film still does not exist for truly cultivated people. After all, there still is not an ideal copy of noble gilt-edged celluloid that one can collect."²²

In order to attract the educated middle class and turn them into filmgoers, movie houses were designed to resemble theaters or palaces (*Zoo Palast, Gloria Palast, Ufa Palast*), wherein extravagant premieres were staged, accompanied by full orchestras, variety acts, and brief *Kulturfilme*. Famous stage actors were called upon also to lend stature to cinema, replacing the *Varieté* actors who were used in many early films. The well-respected stage actor Albert Bassermann's acceptance of a role (an offer many of his colleagues initially refused) in Max Mack's 1913 film *Der Andere* (the other) was a milestone in changing the face of cinema for middle-class consumption and thus eroding the barrier between theater and film.²³ Other attempts to entreat the middle class were "author's readings" at movie theaters.

In a further effort to lend pedigree to cinema, literary adaptations were used to draw the middle class to the box office. Reputable authors were enlisted to establish an *Autorenfilm*, lending seriousness to cinema as an art form, as opposed to mere popular entertainment and kitsch. Works of such well-known German and Austrian authors as Gerhart Hauptmann, Hugo von Hofmannsthal, and Arthur Schnitzler lent respectability to the cinematic fare. At the same time, cinema had the potential of sharing with art the aura of the creative process that privileged the "auteur" or filmmaker over stars. Von Sternberg's own account of his filmmaking experience in Berlin during the making of *The Blue Angel* reveals the status that filmmakers were bestowed, which owed itself largely to a market that was intent on selling its directors as "auteurs." Film and its directors garnered a cultural prestige that was deemed foreign in the United States. Admittedly, von Sternberg reveled in the mystique attributed to the filmmaker in Germany—that same mystique that writers and other artists already enjoyed. In Germany, the status of the author throughout the 1920s evoked the notion of the artist as genius—a concept that the Romantics cultivated in the early part of the nineteenth century, but that modernists, like the playwright Bertolt Brecht, resisted. In an effort to ennoble film, filmmakers began falling into the same league, as von Sternberg recounts:

> The premier of a film, such as the one mine had last week, is the Mecca for the highest society, the biggest statesmen and public personages, and the most famous names. To go to the movies in Germany bespeaks intelligence and culture. Pictures are taken with more seriousness and with more dignity than they are here. Criticism is more venomous and much more honest. That same attitude of seriousness and culture is apparent in the studio. In Germany, the director is all-important, even the biggest star is secondary. While I was working on *The Blue Angel*, the set was being visited continuously by the best-known writers, painters, and musicians. One of them painted my portrait, another modeled my head in bronze; all of them were vitally absorbed in the artistic potentialities of the picture.²⁴

The review in the *Los Angeles Times* on the successful premier of *The Blue Angel* in Berlin also poignantly exemplifies the different perception of the status of film and filmmaking in Germany from an American perspective. The European trademark, in contrast to Hollywood's fare, presumed (however erroneously) a more sophisticated product and an audience with more refined taste. European films were more closely aligned to art than Hollywood productions. The review reads: "Moving pictures in Germany are not made for the masses, one big distinction between there and Hollywood. They are made for the intelligentsia and the cultured and, therefore, allow the director and the actor to more nearly approach an ideal."[25] This perception in all likelihood was based on the types of German films marketed abroad as well as a marketing strategy that set European products apart from Hollywood commercialism. Ironically, *The Blue Angel* plays off of such distinctions within the German context.

By the 1920s, German film studios successfully produced films for both national and international mass consumption, in addition to promoting innovative, avant-garde cinema, and in spite of a film's precarious position between art and commodity. Under the direction of Erich Pommer, the most acclaimed producer of the period, commercialism and art successfully merged, turning German films into some of the most recognized films in Europe and abroad. The period saw the production of such classics as Robert Wiene's prototypical expressionist film, *The Cabinet of Dr. Caligari* (1919), Friedrich Murnau's *Nosferatu* (1922) and *The Last Laugh* (1924), G.W. Pabst's *Joyless Street* (1925) and *Pandora's Box* (1929), and Fritz Lang's *Nibelungen* (1924) and *Metropolis* (1927). Despite film's initial tenuous relationship to high art, these films eventually gained canonical status, reflecting a more expansive understanding of high culture in a postmodern period—one that has come to include cinema, and especially "auteur" cinema, as partner in the creation of high art.

These art films may be contrasted with Dietrich's earlier commercial films, which have aroused recent interest and survived because of Dietrich's mythic stature (on and off screen) since her performance in *The Blue Angel*. Dietrich's earlier films were virtually unknown, despite respectable reviews. Kurt Bernhardt's *Die Frau, nach der man sich sehnt* (The woman, for whom everyone longs), based on a novel by Max Brod, premiered in Berlin on April 28, 1929.[26] In her starring role, Dietrich seduces an unsuspecting newly-wed to escape her criminal accomplice. Robert Land's partial sound film *Ich küsse Ihre Hand, Madam* (*I Kiss Your Hand, Madam*), which premiered on January 17, 1929 at the Tauentzienpalast, is much lighter fare—a comedy of errors and mistaken identities. Here too, Dietrich plays the seductive modern woman who this time meets her match in the charming and dignified Jacques, played by German film favorite Harry Liedtke. Richard Tauber, of opera and operetta fame and longtime friend of Dietrich, sings the title song that Liedtke lip-syncs. Also of note is the first appearance in this film of the black doll that became Dietrich's mascot.[27] Renewed interest in Dietrich has led to the redistribution of *Die Frau, nach der man sich sehnt* and *Ich küsse Ihre Hand, Madam*, as well as the Austrian film *Café Electric* (1927, Gustav Ucicky). In retrospect, these films already reveal Dietrich's provocative style and the camera's fascination with her face and understated mannerism. The camera lingers to emphasize especially the seductive drama of her eyes. Retrospectively, it is even easy to find traces of Lola Lola in these performances. Reviewers of Dietrich's early films compared Dietrich to Garbo (a comparison that followed her to Hollywood, which Dietrich reportedly detested).[28]

While conflicting attitudes toward high culture and mass culture and the questions of their function and meaning significantly charged cultural debates during the Weimar Republic, discussions on the effects of cinema and differing valuations of text and image have persisted universally since cinema's invention. Timothy Corrigan contends: "Twentieth century history, perhaps more than any other epoch in history, has positioned itself between the 'traditional word' and 'technological image,' and tracing the directions of this debate throughout this century as it works through movies, books, and culture dramatizes one of the most pressing motifs of these times."[29] Preoccupation with mass or popular culture, its proliferation, its social function and impact remains, as Corrigan notes, as pertinent today as during the Weimar Republic, and as charged by such varying questions as the relationship of image to spectator, the impact of images on national and even global identities, and the social function of high art and mass cultural production. The definition of the *Bildungsbürger*, as Martin Mosbach writes, who had "a concert, an opera, and a theater subscription, and who sent their children to humanistic preparatory schools, who lived at a distance from the hallowed spheres of high culture but sought them in contemplative hours and thought culture was important" has vastly changed, and with it, pressing issues of cultural literacy have followed.[30]

The increasing domination of visual culture and its popular venues has some critics today lamenting the loss of traditional cultural knowledge and subsequently scrambling to revive and define a body of canonical texts to secure a "German" identity. On this scale, images have acquired a troubled reputation. Indeed, W.J. Mitchell identifies the persistent attitude toward images, especially those that popular culture produces, as "all-powerful forces, to blame for everything from violence to moral decay—or they are denounced as mere 'nothings,' worthless, empty, and vain."[31] Hollywood's Tim Burton provides a contemporary tongue-in-cheek answer to the question of the relationship between mass or popular and high culture in his 1989 *Batman*, based on the comic book, with sets reminiscent of Fritz Lang's *Metropolis*. The Joker (played by Jack Nicholson), a pop archetype with green hair, prances through a museum in Gotham City, a pantheon of high art, irreverently slashing masterpieces as one of his evil deeds. Seen in light of what seems to be an unresolved self-conscious struggle of competing art forms, *The Blue Angel* acquires heightened relevancy.

This cultural history of *The Blue Angel* therefore begins with the early debates on cinema by returning the film to its historical setting. Chapter 1 places *The Blue Angel* into a larger cultural context on the debates on cinema, mass culture, and national identity and shows how these conflicts between mass culture and high culture, which persisted throughout the 1920s, are played out in the dramatic trajectory of the film, in the configuration of its characters, and in the conflicts and contradictions that define multiple narrative layers. Even though the *Kino-Debatte* for the most part receded by the end of the 1920s, discussions over the social function of film and its value did not. Since film retained its status as a lesser or more popular art form, it constantly existed within the tensions inherent in definitions of high and mass culture until the end of the Weimar Republic, despite being able to claim a number of "artistic" productions. Even the reception of *The Blue Angel* largely rehearses the debate on culture that preoccupied many cultural critics during the Weimar Republic and later on. Thus I look at the intersection of a variety of discourses that are layered and potentially contradictory in nature. Additionally, I argue here that the film reveals as much about the social and cultural transformations that defined the interwar period as it does the anxieties associated with these cultural changes. It raises questions about perception and the new dispositions associated with the Weimar Republic, which are linked to an epistemic crisis that profoundly affected notions of culture.

Chapter 2 explores the spectator's (more specifically, Rath's), relationship to the image—that is, popular visual culture—and his unconditioned gaze. Here image is understood in its full complexity both as material object and as psychological phantasm, which means the source of dreams, desires, and longing. I look at the irresistibility of the image, its desire to be absorbed, loved, owned, and consumed, and at the "magic of the image" derived from its aura.[32] More specifically, I explore Rath's submission to the image as testimony to its power and to the masochistic relationship inherent in the cinema-viewing experience of von Sternberg's film. Here, I expand on Gaylyn Studlar's argument by subscribing to a reading of *The Blue Angel* as a masochistic text, but additionally frame Rath's experience historically, by arguing that his extreme disavowal of reality—that is, his uncensored desire for the image of Lola—stems from misapprehension of the conventions of mass media. He allows himself to be absorbed by the image and is caught within the swirl of his own projections. Thus, as a representative of nineteenth-century middle-class educational values, he embodies both the pleasures that mass culture promises and the dangers of total absorption and submission. Rath's decline is read as a symptomatic breakdown of the cultural norms he embodies, and as a paradigmatic shift in the values and modes of reception linked to modernity.

Chapter 3 discusses the modern woman as image, modern phenomenon, and historical figure. Lola is viewed as the modern woman, a figure that fueled discussions intricately linked to those of modernity and mass culture. I argue that despite von Sternberg's guard against history through his highly calculated, aesthetic construction, history invariably appears as a powerful subsidiary text. Rendering a historical reading of gender, and taking into account the convergence of discourses on the modern woman, and especially on marriage and female employment (two themes often disregarded in most interpretations of the film), opens the film up to a more nuanced understanding of the relationship between Rath and Lola. The historical "punctures" the aesthetic illusion of the all-powerful image of desire, meaning that historical discourses on gender reside as powerful peripheral texts within the narrative and challenge on occasion the masochistic aesthetic of disavowal.

Chapter 4 investigates sound and the seductive combination of the visual and the aural spheres. The introduction of sound film challenged existing definitions of art and cinema, mass culture and high art, which becomes apparent in von Sternberg's use of film music to amplify the conflict between his main characters and the spheres they represent. The tension is expressed by contrasting the serious classical tradition with popular song (Schlager), a signifier of modernity. Accordingly, Rath is defined through art songs and Romantic music conventions, while Lola's songs, self-consciously and self-reflexively performed, belong to the realm of mass culture and cabaret. At the same time, sound signifies the "real," which further blinds Rath to the deception of the performance and allows for complicated operations of disavowal. He relinquishes the boundaries of his identity to the promise of love and erotic pleasure—even though the promise is a deceit. Sound underscores the masochistic aesthetic since pleasure does not derive from mastering or sequestering the threatening female but from submitting to her voice and her gaze to attain immediate symbiotic bliss.

Chapter 5 turns to the revivification of Dietrich as "The Blue Angel" and the transformation of Dietrich into a cultural icon in the narrative of a newly unified Germany. Her "comeback" has a symbolic quality that allows for an atonement of Germany's Nazi past and a celebration of its glorious roaring and experimental 1920s. Dietrich's popularity compellingly attests to a shift in the cultural forms that conceptualize national identity and national culture. Based on the fetishization of stars like Dietrich, it could be argued that a new *Bildungsbürgertum* emerges in the twenty-first century, one that embraces select exemplars of popular culture, with film literacy figuring as a sign of the "educated" citizen.

Lastly, an appendix provides short biographies of the many figures that contributed to the making of *The Blue Angel*. These biographies intimately illustrate German film history and represent the many directions that lives took in Germany's film industry after 1933—some ending in success stories, others in unfathomable tragedy. The film premiered three years before Hitler's rise to power and stands at the juncture of German history. It also provides evidence of the deeply entrenched affiliation between film and German political and cultural history.

As cultural theorists continue to wrangle with definitions of culture and with the ever-expanding surplus and marketing of images that the "culture industry" produces (as the term was coined by the Frankfurt School, deeply influenced by the ideals of the *Bildungsbürgertum*, which cautioned against mass media's disempowerment of the individual), they have come to acknowledge mass culture's potential to empower its audiences, in addition to its seductive and addictive pleasures that disable individuals. Furthermore, the boundaries between contemporary popular culture and high art have blurred progressively since early debates on mass culture and high art, and concepts of textuality and culture have undergone dramatic transformations, all adding new dimensions to a contemporary reading of *The Blue Angel*. This, however, does not mean that these distinctions do not continue to reside in the cultural subconscious. The initial tensions between mass culture and high culture still inform cultural understanding and can be seen in the spaces these various expressions of culture inhabit. Certain films still aspire to set themselves off from mere entertainment; the trade-off often is attracting smaller audiences and settling for less revenue.

Despite film's dependence on technology, art cinema, often equated with experimental cinema and the avant-garde, successfully wedged itself between the towers of high art and the channels of mass culture, leaving other forms of filmmaking (like the films of von Sternberg) precariously positioned between art and entertainment, culture and industry. Yet other, more "popular" films since then have been considered products, variously, of popular culture and of high culture, and have come to elude the overdetermined, binary, and modernist designations of "high" and "low culture." The instability of attribution attests to the now-fluid boundaries between these designations. In spite of his mordant critics, Sternberg prophetically regarded his film as a work of art.[33] He recognized early on (and perhaps by necessity because of his own status within Hollywood's industry and the perception of himself as artist) the permeable boundaries between high art and mass culture and between various forms of artistic expression in his own work as a filmmaker. The camera, he said, was his "paintbrush," the *mise en scène* his still life, and the film his creative vision. In a letter to Curtis Harrington (1949), von Sternberg writes: "Poetry is not exclusive to any single medium of expression, and you will find a clue to much of my work, if not to all of it, in noting that I use images and sound like others have used words."[34] Profound in his understanding of images, von Sternberg calls for a poetics of images and sound.[35] Dependent on technology and on multiple contributors (director, actors, screenwriters, set designers, and so forth) rather than a single author, filmmakers have challenged film's standing within the artistic arena as von Sternberg expresses in his insistence of his poetic vision. His films are documents of personal expression, unique in their intricate play of shadow and light. Setting himself off from those who produce mass culture films, von Sternberg claims for himself the role of the artist, so much so that he maintained he knew nothing of the political strife that beset the Weimar Republic during the time he spent there: "I went to Germany to make *The Blue Angel* without any knowledge of the conditions there—mine was an artist's pilgrimage, and no more."[36] Since that time, von Sternberg has gained canonical stature, and his name has been added to America's most significant *auteur* filmmakers—his films proudly bearing his unique signature. Although an anomaly among his oeuvres, *The Blue Angel* is regarded as one of his masterpieces.[37]

In light of the cultural wars of the Weimar Republic, and cinema's precarious position between art and mass culture, along with many filmmakers' intense struggle to assert themselves as poets, as von Sternberg did, it may be helpful to consider W.J. Mitchell's provocative question, "What do pictures want?" "The question to ask of pictures from the standpoint of poetics," he proposes, "is not just what they mean or do but what they want, what claim they make upon us, and how we are to respond."[38] Beyond wanting that their individual meanings be understood, the answer may be that images simply want to capture and awe their beholders and be recognized for their art. What they also want, according to Mitchell, is closely linked to what they lack. In short, they are a composite of what they have and do not have. Thus, the spectator must learn to recognize what the image does not have in order to decipher what it wants. When seeing *The Blue Angel*, and its display of richly textured images, its luscious close-ups of Lola surrounded by posters that powerfully multiply her image; and when considering the emphasis on the spectacle and the choreography of looking and of being seen; and when witnessing Rath's surrender to the image with the ill-fated promise of possessing it, his sever punishment for wanting to see, and his tragic demise, we could conclude that what these images want is to be accepted as art. They long for the suspension of judgment on products of mass culture and high art, and to be taken seriously. What these images *want*, on a meta-narrative level, is legitimacy as an art form. They speak to cinema's desire for recognition, for an admiration of their artistic expression and poetic vision. At least, this seems to be what von Sternberg's highly aestheticized and self-reflexive images want. Lola Lola says as much when she crosses the cultural divide and claims, "I am an artist."

To engage in images on multiple levels in the way Mitchell suggests (whether they are the product of von Sternberg's poetics, the New German Cinema or mainstream Hollywood), calls for an astute reader, a reader who is at once absorbed and distant. Yet, despite the dominance of visual culture in contemporary society and its forceful shaping and informing of our lives, we seem to be far from achieving a truly sophisticated visual literacy. Perhaps Professor Rath serves as an example of the grave consequences of misreading what the image means, and more provocatively, what it wants.

## Notes

1. My study is based on the uncut German version of *The Blue Angel*, which is longer (106 minutes) than the contemporaneous American version (94 minutes). For a discussion on the difference between the American and German versions, see Peter Hogue, "True Blue," *Film Comment* 30, 2 (March 1994), 38–43. Hogue argues that the American version lacks the emotional complexity that saturates the German version.
2. Marlene Dietrich with Maximilian Schell, "Nee, die alten Kramfilme," *Der Spiegel* 9 (February 27, 1984), www.spiegel.de/spiegel/0,1518,269337,00.html. See also Dietrich's autobiography, in which she claims that the costumes she created for *The Blue Angel* have become a symbol of her persona. Marlene Dietrich, *Ich bin, Gott sei Dank, Berlinerin* (Berlin: Ullstein, 2000), 85.
3. See Donald Spoto, *Falling in Love Again: Marlene Dietrich* (Boston and Toronto: Little, Brown and Company, 1985). Other biographers concur with the significance of *The Blue Angel*; see Steven Bach, *Marlene Dietrich: Life and Legend* (New York: William Morrow, 1992) and Ean Wood, *Dietrich: A Biography* (London: Sanctuary, 2002).
4. See "$94,700 for 'Lightnin,' Roxy; 'Morocco' and 'Blue Angel': Only Other Standout Films on B'way," *Variety* (December 10, 1930), 9. The review continues to laud the film as an "excellent picture probably classing it as the best foreign version made to date by any country." The film was enthusiastically reviewed on both US coasts.
5. Richard Firda, "Literary Origins: Sternberg's Film *The Blue Angel*," *Literature/Film Quarterly* 7 (1979), 127. See also Ulrich Weisstein, "Translations and Adaptations of Heinrich Mann's Novel in Two Media," *Film Journal* 1, 3–4 (Fall/Winter 1972), 53–61.
6. G.W. Pabst adapted Frank Wedekind's play for his film *Die Büchse der Pandora* (1929, *Pandora's Box*) starring the American actress Louise Brooks as Lulu.
7. See Maria Tatar, "1905, Eroticism and the Femme Fatale," *A New History of German Literature*, edited by David E. Wellbery et al. (Cambridge, MA: Harvard University Press, 2004), 658. Of interest is that Dietrich's first "legitimate stage performance" was in Wedekind's play *Pandora's Box* on September 7, 1922.
8. Andrea Slane, *A Not So Foreign Affair: Fascism, Sexuality and the Cultural Rhetoric of American Democracy* (Durham, NC: Duke University Press, 2001), 226.
9. Slane, 227 and 247 respectively.
10. See Gerd Gemünden and Mary R. Desjardins, eds., *Dietrich Icon*, (Durham, NC: Duke University Press, 2007).
11. Janet Staiger, *Perverse Spectators: The Practices of Film Reception* (New York: New York Press, 2000), 77.
12. Peter Jelavich, *Berlin Alexanderplatz: Radio, Film, and the Death of Weimar Culture* (Berkeley: University of California Press, 2006), xi.
13. Béla Balász, "The Visible Human," *German Essays on Film*, edited by Richard McCormick and Alison Guenther-Pal, translated by Lance W. Garmer (New York: Continuum, 2004), 70.
14. Anton Kaes, ed., *Kino-Debatte: Texte zum Verhältnis von Literatur und Film, 1909–1929* (Tübingen: Niemeyer, 1978), 16 (my translation).
15. I wish to retain this term in order to emphasize its technological aspect and its historicity, despite the negative connotations it has gained through the works of the Frankfurt School and, specifically through the work of Theodor Adorno and Max Horkheimer.
16. Georg Bollenbeck, "German Kultur, the *Bildungsbürgertum*, and Its Susceptibility to National Socialism," *The German Quarterly* 73 (Winter, 2000), 69.

17. Wolfgang Jacobsen, Anton Kaes and Hans Helmut Prinzler, eds., *Geschichte des deutschen Films* (Stuttgart: Metzler, 1993), 18.
18. Heinrich Mann, *Professor Unrat* (Frankfurt am Main: Fischer, 1994), 10 (my translation). The only allusion to the new medium in the novel is Mann's description of the abrupt change—much like a jump cut—in the facial expression of the cabaret singer, Rosa Fröhlich, who later becomes Lola Lola of film fame: "Und jetzt geschah es allerdings, dass ihre wohlaufgelegte, dienstfertige Miene ganz unvorbereitet in eine bittere und böse hinüberglitt, mit einem kleinen Ruck, wie beim Kinematographen." ("And thus it happened that her composed and compliant expression unexpectedly changed into a bitter and angry expression as if effected by the slight jerk of a cinematographer.") The changed facial expression here presumably refers either to editing or the reaction on people's faces when they noticed a camera set up on the street to arbitrarily film passers-by—a common practice.
19. The spelling of Rath's name differs in Mann's novel, where it appears as Raat. Heinrich Mann, *Professor Unrat* (Hamburg: Rowohlt, 1969). ("Da er Raat hiess, nannte die ganze Schule ihn Unrat.").
20. Tatar, "1905," 659.
21. Josef von Sternberg, *The Blue Angel: The Novel by Heinrich Mann, The Film by Josef von Sternberg* (New York: Frederick Ungar, 1979), 259.
22. Adolf Behne, "Die Stellung des Publikums zur modernen deutschen Literatur," *Kino-Debatte: Texte zum Verhältnis Literatur und Film, 1909–1929*, edited by Anton Kaes (Tübingen: Niemeyer, 1978), 163 (my translation). ("Für ganz feine Leute existiert er doch nicht. Es gibt ja noch keine Vorzugs-Kopien auf Edel-Celluloid mit Goldschnitt, die man sammeln könnte.").
23. See Jerzy Toeplitz, *Geschichte des Films 1895–1928*, I (Berlin: Henschelverlag, 1984), 134–35; Klaus Kreimeier, *Die Ufa Story* (Munich: Hanser, 1992), 26–27.
24. Elena Boland, "UFA Film Wins Plaudits: Von Sternberg on Return Contrasts Problems of Producing 'The Blue Angel' in Germany," *Los Angeles Times* (April 6, 1930), B9.
25. Ibid.
26. In this film, Dietrich plays Stascha, a woman who has her husband killed in order to free herself from his tyranny but whose complicity binds her to the murderer, Dr. Karoff (Fritz Körtner). Desperate to free herself, she draws into her web of intrigue Henri Leblanc (Uno Henning), an unsuspecting newly-wed who is just boarding the same train as Stascha for his honeymoon. Here the street film genre is unleashed spatially with the streets of the metropolis expanded to more radical representations of mobility. The catalog of settings includes a train, a hotel, a factory, and an encounter with foreigners, namely, Russians. Stascha passes off Henri as her cousin, and arranges in vain to flee with him during a New Year's Eve party. With the arrival of the police who apprehend the criminals, Dr. Karoff kills Stascha at her request and turns the gun on himself unsuccessfully. The despondent Henri who witnesses the killing and learns of Stascha's past, replies when asked about his plans: "I am going home" ("Ich fahre nach Hause"). Much like Rath and his other "street film" predecessors, who have fallen to sexualized women, Henri is absorbed by the image of promised sensuality when he first lays eyes on Stascha, who draws open the curtain of the train and invites his gaze. Her image is framed doubly: first by the window frame and second by frostwork that lends an ethereal sense to the image. It is this static, yet emotionally moving portrait of Stascha (Dietrich) that "arrests" Henri.
27. The beautiful divorcée Laurence Gerard (Marlene Dietrich) falls in love with an exiled Russian count, Jacques Lerski, who works as a waiter in a chic hotel. Even though he introduces himself to her as a count, the Dietrich character believes he has tricked her when she learns of his job. Avenging herself, she tries to humiliate him and spitefully causes his firing. Demoted to room service, Jacques accepts his new post with dignity and becomes the darling of the third floor, with flocks of women booking rooms. Finding out the truth about Jacques's actual title, Laurence pursues him. He fights his attraction

to her and exposes her for her superficiality. The film, however, ends happily with their union and a moral that the short "Dickerchen" (Karl Huszar-Puffy), who has been her loyal and wishful companion, humbly accepts: "You have to be lucky and you must be attractive" ("Glück muss man haben und schön muss man sein").

28. See Ralph Flint, "Hollywood Happenings," *New York Times* (June 1, 1930), X6; "Marlene A Chameleon with Personal Charm," *Variety* (December 10, 1930), 52; "What Led to Dietrich's Great Success?," *Los Angeles Times* (August 16, 1931), B11.

29. Timothy Corrigan, *Film and Literature: An Introduction and Reader* (New Jersey: Prentice Hall, 1999), 5. It is interesting to note how "literary" was the New German cinema—a movement that spanned the years 1961–82 and beyond. The return to a "textuality of cinema," aspiring to close the gap between literature and film while exploring the aesthetic (and didactic) possibilities of film, may be read as an effort to diminish the "inherent" antagonism between literature and film that was felt well into the 1980s. Rainer Werner Fassbinder, for instance, one of postwar Germany's most prolific filmmakers, felicitously adapted Theodor Fontane's novel *Effi Briest*. His own sixteen-hour magnum opus *Berlin Alexanderplatz*, produced for television in 1979, was based on Alfred Döblin's 1929 Weimar novel. In turning to these literary texts, Fassbinder sought to develop an alternative aesthetic, to counter mainstream cinema's absorption of the spectator and to develop a critical public sphere by bridging mass and high culture.

30. Martin Mosbach, "Willkommen im Paradies der Furchtlosen," *Die Zeit* (September 25, 2003), 40. In Germany, the discussion of loss of a common national cultural identity in today's multicultural society has given way to suggestions of a "Leitkultur," a guiding culture among cultural conservatives.

31. W.J.T. Mitchell, *What Do Pictures Want?: The Lives and Loves of Images* (Chicago: University of Chicago Press, 2005), 77.

32. Mitchell, 9.

33. Von Sternberg seems to have had aspirations similar to Lola—that is, to be assigned the title of artist. B.G. Braver-Mann, one of Sternberg's acerbic critics, claims: "From the time Sternberg made *Salvation Hunters* down to the present day, he has persistently posed as an artist, an affectation which afflicts a considerable number of Hollywood's 'leading' directors, among them such over-rated men as King Vidor, Frank Borzage, C.B. De Mille, Clarence Brown and others whose chief claim to film leadership is rooted in their talent for *Kitsch*." Quoted in Peter Baxter, *Sternberg* (London: British Film Institute, 1980), 29.

34. Herman G. Weinberg, *Josef von Sternberg* (New York: Dutton, 1967), 135.

35. The story of his search for the perfect Lola, inspired by the images of Félicien Rops, casts von Sternberg as a cinematic god. This tribute is not that far-fetched, since von Sternberg evokes the myth of Vishnu (who churned a sea of milk to have woman surface from the agitated waters to charm the world) to describe his work. See *Fun in a Chinese Laundry*, 227.

36. Weinberg, 54. Sternberg, who insisted on full authorial control, claimed that he drew from his own biography in his creation of the film and his experiences as a child in an orthodox Jewish household with a strict (yet often absent) father. Rath, Sternberg maintains, is based on his Hebrew teacher in Vienna. While Sternberg's biography is interesting in its own right, what makes it all the more fascinating in terms of *The Blue Angel* is von Sternberg's position as intercultural interlocutor, despite his denial of interest in Germany.

37. Peter Baxter revisits the discussion of von Sternberg's rise to fame in his book *Sternberg*. Some critics referred to von Sternberg as a "genius," thus resuscitating the Romantic notion of the artist within the context of filmmaking; others claimed that the symbiotic relationship between Dietrich and Sternberg led to their success.

38. Mitchell, 24.

*Chapter 1*

# Mass Entertainment and "Serious" Culture

> Our taverns and our metropolitan streets, our offices and furnished rooms, our railroad stations and our factories appeared to have us locked up hopelessly. Then came film and burst this prison-world asunder by the dynamite of the tenth of a second, so that now in the midst of its far-flung ruins and debris, we calmly and adventurously go traveling.
> **Walter Benjamin, "The Work of Art in the Age of Mechanical Reproduction"**

> Not so long ago it was still difficult to convince the Philistines that the film was an independent, autonomous new art with laws of its own.
> **Béla Balász, *Theory of Film: Character and Growth of a New Art***

The story of Josef von Sternberg's filming of *The Blue Angel* often begins with the account of von Sternberg's search for the perfect Lola, and his fateful discovery of Marlene Dietrich. She allegedly had a minor role in a theater performance of Expressionist playwright Georg Kaiser's *Zwei Krawatten* (*Two Bow Ties*) in the Berliner Theater, where she played an American and had one line—"May I invite one and all to dine with me tonight?" Delighted with Dietrich's nonchalant stage presence, von Sternberg immediately arranged an audition.[1] In Dietrich he found his perfect Lola, whose image reminded him of images of women he liked in paintings by Félicien Rops and Toulouse Lautrec.[2] This intricate relationship between art and life would play a key role in their future collaboration.

Yet the story of *The Blue Angel's* filming begins long before the director selected his cast. It begins with the relationship between Hollywood and Berlin, and with Emil Jannings's star role in the film *The Last Command*, which von Sternberg directed in 1928. Emil Jannings's performance not only earned him an Oscar for best actor but occasioned yet another collaboration between film giants. Hollywood's Paramount studio and

Berlin's Ufa chief business manager, Ludwig Klitzsch, brought the successful producer Erich Pommer back to Berlin from Hollywood to lead a production company with Ufa. Since Jannings was eager to make the passage into sound film, he and Pommer invited Austrian-born von Sternberg, who was versed in the new technology of sound, to Berlin, where von Sternberg would smooth the path for Ufa's inevitable transition into sound and secure the German studio's position as a viable competitor to Hollywood. The film studio hoped to duplicate the success of von Sternberg's and Jannings's previous collaboration, as well as that of von Sternberg's first sound film, *Thunderbolt*; to that end, it was willing to pay the director handsomely and to give him free rein. In fact, Dietrich got the part only at the insistence of von Sternberg and because Pommer wished to retain him. Based loosely on Heinrich Mann's 1905 novel *Professor Unrat* and filmed in both German and English to gain an international market, the Berlin production would be exemplary in its synthesis of art and commercialism. Although originally intended to launch the career of Jannings in the new medium, once retitled and transformed into *The Blue Angel*, the film instead gave birth to the legend of Marlene Dietrich, whose performance captivated her audience.[3]

*The Blue Angel* premiered on April 1, 1930, at the Gloria Palast in Berlin, and was met with great enthusiasm. Critics lauded the performances of both Jannings and Dietrich; the *Reichsfilmblatt* reported: "One is downright overwhelmed by Miss Dietrich's performance. Her ability to dominate scenes without great effort, yet with simple and absolute authority is unprecedented."[4] Emil Jannings was recognized primarily for his expansive talent, despite reservations about his theatricality. Kurt Pinthus wrote in *Das Tagebuch* that Jannings "proves himself here as an aggregate figure with a thousand individual traits of incredible genuine talent for characterization, particularly in awakening, in transitions of tragic grotesque feelings."[5] In the *Vössische Zeitung* on the day after the premier, Pinthus particularly lauds Dietrich for a "vulgarity" that derived from filmic presentation alone. "Everything here is film, not theater … Extraordinary!"[6]

Those reviews that did not focus on the captivating performances of Dietrich and Jannings addressed either implicitly or explicitly the relationship between serious culture and mass culture, and especially the relationship between literature and film and between Heinrich Mann's novel and its filmic adaptation. To a great extent, these reviews rehearse the divergent understandings and expectations of "culture" and cinema that shaped public debate during the Weimar Republic. These polarized definitions of serious culture and mass culture, as I will show, are at the heart of *The Blue Angel*. Indeed, these debates resonate in the encounter of Rath and Lola, an encounter that rests on the divide between high culture and mass entertainment, and in attitudes toward cinema, and highlights the assumptions underlying—and vulnerabilities of—interwar Germanness. Having found there was far more to the film's success than Miss Dietrich's naked thighs, as Heinrich Mann famously proposed, I contend that discourses on mass culture and "serious" culture of the *Bildungsbürger* are integral to the film's thematic and narrative structure.[7]

It was in the discussion of the adaptation of Mann's novel that critics were politically divided in a climate that was moving increasingly toward the right. Prone to a sense of cultural despair, verging on disenchantment with everything modern, the right only partially was relieved to see that von Sternberg had sanitized the film of any political content, sparing German educators the condemnation of the tyrannical Wilhelminian schoolmaster that Mann develops in his novel. While cultural conservatives applauded the film version, they did not miss the opportunity to condemn Mann's novel as an affront to long-cherished national institutions that laid the foundation of German national identity. The Nazi press was less appeased by the changes, and the right-wing *Völkische Beobachter* branded the film a product of "Jewish erotic thinking ... a conscious Jewish subversion and denigration of German character and of German educational values; Jewish cynicism shows itself here with a baseness that is seldom seen so openly."[8] Measures taken against the film during the Third Reich were anticipated in this diatribe against the film, in which the author commemorates a teacher's conference day in Bavaria, decrying the slanderous representation of Professor Rath. Once Hitler came to power in 1933, the film was placed into the "*Giftschrank*" (poison cabinet).

No less critical of the film, the left claimed that it was deliberately directed *against* Heinrich Mann; they reproached von Sternberg for his lack of social analysis, for his failure to critique the authoritarian educational system, and for his "misuse" (Kracauer) of the novel's social consciousness.[9] A review in the leftist newspaper *Die rote Fahne*, purposely playing off of the name of *The Blue Angel* screenplay writer Carl Zuckmayer, accused the writers "of having 'sugar-coated' <*verzuckmayert*>" Mann's novel, indeed of selling out to Ufa owner Hugenberg's conservative party line. The leftist intellectual Carl von Ossietzsky went even further in *Die Weltbühne* and accused the screenplay writers of betraying their calling as writers and intellectuals: "It would have been better, if they had left the vandalizing bowdlerization of an intelligent German novel to Ufa's ghostwriters."[10]

Indeed, in light of his 1928 speech at the Capitol movie theater in Berlin, in which Heinrich Mann, a fervent advocate of cinema, clearly outlined the social function of the medium, it is somewhat surprising that he approved of von Sternberg's revisions. Echoing the sentiments that many leftist intellectuals held at the time, Mann, in other contexts, alerted his audience to the intellectually impoverished state of Weimar's popular film culture, asserting "intellect and taste get short shrift in daily film productions."[11] The majority of films, he went on to say, were based on sensation and denied their audiences a critical commentary of reality.

Cinema had the power to structure perception, and, contrary to popular belief, affect daily life. As an art form, rather than a mere commercial enterprise, film's primary obligation was "to teach <us> to see and think." To that end, it was not necessary for directors, literally "film poets" (*Filmdichter*), as he called them, to turn to literature for their stories. Like many left-wing Weimar intellectuals, Mann looked to Russian film (Eisenstein, Vertov) as exemplifying film's potential to produce insightful poetic narratives independent of literary adaptations.

In step with the social changes the interwar years demanded, and in contrast to his brother Thomas Mann, Heinrich Mann refused to separate art from politics, and harshly criticized the cultural elitism of the *Bildungbürgertum*. In "Geistiges Gesellschaftskapital" (Intellectual social capital, 1924), he addresses the ineffectiveness of past cultural ideals and the insular society that emerged from them: "What should society do with the intellectual education of the prewar years, with culture that was considered a privilege and that was espoused by a few thousand snobby bearers of culture, that they never imparted to others? That type of culture did not advocate the politicization of the nation, but rather hindered it, it was against the democratization of culture."[12]

Despite his pointedly laid out expectations of film, Mann agreed to radical changes in both the substance and in the title of his novel (even though it was said he complained privately); during the filming of *The Blue Angel*, he even visited the set regularly and enjoyed an amicable working relationship with von Sternberg. Pommer also arranged a screening of the final version for Mann in Nice, France before premiering the film in Berlin.[13] All of this allowed Pommer to counter critics and claim that the script was written *with* Mann. S.S. Prawer suspects that Mann was motivated by the sizeable payment Ufa offered him and the prospect of improved book sales.[14] Other critics have speculated that Mann had too much respect for his colleagues Zuckmayer and Liebmann to interfere with their work.[15] More to the point, however, had von Sternberg *not* made the changes he did to the original story, it is doubtful whether the film mogul Alfred Hugenberg, an extreme right-wing nationalist, would ever have accepted Mann's novel for the film. Even as changed, the film had to maneuver its way through a politically volatile period in German history, and through the intense debates on the relationship between mass culture, literature, and national identity.[16]

More critical than Mann of the discrepancies between the literary work and its filmic adaptation, Siegfried Kracauer, in his 1930 review in *Die Neue Rundschau*, joined others in objecting to the film's content, whose vacuity and superficiality he saw as only thinly veiled by its ornamentation. While acknowledging the talent of both Jannings and Dietrich, and mentioning especially Dietrich's attractive legs and voice, Kracauer provocatively queries, "But to what purpose the legs, the effects, the technique, and the enormous fanfare <Riesentheater>?" The purpose, in his estimation, is "to forget reality and conceal it."[17] Given that the film was made during a time of great economic instability and great political uncertainty in Germany, with the right gaining popularity, his words carry a weight missing from the haughty dismissal of mass culture on the part of many Weimar intellectuals. Indeed, as an intellectual who, during the 1920s, appreciated the democratizing potential of mass culture and saw in it an implicit critique of a bourgeois culture that promoted authoritarian structures and paid homage to the arts as a sign of social status, Kracauer may be counted among Weimar's most ardent proponents of mass culture, modernity, and Americanization. In Miriam Hansen's words: "Like many Weimar intellectuals, Kracauer welcomed mass culture as a practical critique of the remnants of bourgeois high culture and philosophical attempts to patch up the actual state of disintegration and disorder."[18]

While Kracauer understood the need for people in modern society to seek diversion from their tedious working conditions, the state of distractedness was at once an integral element of modernity and a sign of disarray. "The Berlin public," Kracauer wrote, "behaves in a profoundly truthful manner when it increasingly shuns <conventional forms of high art>... and shows its preferences for the superficial luster of stars, films, revues, and production numbers. Here, in pure externality, it finds itself; the dismembered succession of splendid sensory perceptions brings to light its own reality."[19] Even though mass culture could offer crucial insight into the problems of modernity, more often it disappointed its advocates and simply blinded its audiences. For Kracauer, distraction ultimately robbed the individual of psychological and social insight and the possibility of reflection. Thus, reading Kracauer's 1930 critique of *The Blue Angel* beyond its function as a review reveals his expectations of the cinema, or, for that matter, any art form. Art and cinema should comment on the increasing disaffectedness of the modern condition and the growing sense of isolation from a chaotic, fragmented world; they should explore individual psychologies since "don't individual destinies and psychology exist now after the war as they did before?"[20] Indeed, where mass culture was not invested in its innovative potential, it was no more than an obstruction to cultural progress, an escapist and inferior form of cultural expression.

In 1952, and five years after coining the term "culture industry" with Max Horkheimer, Theodor Adorno was even less convinced than Kracauer of *The Blue Angel*'s worth. Echoing the objections of critics before him, Adorno submits that the film falls short of the aesthetic quality of the novel and undermines its social relevance. The ultimate adoption of the film title for the book title served as yet another example of "earnest culture" suffering a kind of putrefaction in the modern world, with modern mass culture as instrumental in bringing about this decomposition. Indeed, mass culture seemed to compromise the very integrity of an elite ennobling culture, which Adorno, according to Robert Witkin, identified with the intellectual and aesthetic systems that developed in the eighteenth century; those grand systems of Enlightenment ideas and of speculative metaphysics that constituted, for example, the culture of German Idealism, together with the aesthetic ideals embodied in the literature and Culture in this larger sense secures for the individual some degree of autonomy and integrity at the level of agency.[21]

The cinema's indiscriminate use of highly regarded literary texts confirmed for critics of mass culture the decline of literary culture, which they foresaw as soon as cinema developed narrative sophistication and became popular. In fact, early critics of the cinema saw mass culture encroaching on all art forms. In reaction, they theorized mass culture's limitations, doggedly drawing sharp distinctions between high and mass culture and installing a cultural divide that would be both reinforced and challenged throughout the twentieth century. As an alternative to popular cinema, a number of leftist intellectuals proposed a *cinéma pur* to protect art from its predatory "other," and to secure the distinct nature of art as opposed to entertainment. They, in effect, attributed the dictates of authenticity and superiority to art as opposed to culture for mass consumption, that is, for profit. Underlying the assumptions about art and mass culture that these reviews of *The Blue Angel* convey is a concept of Germanness deeply rooted in notions of high culture and education (*Bildung*) as cultivated by the Enlightenment and borne by the educated middle class (*Bildungsbürgertum*).

To begin exploration into the relationship between the arts—that is, culture and the concept of the German nation—is to start with the rise of bourgeois society (*Bildungsbürgertum*) during the eighteenth century; with the rise of a class that was excluded from the spheres of the aristocracy and their absolutist power, and, in concert with Enlightenment ideals, establishment of a private sphere of civil society focused on the family and the greater, albeit homogeneous, community. Access to education during this period reflected the increased wealth and significance of this class, with education viewed as a means to empower the individual, if not politically then morally and intellectually. The path toward enlightenment was through *Bildung*, a term denoting education and self-cultivation (but also culture and breeding) derived from the verb *bilden*, to shape or form. Beginning with the weakening of the aristocracy, the *Bildungsbürger* were the non-aristocratic producers, consumers, and patrons of the arts. High art served to establish a critical public sphere and a community of like-minded citizens with common "taste," and to fortify an identity apart from the corrupt nobility. Culture enabled the middle class to empower itself as aristocrats of the spirit to rule, or at least to administer in limited capacities. This refined, educated elite was arbiter of opinion and cultural debate, enjoying cultural authority and shared ideals that were believed to be linked to a common identity and German mission. For the new bourgeoisie (scholars, businessmen, and the educated—that is, the literate middle class), art and music, in addition to providing meaningful entertainment, provided both an empowering sense of moral superiority and moral orientation and a cultural identity to substitute for a lacking national identity. In this vein, as Georg Bollenbeck contends, "The arts not only functioned as a demonstration of one's own learnedness, they also testified to a 'German greatness,' as Schiller, one of the more significant prompters, expressed it—originally to a national or cultural greatness, invoked repeatedly, both to compensate for the enduring lack of a nation-state and to promote its realization."[22]

Adorno's concept of traditional culture provides an idea of the contours of this Germanness. In contrast and closely associated with modernity and Americanism, mass culture, which for the most part meant cinema, was perceived by cultural conservatives as a foreign import that compromised "true" German values. Others saw mass culture as undermining the goals of *Bildung*. Referring to intellectuals of various political persuasions, Patrice Petro observes: "Many German artists and intellectuals directed their attack against the cinema by way of an attack on the U.S. film, that form of cinematic representation not only emblematic of mass industrial culture, but also most threatening to the maintenance of a uniquely German cultural heritage."[23] There is a particular irony then in von Sternberg coming to Berlin, himself an "American" import from Hollywood, to bring with him the technology of the sound film and the tools of mass culture to transform a German novel of great social and literary value into film and "creating" one of Germany's most renown cultural icons.

Given the vitality and complexity of the cultural debates that profoundly shaped the Weimar Republic and that persist today, it is curious that scholars and critics have failed to investigate the significant ways in which *The Blue Angel* participates in these debates, which, as I mention above, the film reviews symptomatically reproduce. In contrast to Kracauer's assessment that *The Blue Angel* offers "a distorted image of the German way of thinking <*Denkart*>," I wish to show that the film strikes at the very heart of a way of thinking about culture that was cultivated in Germany before and long after becoming a nation.[24] The conflict between mass culture and high or national culture surface, above all, in the relationship between Lola and Rath, in the institutions they represent, in the spaces they inhabit, in Rath's displacement and in Lola's rise to stardom. Furthermore, it surfaces in the intertextual structure of the film, and even in the choreography of sound, which I discuss in Chapter 4. However much the film may conceal about the social realities of the Weimar Republic, the desperate years of economic instability and political turmoil (a point I will return to later), at a deeper level it reveals as much or more about the transformation brought by sweeping technological advances, by urban development, by changing gender roles arising from new employment opportunities, and by the emergence of a vibrant mass culture that transformed both the private and public sphere and, with them, ways of experiencing and seeing the world.

Thus, when critics ask how German is *The Blue Angel*, they call for placing the film into a historical trajectory that addresses a dense network of discourses specific to its national context. Gertrud Koch (in 1986) sees the film's greater success in Germany than abroad as a sign of its Germanness. She looks for evidence of its Germanness in the contradictions that inevitably arise in a production authored and directed by an Austrian-born American and filmed by a team of Germans who were experiencing Germany's violent political turmoil and the increasing popularity of the right (especially those who were involved in Berlin's liberal cabaret scene). Presumably, German film audiences were more knowledgeable about the opposing character types and social milieus that Rath and Lola represented, as well as the risk that Rath ran when these collided.[25] Commenting on *The Blue Angel*, filmmaker Sanders-Brahms (in 2000) suggests: "The pain of a failed school teacher is more difficult for US audiences to relate to than German audiences."[26] Equally interested in identifying the film's Germanness, Richard McCormick highlights its indebtedness to cinematic styles that characteristically bear the Ufa signature under Erich Pommer, and which range from German expressionism to the street film genre.[27] An avid fan of early German cinema, von Sternberg makes extensive use of expressionism's shadows in his favored *mise en scène* of dark, menacing, labyrinthine cobblestone streets, which art director and set designer Otto Hunte claimed von Sternberg was loath to tear down. *The Blue Angel* also references the classic street film plot of an unsuspecting bourgeois male who ventures onto the street and falls prey to a sexualized female, as happens in Karl Grune's *The Street* (1924), in Bruno Rahn's *The Tragedy of a Prostitute* (1926), starring Asta Nielsen as an aging prostitute, or in Joe May's *Asphalt* (1929), featuring the German-American actress Betty Amann as a jewel thief. *The Blue Angel* cites as well the traditions of the *Kammerspielfilm* (chamber film drama), a subgenre of melodramas known for its intimate, closed settings and psychologically nuanced acting. Dietrich's idol, the German actress Henny Porten, starred in a number of early melodramas of this type.

While one can derive *The Blue Angel*'s Germanness from the stylistic traditions of Weimar cinema or from its more enthusiastic reception at "home," an entirely different response is possible when the film is placed into the context of debates on high and mass culture in the interwar years. Indeed, Dietrich's supersensual presence in the film, produced by the focus on her body, legs and voice, which unmask Rath's inadequacies, may explain critics' blindness to the larger cultural struggle that the film stages, and which the sexualized body conceals or displaces, and that many critics stop short of naming. At stake is a sense of traditional Germanness, which lies at the very heart of the narrative when mass culture, setting on a small German community and disrupting its internal working, snares one of the town's respectable citizens, an educator and representative of Germany's cultural traditions, who abandons himself (for better or worse) to mass culture's allure.

The development of mass culture in Germany brought about new forms of experience and perception that challenged traditional notions of subjectivity, expanding the experience of time and space, as well as of the cultural repertoire and social identities. Walter Benjamin's epigraphic observation on cinema captures the dramatic change that occurred when moving pictures burst onto the scene of modernity, liberating its social actors from the confines of their limited worlds. "The film," he proposed, "is the art form that is in keeping with the increased threat to his life which modern man has to face. ... The film corresponds to profound changes in the apperceptive apparatus—changes that are experienced on an individual scale by the man in the street in big-city traffic, on a historical scale by every present-day citizen."[28] If film best captured and resembled modernity's pace and experience, then it simultaneously challenged institutions such as literature and theater to reinvent themselves.[29] *The Blue Angel*, then, raises additional questions about the profound changes to the perceptual apparatus brought about by mass culture, specifically the cinema, first by silent film and then by sound film. It raises questions of perception and the new dispositions associated with the Weimar Republic, which are linked to an epistemic crisis that impacted notions of culture.

Given the apparent antagonism between high (that is, national) culture and mass culture, each deeply implicated in definitions of art, class, and gender, it may seem somewhat ironic that von Sternberg liberally loads *The Blue Angel* with intertextual references to classical texts and "mines" high culture to create a complex layering of citations that the text incorporates and transforms. He places *The Blue Angel* into a lineage of past and present works of art and, as a result, raises the stakes of the cultural "war" in his pairing of Lola and Rath and in his near irreverent evocation of "high" or "serious" culture texts, and thus challenges its boundaries and any facile polarities. He references Greek mythology, Wagnerian opera, Shakespearean drama, and Roman history, just to mention a few. Perhaps the Austrian-born von Sternberg who returned to Europe from Hollywood wanted to battle his own demons produced by the years he spent under the tutelage of strict educators in his native Vienna. Be that as it may, von Sternberg's intertextual ensemble bespeaks an ambition to become partner to the realm of high culture, since it seems that the popular is always aware of its status as second-class citizen when measured against its privileged and lauded better other. In more ways than one, Lola's and the magician Kiepert's wish to call themselves "artists" resonates with the director's desire to ennoble his own profession and product.[30] Notably, no other von Sternberg film relies as heavily on intertextual references to create a narrative of counterpoints as does *The Blue Angel*.

In light of the film's allusion to the embattled definitions of culture during the Weimar Republic, it is no wonder that Andrew Sarris (1966) perceives *The Blue Angel* as von Sternberg's most violent film. Violence erupts from the collision of irreconcilably conflicting spheres of experience, interests and ways of knowing: the "demands" of a national identity rooted in traditional concepts of culture and the "seductions" of popular entertainment and modernity. These divergent spheres are conveyed in various ways that range from Rath's and Lola's class backgrounds as expressed through language, Rath speaking in a refined high German and Lola in a Berlin vernacular dialect, to Jannings's and Dietrich's different acting styles, with Jannings employing an exaggerated, emotionalized theatrical delivery to impart a sense of the vulnerable and sentimental, and Dietrich playing the detached, cool entertainer and modern type, a product of the New Objectivity.[31] Dietrich's understated acting style largely reflects the post-World War I generation's skepticism of what Béla Balász calls "the forms of expression brought along from the feudal and old-fashioned bourgeois ways of thinking."[32]

So, although Sarris astutely identifies the underlying mood of the film, he oversimplifies the cause for conflict, when he asserts, "<von Sternberg> felt that the conflict between order and nature would be more violent in a German setting than in any other."[33] Relying on the terms "nature" and "order," Sarris evokes the conventional dichotomy of female as nature and male as order, effectively dismissing the film's more complicated commentary on the late 1920s, and its reluctance to reestablish Rath's authority, that is order, at the end. That said, Sarris correctly locates the film's violence within the arena of gender, which, as discourses on the modern woman during the Weimar Republic illustrate, more often than not stands in for a myriad of issues related to social upheaval. Gender becomes a symbol for the larger social and historical changes that modernity demanded, and which were either welcomed or resisted. More specifically, *The Blue Angel* employs gender both to assert cinema as a new art form and to work through the anxieties occasioned by the prospect of losing German identity, an identity as much a product of *Volkslieder* as of *Bildung* in the vortex of American mass culture.

To be sure, as Patrice Petro notes, "it is remarkable how theoretical discussions of art and mass culture are almost always accompanied by gendered metaphors that link 'feminine' values of consumption, passivity, and distraction with mass culture."[34] In numerous renditions, mass culture is turned into the other in order to secure the position of (masculine) high art—the realm of production as opposed to reproduction. Put differently, mass culture is the monstrous or uncanny underside of high culture and, as John Storey writes, "it is seen as the dangerous shadow which haunts and tempts the progress of the real thing," playing off the bourgeois fear of mass culture's predatory potential.[35] In its worst manifestation, mass culture is seen as undermining the life of high culture. At the base of such designations is a valuation of culture as superior and inferior: culture that appeals to the mind and culture that appeals to raw, basic instinct. Given these designations, the conflation of women with mass culture is easily traced to women's position in the social order and the value attributed to the spheres they inhabit. The conflation of mass culture and gender also results from the commodification of the female image and women's role as consumers and vulnerable spectators. While *The Blue Angel* develops and plays with both of these female roles (Lola on stage and the opening scene of the female worker), it establishes a more complex, antagonistic relationship between the mutually reinforcing modalities of mass culture (films, advertisements, and variety shows) and notions of bourgeois high culture. Thus, at the risk of conjuring up old ghosts, I would like draw on the terms familiar to cultural theory and place *The Blue Angel* into larger ways of thinking about mass culture at the twilight of the Weimar Republic.

## Cinema—the Arena of Illicit Sensations

Since *The Blue Angel* evokes the complexities of a debate that throughout the twentieth century involved the relationship of literature and cinema, art and mass culture, and cinema's struggle to gain legitimacy, it is critical at this point to examine initial reactions to the cinema in Germany before it became an accepted, even a respected, form of entertainment, a work of art in its own right. It is necessary to reflect on the cultural debates that accompanied cinema's emergence because they serve as a barometer for the pressures that national identity, class identity, and culture faced during the Weimar Republic. More significant for my purposes, such examination sheds light on the powerful subtexts that structure *The Blue Angel*. Even though the cinema had become the most popular form of public entertainment by the 1920s, it is well known that its beginnings met with resistance that sparked wide-ranging public debates in Germany as to cinema's virtues and vices. First and foremost, early cinema was associated with amusement parks and seen as a form of cheap entertainment for the urban working class. It was associated with music or dance halls and nickelodeons that packed in large numbers of thrill seekers to distract the experience-starved working masses from the drudgery of daily life. Dubbing cinema "The Theater of the Little People" in 1913, Alfred Döblin describes its clientele: "Asthmatic children breathe shallowly and shake quietly with an evening fever; the eyes of foul-smelling workers pop out of their sockets, women with musty clothes and prostitutes with heavy makeup." He ends his essay with: "The highly educated leave the movie theater, happy that the cinema … is silent."[36]

The emergence of cinema marked a break between a more rarefied nineteenth-century concept of culture and the aesthetic adventures of modernity and a culture industry. Members of the educated middle class

(*Bildungsbürgertum*) thus reacted with uncertainty toward the new medium, viewing it, at first, as crude and offensive. Their sympathies were predominantly with the past, and with the "civilized" literate life that lent stature to their class and set them apart from the populace. For them, art was the product of a higher intellect, and it demanded an educated audience in order to properly appreciate the evocations of the sublime and genius. In contrast, popular culture was seen as appealing to the more basic human instincts, the inferior and uncontrolled sensations of the body.[37] Jörg Schweinitz notes: "What counted was the intellect's activity in the appropriation of artistic material, fantasy, empathy and illusion. Sensuality, in contrast, received little attention in this sphere, unless it served in reduced and in well measured quantities 'a higher purpose' of contemplation, of immersion in the ideal."[38] The identification with such high cultural ideals became ever more existential with the threat of eroding class boundaries during the Weimar Republic—through industrialization, increased social mobility, and Weimar's unstable economy, and a new way of life. Emanating from such battle cries against cinema was a deep misgiving of egalitarianism, a discomfort with Germany's new democracy and a mistrust of the emerging working class. Movie theaters invited its audiences to shed their identity and enter the liminal space of unlimited possibilities.

Among cinema's staunchest opponents early on were those who feared the inevitable temptation to break social taboos in dark movie theaters, hidden from society's watchful eye.[39] The physical space of the cinema thus became associated with sexual transgression, reinforced by sensational narratives that relied on images of adultery, prostitution, and seduction to arouse and overstimulate the senses. And if that were not enough, reformers decried the power of moving pictures to hypnotically transfix spectators, to lead them down the path of addiction, disease, and emotional and spiritual corruption. Besides worrying about cinema compromising the moral fiber of German society in general, teachers in particular expressed concern about the impact of movies on young sensibilities. Sabine Hake quotes one such teacher as asking: "Are we producing a generation of movie-children who will be superficial, lazy, fussy, and too spoiled to work?"[40] With the establishment of cinema and its exorcism unthinkable, reformers made a case for censorship to protect the nation's youth.[41] Concerns with cinema's effect on the masses, with the quality of its narratives, and with its impact on German culture were heard outside of the reform movement, not least among the educated middle class and intellectuals.

Even though film culture by the early 1910s had become an integral part of daily life, restructuring the physical as well as the psychic landscape, the relationship of the masses and culture writ large remained incompatible, if not outright adversarial. Critic and architect Adolf Behne succinctly identifies the intense antagonism between art and the masses:

"There is only one way to describe the relationship between the multitude and art for the European: hatred."[42] Thomas Mann, a passionate filmgoer and icon of the educated middle class, succinctly summed up the ambivalence that many intellectuals felt toward the cinema: "I despise it myself—but I love it too."[43] He refused to entertain the notion of film as art, calling it "a way of life" (*eine "Lebenserscheinung"*), and drew clear distinctions between the two cultural spheres; "<film> is life and reality, and its effect lies in its moving muteness, crudely sensational compared to the intellectual effects of art."[44] Although the cultural elite tolerated and even enjoyed films, they were not about to award the cinema its rightful place among the muses of culture. On the contrary, they tenaciously upheld their notion of difference (and superiority), guarding the boundaries of class, tradition, and taste, and protecting themselves against the dissolution of "their" cultural sphere.

Inasmuch as the cultural elite during the Weimar Republic frowned on the standardization and trivialization of culture through film, there is more at stake in the attitude toward mass culture, as *The Blue Angel* shows, than mere aesthetic judgment, matters of "taste," or the belief in the values of the Enlightenment. At the root of such valuations discerning between mass culture and art are issues of class, gender, and national identity, and also notions of the individual subject as opposed to the masses.[45] When vested interests in social status are intertwined with definitions of art and artifact, these distinctions are differently appraised. In his essay exploring the association between class distinctions and the various means of cultural consumption and appropriation, Pierre Bourdieu perceptively reminds us that "art and cultural consumption are predisposed, consciously and deliberately or not, to fulfill a social function of legitimating social differences."[46] The presumption that standards of taste, aesthetic judgment, and value are a function of class and education in part explains the great divide between high art and popular culture and the interests invested in this gap. It also explains the "efforts <in the 1920s> by film reformers, censors and champions of film art to preserve bourgeois cultural hegemony and inherited artistic values," as Thomas Saunders notes, "<which> reinforced the tendency for cinema to fracture along class lines."[47] Even so, the cultural elite was not immune to the pressures of the new medium and modernity, which forced them to redefine themselves according to the changing cultural landscape. With the introduction of mass culture, the institutions of art, literature, and theater had to take into account the changing values of culture and to reassess their cultural place and purpose. Thus what was considered at the margins and outside the domain of "legitimate" culture took center stage in *The Blue Angel*.

Emerging at a time when rapid social and cultural changes challenged traditional bourgeois values and notions of culture, cinema effected a reevaluation of cultural norms. In response to modernity's malcontents who forecasted the decline of civilization and a culture of reading, Hans Siemsen defined cinema as the *"Biblia pauperum* of our time."[48] Similarly, Behne, who enthusiastically endorsed cinema in 1926 as a democratizing force, declared the end of a tyrannical elitist culture that discredited the populace. "The book," he professed, "or the possession of a book was an attribute of a class. The public is no longer interested in books. But it sits evening after evening in front of the modern book and learns to see, think and feel through film—the book that millions read and no one 'possesses.'"[49] Behne astutely acknowledged cinema's new "reading public," and a new form of literacy that Weimar visual culture required. While cinema's advocates applauded the new medium's potential for the dissemination of texts (Behne called Edison "the new Gutenberg"), the fear that film would displace literature and theater provoked ongoing attempts to reformulate the properties of the various media and solidify their unique qualities.

The introduction of sound further strained the relationship between mass culture and serious culture and between literature, that is, theater, and film. In order to dignify sound film and produce quality dialog, producers like Erich Pommer recognized the growing need to enlist well-known authors and establish a new working relationship between authors and filmmakers despite the perception that sound would compromise the artistic potential of silent film and jeopardize the innovative breakthrough that silent film had achieved. A commentary in the conservative magazine *Kunstwart* on the employment of authors as scriptwriters for *The Blue Angel* shows that this new union between literature and drama, on the one hand, and film, on the other, much like the marriage between Lola and Rath, aroused deep suspicion: "When the Ufa gets literary, it takes at least three authors for one film."[50] Implied in this quip is that despite the deployment of an ensemble of reputable authors such as Robert Liebmann, Karl Vollmoeller, and Carl Zuckmayer, the film culture industry could only attempt to emulate the quality literature inherently possessed. At the same time, there was a sense of promiscuity associated with the production of sound film in its need for a multi-authored text in order to achieve its creative outcome, in contrast to the singular (monogamous) relationship between author and text that art demanded.

Fearing that he may have compromised his reputation as novelist, Carl Zuckmayer, who participated in writing the screenplay of *The Blue Angel*, sought to distance himself from the production of *The Blue Angel*. "Shortly before the premier he <Zuckmayer> quickly wrote a feuilleton in which he assured, 'that no one actually knows which idea, which turn of phrase or transition belonged to whom.'"[51] After the film's success, however, individual members of the scriptwriting team alleged authorship with von Sternberg, who resolutely claimed his role as sole creator. While the various versions of the script, along with Zuckmayer's novella, attest to the participation of various authors, their exact contribution, as

Zuckmayer initially contended, remains indistinguishable.⁵² Nevertheless, *The Blue Angel* indisputably bears the director's personal signature, not only in his use of light, shadow, composition, texture, and mood, but in his construction of Lola, an icon of mass entertainment, who challenges the despotic notion of culture that Behne criticizes.

## The Blue Angel

In numerous films made during the Weimar Republic, the allure and the vicissitudes of modernity (often embodied by the female) are typically played out in an urban setting. In *The Blue Angel*, the conflict is displaced onto the provinces when a traveling cabaret troupe featuring the irresistible performer Lola Lola descends on a quiet Hanseatic harbor town. In contrast to the representations of urban areas, which was the stage for many backstreet dramas, the provincial town represents the heart of Germany (and Rath), still to be vanquished by modernity, this time too embodied in the female character. Mass culture, feminized, sexualized, and commercial, alights on the "organic," harmonious, and repetitive rhythms of a town characterized by a market woman placing her squawking geese into a cart. A young, working-class woman raises a shutter to reveal a display window with the Ufa insignia, which fades into a poster advertisement of Lola Lola, thus inscribing the female image and, more importantly, securing her cinematic identity. Opening like a curtain to reveal the world of cabaret and popular entertainment, the shutter evokes the kinship between the cabaret and cinema. Thus is the practice of seeing and consuming the female image—that is, visual mass culture— privileged at the beginning of the film.

The poster shows Lola with her head tilted to one side, legs spread apart, and her hands planted on her hips. The stiff petticoat she wears tilts upward to reveal the top of her stocking and the space between her stocking and thighs. A cupid is wrapped around her left leg and the inscription "Lola Lola" adorns her right leg. Lola's provocative and spirited pose is open and inviting. The image evokes the realm of the imaginary in which wishes and libidinal desires are mirrored and reflected back to the spectator; it capitalizes on the unconscious processes of identity formation and alludes to the psychoanalytical properties of cinema spectatorship—a complex relationship of infusing the image with desire. Lola's alliance with the realm of mass culture in her role as a cabaret performer in a working-class milieu calls to mind cinema's origin in a long tradition of popular cultural venues (fairground, magic shows, and cabarets). Indeed, the most popular form of urban entertainment before the arrival of film, cabaret, with its presentation of short skits, song and dance, reflected modernity's fast pace, and appealed to urban sensibilities accustomed to heightened sensory stimuli, temporal fragmentation, and a feeling of excitement or nervousness characteristic of modern life. Notably, many members of *The Blue Angel* cast and crew, like Rosa Valetti, who plays Guste, and Kurt Gerron, who plays the magician Kiepert, had long-standing careers in cabaret, as did the composer Friedrich Hollaender, along with one of Berlin's leading jazz bands the Weintraub-Syncopators, which sit in the orchestra pit in von Sternberg's film.

Once Lola's identity and cultural context, and the slippage between her identity as image and stage presence, have been established through the poster advertisement in the opening of the film, the scene moves from the streets to the interior corridor of a boarding house. The camera travels up the stairs and alights on the plaque bearing the name and title of the provincial high school teacher, "Dr. Imm. Rath." Powerfully contrasted with the corporality of the image and its culture, the culture and authority of the word is privileged in this realm.[53] Indeed, the writing on the plaque defines Rath's social position and aligns him with paternal law and institutional authority. As we shall see, however, Immanuel Rath is a relic of the nineteenth century in habit and costume, an anachronism (as well as a commonplace) in the heyday of the Weimar Republic. Tightly framed (and restrained) when he sits down to breakfast by shelves of books and a globe, the symbols of his trade, he represents notions of *Bildung* rooted in humanistic ideals and a notion of *Kultur* based on a tradition of the autonomous work of art, which had been one of the pillars of bourgeois cultural hegemony since the mid-nineteenth century. The assumptions that this *mise en scène* evokes can be read in a 1930 review of the film: "That he is a voracious reader is understood through the fact that the walls of his den are lined with books. One can readily imagine that he spends his evenings and holidays pouring over the volumes."[54]

Yet, as can be deduced from a contemporaneous article on the state of the new generation and the educational system, which places Rath at odds with his time, his identity already rests on precarious ground, owing to the status of the word vis-à-vis the image and the pressures of modernity. In addition to the generational conflict between Rath and his students, a definition of culture is at stake, which can be gleaned from a 1929 essay entitled "Die Not des Literaturunterrichts in der grossstädtischen Schule" (The crisis of the study of literature in urban schools). Its author, Walter Schönbrunn, bemoans the loss of the "treasures of German literature" and lists external reasons for fading interest in Germany's classical texts. (Understandably, in order to address an international audience von Sternberg substitutes English-language classics for Friedrich Schiller's 1801 drama *Die Jungfrau von Orléans*, a staple of the German curriculum.) While the more comprehensive "modern" curriculum (art history, speech, and sports) had significantly detracted from teaching literature, the true culprit of the lack of interest in the classics is "the new spirit of today's youth," which Schönbrunn accuses of being "unromantic, untraditional and unsentimental." As a result, "the heartfelt petit bourgeois cozy and sentimental attitude of the last century finds no mercy." He specifically cites *Heimat* authors (Storm, Raabe, and Reuter) among those no longer appreciated or understood and regrets the passing of a literary canon that reflected a pre-World War I generation's "spirit."

Notably, Schönbrunn blames the blatant rejection of his generation's prized literature on modernity's changed sexual mores and sensibilities. Of particular significance is the role he attributes to the modern girl in his apocalyptic account of the state of German education. Her more libertine sexual attitude threatens traditional cultural values, and even imperils epistemologically the ability to understand the classical narratives of sexual transgression such as Gretchen's seduction in Goethe's *Faust*, a narrative that is celebrated as an integral part of Germany's cultural heritage and German identity. Thus, the altered sense of eroticism and the new sensibility and morality, in Schönbrunn's words, "undermines the interest and understanding of earlier literature, which stood at the center of the German middle class. The Gretchen tragedy is pallid."[55] Indeed, writing one year before the premiere of *The Blue Angel*, Schönbrunn breathes a sigh of relief that outlying provinces, namely small towns, in contrast to urban areas have been spared the high price of modernity.

Yet Rath, as we know, is not spared. Despite the prestige of his professional standing, the state of his living quarters suggests that the terms of his identity and the culture he represents are already distressed. The *mise en scène* alludes to obsolescence rather than patriarchal mastery. The room is cluttered and claustrophobic; the books and the globe, the icons of knowledge and worldliness that decorate his sphere, seem musty and neglected. Even the housekeeper who brings in his breakfast complains about a stench in the room ("alles verpestet"). Moreover, Rath's repressed body language, his tight movements, clenched fists and the performance of his daily rituals convey a life pent up and stifled by pedantry. When he enters the room for breakfast, the visual weight of the stovepipe that runs across the ceiling just above his head further diminishes his stature, both psychologically and socially. And with the death of the caged bird, the absence of life (potency) in his surroundings is symbolically underscored.

As an apostle of high culture—literature and history being the instruments of humanist and therefore "universal" knowledge—Rath naturally subscribes to the classical traditions: history as a *grand récit* (Julius Caesar) and the literary canon (Shakespeare). His classroom is the arena of high culture, where bourgeois practices and cultural elitism are rehearsed in the service of training honorable German citizens. Yet, one can sense the fragility of Rath's authority within the classroom even in the routine with which he begins the class, demonstratively blowing his nose and superciliously surveying his students. His ungainly posture and the repetition of the line "to be or not to be" from Shakespeare's *Hamlet*, along with the malleability of his name, the slippage from Rath to Unrat (rubbish or refuse), reflect his vulnerability and question the very foundation of his identity.

Rather than strengthen their moral character, as the principles of the Enlightenment intended, Rath deploys the curriculum to impose the will of the institution on his students; wielding his black notebook like a tyrant, he checks off his students' infractions with sadistic pleasure. When Rath forces a pencil between a student's teeth to improve his pronunciation of the English "th," he literally assaults the learner. Leavening the violence of Rath's pedagogical approach is the comical interplay between teacher and student in their attempts to reproduce the English "the." The implicit critique of his traditional approach resonates with cultural liberal assertions of the time that traditional pedagogy was no longer relevant to the everyday needs of the Weimar Republic and that educational reform was urgently needed (a point raised to great effect in Leontine Sagan's 1931 film *Girls in Uniform*).

Even though Rath's identity as a teacher aligns him with a prescriptive canon, it would be amiss to place Rath solely on the side of highbrow German culture. A line from Ludwig Hölty's poem "Üb immer Treu' und Redlichkeit" (Always practice loyalty and honesty) and snippets of folk music additionally delineate his cultural and religious bearings. This point was not lost on Weimar's attuned film critic Kracauer, who stated that "an old church-clock chimes a popular German tune to the praise of loyalty and honesty," is "expressive of Jannings's <Rath's> inherited beliefs." These beliefs will be sorely tested by the power of visual mass culture and the modern woman. Just as the poster advertisement intruding on the town attracts and captivates the eye of the viewer, so do the postcard images of Lola that Rath's students smuggle into the classroom set in motion the temptation and downfall of Rath and the cultural values he represents.

Thus, when Rath strays from the path by acquiescing to the popular, he performs a series of betrayals to his class, to his calling, and, by extension, to his nation. Lola and Rath's misalliance exceeds sexual transgression. It violates the boundaries of class integrally linked to notions of art, culture, and national identity. Unlike most bourgeois sons in street films who leave the sanctioned path and seek penance when they recognize their moral failure, Rath never returns to the fold. His journey into an unfamiliar world of sensual and bodily pleasures takes him down a treacherous, sexualized street marked by two prostitutes, one standing in the shadows and another leaning on the window ledge, both watching him negotiate the expressionist scene (indeed, jagged lines of the sets designed by Otto Hunte and Emil Hasler evoke the expressionist paintings of George Grosz and Max Beckmann or the dangerous streets that Caligari walked in Robert Wiene's 1919 film *The Cabinet of Dr.*

*Caligari*). Neither the policeman standing in front of Lola's poster the first time, nor the foghorns, the second warning against shipwreck, can forestall him on his way to the nightclub. Judith Mayne observes that "his journey is one fraught with obstacles, suggesting an enormous psychic and social distance between his world and that of the cabaret."[56] He cannot decipher the signs at the gates of this "terra incognita."

Rath's first visit to "The Blue Angel," ostensibly to catch his delinquent students there, parallels the reformers' strident attempts to protect Germany's youth from the harmful effects of cinema and popular entertainment.[57] Yet Rath is drawn back to the club a second time, this time unambiguously interested in the performer, as though to confirm the addictive nature of mass culture. After visiting Lola backstage, he is invited to the theater loge, located both physically and symbolically above the general audience, to delight in Lola's performance; indeed, he is seduced by this icon of popular culture when she addresses him with her theme song, "Falling in Love Again." Silently commenting on the disparity and tension between Lola and Rath and on the space that both joins and separates them, the camera follows the clown's gaze from Lola to the balcony above. As though returning the clown's expressionless gaze (establishing a connection between Rath and the clown), Rath looks down, only to notice the figurehead of a naked woman that adorns the balcony pillar, and from which he quickly averts his eyes.

But before Lola openly engages and entrances him, Kiepert, the show's manager and magician (played by Kurt Gerron) proudly introduces Rath as the professor at the local high school and as Kiepert's guest of honor to the working-class audience. Out of place, both figuratively and literally, Rath's presence is used to transform the social space and lend respectability to the entire theatrical enterprise, of which Lola is only a small part. Kiepert promotes the liaison between Lola and Rath, in an attempt to forge a union between mass culture and art and between *Kunst und Wissenschaft* (science). The uncanny doubling of Rath and Kiepert at the beginning of the film through their stature and attire, black cape and top hat, places the two representatives of disparate cultural spheres in such curious proximity that it emphasizes the paradox of similarity and difference. In other words, an "othering" takes place that at once suggests a dichotomous relationship and an interdependence that replicates the relationship between literature and film and popular and high culture. Although an association with the professor promises to lend status to the traveling cabaret troupe, Rath's fragile existence in the world of entertainment becomes a study in downward mobility.

Indeed, Kiepert's interest in Rath reflects an attempt to ennoble the social institution of popular culture and its related art forms. Judith Mayne even contends that the "real" conflict in *The Blue Angel* is located in the relationship between the two characters, Rath and Kiepert. Similarly, Lola aspires to lend her performance the prestige of "serious"

**Figure 1.1** "I am an artist." Still from *Der blaue Engel*, 1930, directed by Josef von Sternberg. Source: *Deutsche Kinemathek*.

art and reinvent herself after her introduction to Rath by calling herself an artist. "Why should I care? I am an artist <Ich bin Künstlerin,"> she haughtily replies when Kiepert enjoins her in front of Rath to drink champagne with the merchant marine who has paid for her company backstage (see Figure 1.1).

Unimpressed, Kiepert puts Lola in her place: "What do you say to that. She has a peculiar concept of her profession." In response, Rath demands that the captain leave the premises and slaps Kiepert for presuming that Lola is "for sale." Evoking the bourgeois code of honor and displaying refined, cultured masculinity, Rath paternalistically steps in—even the captain mistakenly calls him "father." Rath, who typically is aligned with the law ("I have nothing to fear from authority"), is asked to hide when a policeman appears on the scene. Rather than maintain his position of authority, Rath complies with Kiepert's request and enters the cellar through the trapdoor where his students have been hiding. In doing so, Rath becomes complicit with the economy of the popular. Moreover, the descent into the cellar prefigures his fall.

The misalliance between Rath and Lola, despite Rath's attempt to legitimize their relationship through marriage, brings about his dismissal from school and the eventual disintegration of his identity. Once a chivalrous protector of Lola and her image, his acquiescence to her lifestyle reduces him to selling the image of Lola he so prized. He thus capitulates to the utilitarian logic of mass culture, according to which the value of the image lies in its marketability and its reproducibility. The image becomes the source of both his livelihood and his death. As audiences stop purchasing the postcards, Rath defensively derides them as having no taste. His utterance engages an idiom that has no meaning in the world of mass culture associated with the popular and with kitsch. He evokes the modes of valuation familiar to bourgeois culture, in which taste, as Pierre Bourdieu reminds us, is based on the refined, distinguished experience of pleasure forever closed to the profane.[58] The cinema audience's more discriminating taste, however, may reflect a more successful assimilation of mass culture into middle-class culture, as can be seen in Lola's later performance in which she wears a long gown and is accompanied by a female dance troupe reminiscent of the Tiller girls, who were known for their high-kicking synchronized dance and who became synonymous with a mechanized modernity. The proliferation of mass cultural venues, the abundance of movie theaters, stage shows, cabarets, amusement parks, as well as the production of a wide range of periodicals and introduction of radio, arguably cultivated a more demanding audience. Mass entertainment provided distractions from the drudgeries of daily life and transformed both the public and private spheres. In Berlin alone, the number of movie theaters mushroomed, with a total of 148,000 seats by 1921, and 189,000 seats by 1932, thanks to new, larger movie theaters with a seating capacity of 1,000.[59]

When the show returns to Rath's provincial hometown, he is featured as its main attraction—its tarnished star. A banner announcing the arrival of "the professor" pasted across Lola's body on the poster effectively displaces her. Rath reluctantly prepares for the show, applying clown make-up in a mirror. His mute stare reveals an inner disintegration, which culminates in an emotional breakdown in the course of his performance. This time, former students and colleagues, members of the learned middle class, attend the show, presumably aware of the boundary they are crossing and indirectly seeking validation of their own cultural values and social standing by witnessing the fall of one of their own. Rath's appearance only confirms the peril of cultural displacement and of downward mobility, not to mention the danger of surrendering to libidinal desires, and to the realm of the popular and betraying class affiliations. A series of shot/countershots establish and comment on the relationship between the middle-class spectators and Rath. Some protest the unsettling carnivalesque scene of abject humiliation while others applaud in amusement. Arguably, Kiepert, the magician and master of ceremonies, does not seek to humiliate Rath, but rather to use him for entertainment and commercial gain—to practice his "magical art" on the clown August, a comical figure, ironically, taken from Goethe's famous poem *Ein Zauberlehrling*. Although difficult to watch, the scene hardly participates in a critique of the popular, which runs by its own internal rules and truths, to which the magician "innocently" subscribes. Thrilled about the sellout crowd, Kiepert enthusiastically informs Rath before his debut, "This evening will determine your whole career."

The stage, however, transforms into the site of Rath's humiliation when the magician cracks the "laid" eggs on his head and commands Rath to crow like a rooster, a paradoxical proclamation of potency. The scene is humiliating precisely because of Rath's displacement, his impotence and thus feminization. Incapable of identifying with his role or with the milieu, he unwillingly is turned into a spectacle. While the performance itself belongs to the realm of the profane, its tragic, multiply misplaced subject produces an unsightly scene, one of failed masculinity. The final blow occurs during the performance, when Lola flirts with the strongman and escapologist, Mazeppa, (played by the dashing newcomer Hans Albers). Fleeing from the stage and attacking Lola, Rath acts out the role of the jealous Canio, the *Bajazzo* character from Leoncavallo's 1892 opera *I Pagliacci*.[60] Indeed, Lola evokes this image earlier when she explains to Rath: "Anytime I am in a good mood, you have to play the Bajazzo."

When Kiepert frees Rath from the straitjacket that holds together the pieces of his fragmented psyche, he assumes: "All because of a woman. I don't understand. *You are a well-educated man*. Rest for a while. I'll take care of everything." Kiepert interprets Rath's rage as a fit of jealousy, which only partially represents the complexity of Rath's undoing. As Rath steals out of The Blue Angel nightclub, the close-up of his face, magnifying the microscopic facial spasms and the detached look of psychic disintegration, reveals an intimate look at the wreckage of a life. Expressionistic shadows underscore his inner struggle as he retraces his steps through the chiaroscuro, expressionist space of the street that earlier fores*hadowed* his path of destruction. To avoid the dark abyss of the street (the scene recalls the fallen doorman in Friedrich Murnau's 1924 *The Last Laugh*, also a casualty of modernity—an association not altogether accidental since Jannings starred in Murnau's film, and von Sternberg greatly admired the German director), he moves along the wall to retain his bearing. In effect, not only does the expressionist space of the street define its vagrant resident and signify his collapse, but it vividly recalls expressionism, itself an early twentieth-century avant-garde movement whose youthful proponents rebelled against the structures that Rath embodied.

The crosscuts from Rath's dazed flight back to Lola singing and then back again to Rath emphasize the irreconcilable cultural and social divide that separates their two worlds. They have their designated places, which are historically and culturally defined and which neither can successfully transcend. Even though Lola can become a star, she cannot be elevated to the role of the "artist." Her artistry is her deception. And, however burned by modernity's promises, as conveyed through the allure of visual mass culture and the female body, Rath cannot shed his premodern philistine identity.

Seeking solace and safety in his former high school, a symbol of the cultural assumptions that shaped his identity and lent him power and secured his social stature, Rath dies slumped over his desk and clutching it. In the final scene, death is an index of the vulnerability of social and cultural assumptions linked to nineteenth-century notions of *Kultur*, with its inherent modes of perception and experience. The night watchman cannot pry the dead man's fingers from the desk. The camera reverently and silently takes leave, slowly retreating, as it did at the beginning of the film when Rath stood before his class on his own familiar stage.[61] Indeed, the camera movement at the beginning of the film foreshadows Rath's death; it conveys the inevitability of his failure, and, by association, of the broader social and cultural context that defined him. The camera abandons its tragic, archaic, humanist subject—a casualty of modernity and popular culture and a subject wistfully mourned by some critics mentioned before. The penitent professor is denied a happy ending; the narrative withholds the sentimental redemption of bourgeois individuality (while powerfully evoking it aurally) and leaves unresolved the crisis of male vision arising from the emergence of mass culture.[62] Rath's body represents its ambivalent monument.

Contrary to more traditional renderings of damaged masculinity in early German cinema, and particularly in the genre of the street film, which work to contain disruptive sexuality, the sexualized female in *The Blue Angel* goes unpunished. The repetition of the camera's retreat from Rath absolves the self-described "fesche Lola" of the song ("They Call Me Naughty Lola"). While the narrative features Rath as the tragic hero, he appears as a relic; in his return to the school in darkness, there is no sense of nostalgia, no sense of a lost idyll. The camera forsakes him, after focusing on its true object of interest—the starlit Lola, dressed in glimmering sequins. The juxtaposition of these last shots of Rath and Lola epitomize both visually and acoustically the domination of mass culture and the incompatibility of these divergent but mutually dependent cultural spheres. The uninterrupted and steady full shot of Lola, unaltered, unscathed, and unremittingly committed to pleasure, in the scene that precedes Rath's death, indicates the permanence and resilience of cinema, of moving images and sound. Lola appears in a cavalier pose straddling a chair, wearing a carpenter's hat like the one in the poster at the beginning of the film. She is singing the popular theme song "Falling in Love Again."

This time, however, in sharp contrast to earlier performances, she is isolated from her diegetic audience. Elisabeth Bronfen describes the transition from Lola's earlier performance: "The original heterogeneous space of the cabaret, in which the boundary between the performer and spectator was porous is now overcome and substituted by a homogeneously structured theater space, in which she accepts her symbolic mandate to become an international star."[63] With this last(ing) image of Lola, the film celebrates itself and its new technology of sound.

It is no wonder that "what is best-remembered, worldwide, is not the professor's tragedy, but Lola's triumph."[64] Yet, to read this ending in terms of a triumph of mass culture over serious culture would be too reductive an antagonism.[65] Instead, Rath's decline must be read both as a symptomatic breakdown of the cultural norms he embodies and as a paradigmatic shift in perceptual values and modes of reception linked to modernity. The sense of danger that mass culture evokes is tantalizing, rather than apocalyptic. The circulation of images and mass entertainment become the film's "center of value."[66]

*The Blue Angel* was released in the United States only after Dietrich, the newly contracted European Paramount star, had established herself in Hollywood in von Sternberg's 1930 *Morocco*.[67] The cooler image of the femme fatale cabaret singer Amy Jolly in Hollywood's *Morocco* would counterbalance the risqué image of Ufa's Lola. Later on, however, Lola was used to sell Dietrich, as Andrea Slane writes, "after both films were released, a fan card bearing the *Blue Angel* image was distributed in the United States to characterize the star."[68]

*The Blue Angel* survives as evidence of mass culture's power and of the dramatic standoff between mass culture and serious culture, tradition and modernity that was rehearsed obsessively in public discourses during the Weimar Republic. Admittedly, the antagonism between these two valuations of culture has lost its volatility as popular culture and serious culture progressively merge. For the *Bildungsbürger*, however, the pleasures of mass entertainment, and especially the indulgence in Hollywood's fare, while it continues to fascinate, still seems to be mixed with a tinge of bourgeois guilt.

## Notes

1. See Herbert Ihering's September 6, 1929 review of the play in *Von Reinhardt bis Brecht: Vier Jahrzehnte Theater und Film: 1924–1929*, Vol. II (Berlin: Aufbau Verlag, 1959), 425–26. See also Ean Wood, *Dietrich: A Biography* (London: Sanctuary, 2002), 72. Wood claims that the musical was produced with Dietrich in mind. She had a leading role and played a rich American "jazz baby visiting Germany:" "*Two Bow Ties* was for a while the hottest show in Berlin, knocked off the top only by the famous *Three Penny Opera*, which opened a few months later."
2. Marlene Dietrich speaks of her "pygmalionization" in her autobiography. In Rouben Mamoulian's 1933 film *Song of Songs*, Dietrich plays an idealized statue.
3. Andrew Sarris, *The Films of Josef von Sternberg* (New York: Doubleday, 1966), 25. A review in Peter Baxter's *Sternberg* (London: British Film Institute, 1980) is worth quoting: "We have Herman Weinberg's assurance, written in 1932, that *The Blue Angel*'s success in the United States 'was due principally to the presence of the exotic Marlene Dietrich ... and in a lesser, though not unimportant degree to the direction of the American-assimilated Josef von Sternberg, who knew of the enormous reserve of sex-appeal dormant in the hitherto angelic Dietrich with which he pervaded his film'" (6).
4. Quoted in Helma Sanders-Brahms, *Marlene und Jo: Recherche einer Leidenschaft* (Berlin: Argon, 2000), 74 (my translation). "Man ist geradezu überwältigt von Fräulein Dietrichs

Darstellung. Ihre Fähigkeit, ohne grosse Mühe, aber mit schlichter und unumschränkter Autorität Szenen zu dominieren, ist in dieser Form noch nie dagewesen."
5. Kurt Pinthus, *Das Tagebuch*, 11, 14 (May 4, 1930).
6. Kurt Pinthus, *Vössische Zeitung* (April 2, 1930).
7. Peter Baxter, "On the Naked Thighs of Miss Dietrich," *Movies and Methods II*, edited by Bill Nichols (Berkeley: University of California Press, 1985), 557–64.
8. *Völkische Beobachter* 210 (July 29, 1931), 3. The original text reads: "Die glänzende Darstellung eines Spießbürgers verknöcherten, aber grundanständigen Kleinstadtlehrers durch Jannings beispiellose Kunst der Menschenschilderung in Wort und Gebärde darf nicht darüber hinwegtäuschen, dass dieser Film auf eine Reihe grober (aber echt jüdischer) Denkfehler aufgebaut ist, Bruchstellen der Logik, von denen der Jude glaubt, dass der Gojim sie nicht merkt und von der raffiniert ineinander geschachtelten Handlung so umnebelt wird, dass er nicht mehr das jüdische-erotische Denken erkennt, dass den ganzen Film mit seiner zahllosen Schamlosigkeit trägt. Bewusst jüdische Zerstetzung und Beschmützung deutschen Wesens und deutscher Erziehungswerte ist hier am Werk, in dem sich jüdischer Zynismus selten gemein offenbart. Man darf nur den Namen der Macher des Ganzen durchgehen—nichts als Juden mit gällischen Visagen, die als Brechmittel wirken. Selbst in der Klasse, in dem sich der Judenbengel Goldstaub am frechsten benimmt, wird der arisch-blonde Primus als verächtlicher Streber und Feigling hingestellt und lächerlich gemacht. Wir hoffen, dass die gegenwärtiger Lehrertagung die entsprechenden Folgerung zu dieser Art Begrüßung durch einen Judenfilm zieht." ("The dazzling representation of a petite bourgeois, fossilized, but decent small town teacher through Jannings's exemplary ability to portray humanity in word and gesture should not detract from the fact that this film is based on a series of crude (and truly Jewish) flawed reasonings. Breaches of logic that the Jew believes the Goyim will not notice and will be befogged by the sophisticated, interlaced plot, that he no longer recognizes the Jewish erotic thinking, that carries the whole film with its immeasurable shamelessness. A deliberate Jewish destruction and defilement of German being and German educational values are at work here, in which Jewish cynicism banally exposes itself. One only has to go through the names of the contributors—nothing but Jews with Gallic faces that cause one to vomit. Even in the class, where the Jewish urchin Goldstaub behaves the worst, the blond, Aryan Primus is presented as a contemptuous nerd and coward and ridiculed. We hope that the present teachers conference comes to the appropriate conclusion for this kind of welcoming from a Jewish film.") An anti-Semitic caricature in the National Socialist magazine *Die Brennessel* shows Heinrich Mann wearing Dietrich's legs with: "ich bin von Kopf bis Fuss auf Juda eingestellt." See "Zerrbilder als Spiegel der Zeit: MannoMann—eine Karikaturenausstellung im Strauhof," *Neue Züricher Zeitung* (June 12, 2003).
9. Hans Stahl, *Der Montag Morgen* 8, 14 (July 4, 1930).
10. Quoted in Michael Töteberg, "Der blaue Engel," *Ufa Magazin* no. 8, 5 (my translation).
11. Kaes, *Kino-Debatte*, 168. The speech was held at the *Veranstaltung des Volksverbandes für Filmkunst* (meeting of the peoples' association for film art).
12. Heinrich Mann's 1924 essay, "Geistiges Gesellschaftskapital," directly addresses the social changes he perceives: "Of course, society exists now as it always has. It is organized differently now, it functions differently, and has other purposes than it did 10 years ago. Wealth and education are widely separated again, which can happen of course. What should society do with a pre-war humanist education, in which "culture," which was a prerogative that was discussed by a few thousand snobbish bearers of culture, and that never was imparted. That type of culture did not advantage the politicization of the nation but rather hindered it. It worked against the democratization of the nation." ("Eine Gesellschaft gibt es natürlich jetzt wie immer. Jetzt ist sie anders angeordnet, arbeitet anders, hat andere Zwecke als noch vor zehn Jahren. Reichtum und Bildung sind wieder einmal weit auseinandergerückt, was freilich öfter vorgekommen ist. Was sollte ihr &lt;die Gesellschaft&gt; nun die Geistesbildung der Vorkriegszeit, jene

'Kultur,' die ein Vorrecht war, im Munde geführt von wenigen tausend snobistischen 'Kulturträgern,' die sie niemanden mitteilten? Jene Kultur hat die Politisierung der Nation nicht begünstigt, eher mit verhindert, sie war ihrer Demokratisierung entgegen. Damit ist sie gerichtet"). Quoted in Anton Kaes, ed., *Manifeste und Dokumente zur deutschen Literatur, 1918–1933* (Stuttgart: Metzler, 1983), 54. Thomas Mann accused his brother Heinrich Mann of showing hostility toward German culture and of betraying his calling as a writer and moral beacon by aligning himself with the left and with writers who irresponsibly employed their creative genius to promote their political agendas. A great defender of the *Bildungsbürgertum* who initially cautioned against a democracy for Germany, Thomas Mann turned to *Kultur* to advocate for the *Kulturstaat*, in which the state subscribes to the ideals of the Enlightenment. A self-declared cultural conservative, Thomas Mann's support of middle-class culture seemed out of step with the demands of society at large during the 1920s.
13. Erich Pommer, "Erich Pommer zur Hussong-Polemik," *Film-Kurier* (April 1, 1930).
14. See S.S. Prawer, *The Blue Angel (Der Blaue Engel)* (London: British Film Institute, 2002), 12. Heinrich Mann received 25,000 Marks for the film rights and was promised another 10,000 Marks if the film would sell in the United States. See Klaus Kreimeier, *Die Ufa Story: Geschichte eines Filmkonzerns* (Munich: Carl Hanser, 1992), 224. Jannings received 200,000 Marks and Dietrich a paltry 20,000.
15. The position of playwright Bertolt Brecht toward the film studio's understanding of adaptation is less benign: "We have often been told (and the court expressed the same opinion) that when we sold our work to the film industry we gave up all of our rights; the buyers even purchased the right to destroy what they had bought; all further claim was covered by the money. These people felt that in agreeing to deal with the film industry we put ourselves in the position of a man who lets his laundry be washed in a dirty gutter and then complains that it has been ruined. Anybody who advises us not to make use of such a new apparatus just confirms the apparatus's right to do bad work. At the same time he deprives us in advance of the apparatus which we need in order to produce, since this way of producing is likely more and more to supersede the present one." Quoted in Timothy Corrigan, *Film and Literature* (New Jersey: Prentice Hall, 1999), 24.
16. Timothy Corrigan writes that this relationship has "a history of ambivalence, confrontation, and mutual dependence." *Film and Literature*, 1.
17. Anton Kaes, et al. ed., *Weimar Sourcebook* (Berkeley: University of California Press, 1994), 630 (my translation).
18. Miriam Hansen, "Mass Culture as Hieroglyphic Writing: Adorno, Derrida, Kracauer," *The Actuality of Adorno*, edited by Max Pensky (Albany, NY: State University of New York Press, 1997), 98.
19. Siegfried Kracauer, *Das Ornament der Masse*, quoted in Peter Jelavich, *Berlin Cabaret* (Cambridge, MA: Harvard University Press, 1993), 167.
20. Siegfried Kracauer, *"Der blaue Engel," Der verbotener Blick* (Leipzig: Reclam, 1992), 307.
21. Robert Witkin, *Adorno on Popular Culture* (London and New York: Routledge, 2003), 24.
22. Georg Bollenbeck, "German Kultur, the Bildungsbürgertum, and Its Susceptibility to National Socialism," *The German Quarterly* 73 (Winter, 2000), 69. In "German Nationalcharacter," Schiller wrote: "To form a nation, Germans, your hope is of no avail. Instead you can educate yourselves to become a freer people."
23. Patrice Petro, *Aftershocks of the New: Feminism and Film History* (Brunswick, NJ: Rutgers University Press, 2002), 18.
24. Siegfried Kracauer, "Internationaler Tonfilm?" *Der verbotene Blick: Beobachtungen, Analysen, Kritiken* (Leipzig: Reclam, 1992), 322.
25. Gertrud Koch, "Between Two Worlds: Von Sternberg's *The Blue Angel* (1930)," *German Film and Literature*, edited by Eric Rentschler (New York: Methuen, 1986), 60–71.
26. Sanders-Brahms, 68 (my translation).
27. Richard McCormick, *Gender and Sexuality in Weimar Modernity* (New York: Palgrave, 2001), 115.

28. Walter Benjamin, "The Work of Art in the Age of Mechanical Reproduction," *Illuminations*, translated by Harry Zohn (New York: Schocken Books, 1968).
29. Rudolf Arnheim writes in this context about Erwin Piscator's work with film in his theater productions. Rudolf Arnheim, *Film als Kunst* (Frankfurt: Suhrkamp, 2002), 195.
30. "While working as a scenarist and assistant to director Roy Niell on the film *By Divine Right* (1924), the actor Elliott Dexter suggested that Sternberg add a "von" to his name in the credits in order to give the film "artistic prestige." See Herman G. Weinberg, *Josef von Sternberg* (New York: E.P. Dutton and Co., 1967), 18.
31. Herbert Ihering, in his review of *The Blue Angel*, praises Dietrich for her understated acting, calling it a "sensual phlegmatism" that excites viewers, while he criticizes Jannings's acting style as too theatrical, indicating that Jannings regrettably drew on his experience as a stage actor for his part in a talkie. *Berliner Börsen-Courier*, 62, 156 (April 2, 1930).
32. Béla Balász, *Der Geist des Films* (Frankfurt am Main: Suhrkamp, 2001), 10. (First published in 1930).
33. Sarris, 28.
34. Petro, *Aftershocks of the New*, 122. See also Andreas Huyssen, "Mass Culture as Woman," *Studies in Entertainment: Critical Approaches to Mass Culture*, edited by Tania Modleski (Bloomington: Indiana University Press, 1986), 188–207.
35. John Storey, "The Culture and Civilization Tradition," *An Introduction to Cultural Theory and Popular Culture* (Athens, GA: The University of Georgia Press, 1998), 202.
36. Alfred Döblin, "Das Theater der kleinen Leute," *Prolog vor dem Film: Nachdenken über ein neues Medium, 1909–1914*, edited by Jörg Schweinitz (Leipzig: Reclam, 1992), 154 (my translation).
37. Grappling with the question of mass culture, as opposed to "serious" culture, and writing around the same time as *The Blue Angel* was made, Béla Balász locates the extraordinary divide between "intellectual value" (*"geistiger Wert"*) and popularity (*"Popularität"*) in formations of German ideology. Influenced by a materialist critique of German idealism, he concludes: "Great popularity is rightfully suspicious in this country. It is considered proof of banality. It comes from a type of intellectualism that had to evolve in an abstract and speculative direction and has its historical reasons. The idealistic German spirit rose to the clouds because it had been barred from the path on earth." ("Große Popularität ist hierzulande mit Recht verdächtigt. Sie gilt als Beweis der Banalität. Das liegt an der Eigenart einer Intellektualität, die sich in abstrakt spekulativer Richtung entwickeln musste, und hat seine historischen Gründe. Der idealistische deutsche Geist erhob sich zu den Wolken, weil ihm der Weg auf der Erde versperrt gewesen war.") *Der Geist des Filmes* (Frankfurt am Main: Suhrkamp, 2001), 147 (my translation).
38. Schweinitz, 6 (my translation).
39. Drawing on the anxieties of the educated middle class and its general ambivalence toward cinema, the reform movement, for the most part, rallied against cinema's corrupting influence. The 1912 essay entitled "Sexual Danger in the Movies" ("Die sexuelle Gefahr im Kino") reflects the vigilance with which cinema's opponents sought to protect the public from moral corruption. Its author, Ike Spier, rails against cinema's tendency to challenge traditional sexual mores and against the proliferation of narratives of adultery and sexual adventure that chip away at such sanctified social institutions as marriage. "One can only imagine," he reasons, "the number of adulterous affairs that such cinematic screenings have encouraged, not to mention the moral indiscretions of husbands and wives, who live in small, confining circumstances, and who are suddenly enraptured with the colorful life of the cinema plutocracy and society. Discontented with their own lives, they set out to better their lives in some of the worst ways." He draws on his experience as a physician and attributes the increase in sexually transmitted diseases to cinema's profound negative impact on the most intimate spheres of life, causing "a sexual recklessness and an unfortunate demoralization as a consequence of spiritual transformation and with it seductions, children born out of wedlock, infections,

extramarital affairs, prostitution, etc." (196). In addition to the cinema's impact on individual fates, the behavior it is seen to encourage risks the health and well-being of the national body as a whole. Thus Spier, along with other moral watchdogs, targets cinema to explain what the right perceived as a contemporary trend toward moral decadence which harmed the nation and compromised Germany's international reputation. Ike Spier, "Die sexuelle Gefahr im Kino," *Die neue Generation* 4, edited by Helene Stöcker (April 14, 1912), 196 (my translation).

40. Sabine Hake, *The Cinema's Third Machine: Writing on Film in Germany 1907–1933* (Lincoln: University of Nebraska Press, 1993), 51.
41. *The Blue Angel* received exhibition authorization on March 15, 1930, but was restricted for youth.
42. Kaes, *Kino-Debatte*, 161.
43. Harry M. Geduld, *Authors on Film* (Bloomington: Indiana University Press, 1972), 131.
44. Quoted in Kaes, *Kino-Debatte*, 164 (my translation).
45. The disparate understanding of mass culture as opposed to art is intensified by a valuation of the different modes of production. As a product of technology, mass culture is judged as lacking the autonomy that art traditionally enjoys. In sharp contrast to mass culture, art, as it has been defined since the mid-1700s, is unique and authentic and an expression of creative genius (a tradition to which both Thomas Mann and von Sternberg subscribed). For a discussion of the long-standing tradition in German thought and culture that drew the line between "instrumentalism" and "autonomy," see Sara Danius, *The Senses of Modernism: Technology, Perception, and Aesthetics* (Ithaca, NY: Cornell University Press, 2002). She eloquently traces this cultural split back to the accelerated process of industrialization during the mid-eighteenth century when "the production of art progressively had to resort to the laws of the market rather than those of the church and aristocracy" (25). Art was forced to establish its intrinsic value and developed a new meaning associated with creativity, inspiration, and originality, in order to set itself apart from a craft or skill, which was part of its own etymology (in German, the word for art, *Kunst*, derives from the word *können*, "to be able").
46. Piere Bourdieu, "Distinction and the Aristocracy of Culture," *Cultural Theory and Popular Culture*, edited by John Storey (Athens: University of Georgia Press, 1998), 433.
47. Thomas Saunders, *Hollywood in Berlin: American Cinema and Weimar Germany* (Berkeley: University of California Press, 1994), 33.
48. Hans Siemsen, "Die Literatur der Nichtleser," *Weimarer Republik: Manifeste und Dokumente zur deutschen Literatur, 1918–1933*, edited by Anton Kaes (Stuttgart: Metzler, 1983), 255.
49. Kaes, *Kino-Debatte*, 163.
50. Michael Töteberg, *Ufa Magazin*, no. 8, 2 (my translation).
51. Ibid.
52. See Luise Dirscherl and Gunther Nickel, *Der blaue Engel: Die Drehbuchentwürfe* (St. Ingbert: Röhrig Universitätsverlag, 2000).
53. See Elisabeth Bronfen, "Vertreibung aus dem vertrauten Heim: *Der blaue Engel* (Josef von Sternberg)," *Heimweh: Illusionsspiel in Hollywood* (Berlin: Verlag Volk & Welt, 1999).
54. Mordaunt Hall, "Jannings's Audible Film," *New York Times* (December 14, 1930), x5.
55. Walter Schönbrunn, "Die Not des Literaturunterrichts in den grossstädtischen Schulen," *Weimarer Republik: Manifeste und Dokumente zur deutschen Literatur, 1918–1933*, edited by Anton Kaes (Stuttgart: Metzler, 1983), 126, 127, and 128 consecutively.
56. Judith Mayne, "Marlene Dietrich, *The Blue Angel*, and Female Performance," *Seduction and Theory: Readings of Gender, Representation and Rhetoric*, edited by Diane Hunter (Champagne-Urbana: University of Illinois Press, 1989), 32–33.
57. Karen J. Kenkel, "The Adult Child of Early Cinema," *Women in German Yearbook* 15 (2000), 137–60. She argues that the debates concerning child audiences and the cinema had an impact on the ways in which criticism framed the cinematic spectator: "As early as 1907, teachers, clergymen, doctors, civil servants, and representatives of various, often

nationalist cultural organizations, began to band together in a loosely organized film reform movement to address the deleterious effects of film-viewing on children. In so doing, they launched the first public debate on film in Germany" (143).
58. See Bourdieu, 431–41.
59. Kaes, "Weimarer Republik," *Geschichte des deutschen Films*, edited by Wolfgang Jacobsen, Anton Kaes, and Hans Helmut Prinzler (Stuttgart: Metzler, 1993), 62.
60. Leoncavallo's opera *I Pagliacci* is translated into German as *Der Bajazzo*.
61. In Edward Dymytrk's 1956 remake of *The Blue Angel*, the school principal, Rath's former colleague, rescues him and brings him to a sanatorium.
62. Jack Smith takes into consideration von Sternberg's Judaic upbringing and his deliberate use of a "vocabulary that is highly tinged with spirituality" (in Baxter, *Sternberg*, 70). With the exception of *The Blue Angel*, he mentions every one of von Sternberg's films.
63. Bronfen, 139.
64. Prawer, 67.
65. Peter Hogue, True Blue," *Film Comment* 30, 2 (March 1994), 38–43. In the American edit, Hogue writes that the scene of Rath's death is followed by Lola's performance.
66. George Toles, "This May Hurt a Little: The Art of Humiliation in Film," *Film Quarterly* 48 (Summer 1995), 12.
67. In "Chronik zur Entstehung des Films," *Der blaue Engel. Die Drehbuchentwürfe*, 5 December 1930 is listed as the date of the New York premiere of the American version in the Rialto Theater. The film grossed a record-setting $60,000 in one week (69).
68. Andrea Slane, *A Not So Foreign Affair: Fascism, Sexuality, and the Cultural Rhetoric of American Democracy* (Durham: Duke University Press, 2001), 222.

*Chapter 2*

# DISTRACTION, DECEPTION, AND VISUALITY

And now it is again a chest with magical junk that opens: the cinema. ... The dreamer knows that he is awake; he need hide nothing of himself; with everything that is in him, into the innermost recesses, he stares at this flickering wheel of life that eternally turns. The entire person surrenders to this spectacle; there is not a single dream from the most tender childhood that would not resonate with this. For we have only seemingly forgotten our dreams.
**Hugo von Hofmannsthal, "The Substitute for Dreams" (1921)**

"What did you think I am, a pipe dream?"
**Dietrich to a cowboy in Fritz Lang's *Rancho Notorious* (1952)**

In the same year that Walter Benjamin wrote his celebrated essay "The Work of Art in the Age of Mechanical Reproduction" (1935), Marlene Dietrich was making *The Devil Is a Woman*, her seventh and final film with Josef von Sternberg. Dietrich's film takes place in Spain, where Benjamin would commit suicide in 1940. In the film, the alluring performer Concha dashes the hearts of a number of men, among whom is a revolutionary who must flee to France from Spain. Compared to her performance in *The Blue Angel*, in *The Devil* and with each von Sternberg film that follows *The Blue Angel*, Dietrich's persona becomes more stylized and self-conscious in the performance of an insatiable desire to be desired, and thus more deliberate in performing (in this case) for the male gaze and in affecting her male suitor's demise. To produce her irresistible allure and a sense of intimacy and simultaneous detachment, von Sternberg creates an aura around the image through his masterful choreography of lighting, camera angle, and perspective. Dietrich adds to it in her meticulous costuming and makeup. For this film, she frantically sought the perfect, mysteriously exotic face and finally found it after drawing highly arched eyebrows to accompany the inverted question mark made with hair in the middle of her forehead and a carnation hairdo. Her daughter recalls: "The entire

Make-Up Department became involved in the quest to find Dietrich the face she sought," until "she had the look! The magic that had eluded her!"[1]

Admittedly, at first glance neither *The Devil Is a Woman* nor *The Blue Angel* seem to have much in common with Benjamin's essay except to show the ways in which his belief in the revolutionary effect of media technologies and reproduction techniques were compromised or undermined by the narratives dished up by mass culture.[2] Muting his initial enthusiasm for the media, he even admits reservations: "so long as the movie-makers' capital sets the fashion, as a rule no other revolutionary merit can be accredited to today's film than the promotion of a revolutionary criticism of traditional concepts of art."[3] For Benjamin, the path to social change means the divestment of the aura that the mechanically reproduced work may effect, since the difference between high art and one that is mechanically reproduced lies in the historicity, authenticity, and thus authority of the former as opposed to the very lack of an original and its properties in the latter. Benjamin does his best in trying to pry the cinema away from its "bourgeoisified" antecedent. Mesmerized by cinematic images but intent on defining cinema outside of bourgeois categories, he looks to the means of production to distinguish between cinema and other art forms that are entrenched in rituals, first magical and then religious. Distinguishing between technically produced art—that is, art as replica, and thus transitory, as opposed to art as a unique and authentic product with historical value—he argues that technically reproduced art lacks an aura because the reproduced object is detached from the domain of tradition. Additionally, it lacks "presence in time and space."[4] Released from tradition, it allows for "the liquidation of the traditional value of the cultural heritage."[5] What Benjamin tries to pry mechanically produced art away from is the authority of the *Bildungsbürgertum* and its valuations. In fact, Benjamin objects to his "ultra-reactionary" contemporaries whose praise of cinema is clad in the language of rituals: "It is instructive to note how their desire to class the film among the 'art' forces these theoreticians to read ritual elements into it—with striking lack of discretion."[6]

Despite Benjamin's attempts to liberate film from tradition, similar evaluative structures installed themselves. The technically reproduced image became the very object of worship and mystification that Benjamin resisted, especially when those images aimed at producing the aura of the star. Perhaps this is why Benjamin insisted on distinguishing between aura and what he called "the spell of the personality." "The film responds to the shriveling of the aura with an artificial build-up of the 'personality' outside of the studio."[7] Indeed during the Weimar Republic, much like today, actors became commodities on and off screen.[8] Moreover, the cinematic apparatus produced the illusion of a star's presence, presence being the essence of aura, and of the image in general. This is cultivated in the interrelationship of psychic and cinematic mechanisms of looking that are culturally scripted and that are anchored in primal desires, which film theorists, but particularly feminist film theorists, began exploring in the 1970s. Despite Benjamin's attempt to unhinge film from the vernacular of tradition and intervene in film's more conservative appropriation, the categories he sought to challenge are resuscitated especially in the context of the cinematic spectacle of the body. In effect, both *The Blue Angel* and *The Devil Is a Woman*, as well as other Dietrich and von Sternberg productions between 1930 and 1935 (*Morocco, Dishonored, Shanghai Express, Blonde Venus, The Scarlet Empress*), elaborate to a great extent Benjamin's understanding of aura, which mass culture continued to produce and sustain, relying frequently on the image of the seductive female as spectacle. In the case of *The Blue Angel*, the auratic experience is induced through the exhibition of the female body, which serves to interrupt narrative progression so that the viewer can enjoy the state of contemplative looking. Lotte Eisner intuitively refers to the prevalence of a "spell-binding mood."[9] Indeed, Rath and the audience are spellbound and captivated by the aura of the entertainer Lola. After he bursts into Lola's dressing room and sneaks peeks at Lola taking off her stockings, she *knowingly* and rhetorically queries, "You have nothing to say now, do you?"

In *The Blue Angel*, Lola's performance, the aura cast, and especially the slippage between the numerous images of Lola and her stage presence, all infer a "cinematic presence," so that the film performs a self-reflective exploration of the relationship between the spectator and the image. In the last scene of Lola perched on her chair, the narrative, that is, the progression of time, is suspended, and Lola/Dietrich is transformed into an icon that, as we know in hindsight, will gain international currency and become a symbol of glamour, beauty, and fame. Again, the slippage between an image of worship to one uncritically admired implied in the double meaning of the word "icon" reinstates the auratic experience of the image. The formal aesthetic structures von Sternberg thus employs to evoke pleasure establish a cinematic aura, an optical magic that sustains the illusion of presence differently than in classical cinema, which aims toward narrative progression and the reestablishment of order. Von Sternberg's images stop time. Thus, Lola's "presence" depends on projection and on the needs/fantasies the image arouses in the viewer. It depends on the desire for symbiosis with the image, rather than fetishistic distance, and for the sense of excitement that the film's excesses arouse.[10] Lola's stage presence symbolizes imaginary desire—she conveys what cannot be expressed by rational language. She enchants her audiences and speaks to a need for experience in its most basic sense, while establishing herself as an icon of mass culture.

This chapter explores Rath's specular relationship to Lola as performer and image, his introduction to visual mass culture, his masochistic surrender to the aura whose vehicle is the sexualized body of the modern woman, and the blurring of the divide between representation/illusion and "reality," which the medium exploits. As I argue in Chapter 1, unlike his students, Rath does not "master" the idioms required to engage in the conventions of mass entertainment, nor does he successfully negotiate modernity. Instead, he surrenders himself to the pleasures of fantasy and then attempts to draw Lola (unsuccessfully) into his familiar world as defined by nineteenth-century sensibilities. Placed within the context of the Weimar Republic, *The Blue Angel* becomes an intricately designed meditation on the power of images in a time of emergent consumer mass culture, on a fascination with an ever-evolving visual culture, and on the intrinsic pleasure of looking (scopophilia), and the danger of total absorption. Thus, von Sternberg probes the relationship between the spectator and the image. On a meta-cinematic level, he explores the specter of absence that has haunted cinematic production since its inception.

In order to understand the finely nuanced psychodynamic of Rath's submission to Lola's overwhelming presence as sexualized female, as mass culture, and as an icon of modernity, I will turn to Gaylyn Studlar's illuminating study of the relationship between cinema and masochist pleasure, *In the Realm of Pleasure*. Since Studlar focuses exclusively on Dietrich's and von Sternberg's Paramount films and curiously omits *The Blue Angel*, I intend to expand the trajectory of Studlar's study to include von Sternberg's Weimar film in the repertoire of masochistic texts she cites. Insisting on historical specificity, I anchor my reading of von Sternberg's aesthetic and his reference to various regimes of seeing in the social/historical context of the Weimar Republic—a period in which the acceleration of everyday life and the explosion of temporal–spatial limitations led to profound changes in structures of perception and experience. Combining Studlar's observations and consideration of the social/historical context allows for a more complex and nuanced understanding of the viewing, and of Lola as spectacle and image.

Indeed, von Sternberg explores a very nuanced dynamic of looking in *The Blue Angel* that proceeds along various registers. These registers are articulated both within the film as well as outside, turning the spectator at times into the voyeur par excellence. For instance, while von Sternberg's viewer watches visual exchanges among the actors that locate them within different regimes of power and privilege, the film viewer is also constantly being made aware of the process of watching. Von Sternberg achieves such self-reflexivity by, for instance, delaying the view of the postcards of the cabaret entertainer (teasing the viewer), or by obstructing the view of the stage with an anchor or pillar—all of which highlight the process of looking and the interplay of seeing and not seeing. The act of looking and displaying, revealing and concealing thus evolves into a self-reflexive performance that von Sternberg complexly choreographs. It begins with the image of Lola, who constantly is on display. Moreover, von Sternberg gestures toward the centrality of vision over sound, despite the significant role it plays in *The Blue Angel*, and

**Figure 2.1** Dancing Eyes. Still from *Der blaue Engel*, 1930, directed by Josef von Sternberg. Source: *Friedrich-Wilhelm-Murnau-Stiftung*.

toward the cinema as "Augenkunst," literally "the art of the eyes," in the attention he pays to the female performer whose eyes dance to the sound of "exotic" snake-charming rhythms (see Figure 2.1).[11]

Also, Rath's metaphorical vulnerability and "blindness," emphasized in the overt play with his glasses, or the obstruction of vision when Lola blows powder in his face, live in tension with the conventions associated with the gaze.

In addition to stressing the primacy of looking, von Sternberg inflects looking according to the social, generational, and gendered specificity of the viewing subjects. He delivers a medley of perspectives that establish spatial divisions that at once connote social and cultural disparities and power positions. The gaze then is a composite of meanings influenced by factors ranging from historical context to class, age, gender, and sexual preference, to name only a few. Furthermore, von Sternberg perceptively stages an intricate interplay of visual and projected desire, which must be analyzed in all of its psychological, historical, and sociological complexity. Pierre Bourdieu reminds us that the "eye" must be assessed as "a product of history reproduced by education," which suggests that ways of looking and seeing are culturally informed, dependent on convention and that we *learn* to decipher the world that we believe we are seeing.[12] These various registers of looking manifest themselves, for instance, in the relationship between the professor and his students. As they gather around a postcard, blowing at Lola's feathered skirt, Rath's students take rebellious pleasure in looking at the forbidden image of the scantily clad entertainer. As though incited by the image that unleashes mayhem, a student defaces Rath's notebook and affixes the German prefix "un" to Rath's name, turning it into Unrat (garbage), literally "trashing" his name and authority. Additionally, the student draws a clown-like figure under the name, prefiguring Rath's own demise, which suggestively begins with the illicit image of Lola in the classroom. Later on, the image of the cabaret singer will take Unrat into the realm of the abject (both socially and psychologically) and cause his banishment from bourgeois culture.

## Looks Deceive

Entering the classroom with full sovereignty, Rath takes a seat at his desk raised on a platform—his own stage and symbolic home. He notices the insolent graffiti on his notebook and calls upon his star pupil, Angst, to erase it—unaware, of course, that the realm of the visual will alter his identity. Yet, for now his gaze continues to exert the authority demanded of his calling; it is emphasized repeatedly when he cleans or peeks over the rim of his glasses to survey his students. Afraid of being locked in the professor's gaze, his students quickly divert their eyes to avoid being called on to recite the phrase from *Hamlet* "to be or not to be" (given the emphasis on looking, one is tempted to say "to see or not to see"). Later on, while his students write essays on a purely hypothetical historical event, Rath prowls about the back of the classroom, adjusting his glasses only to spy a student engrossed in the forbidden postcard of Lola. Angered by this bold violation of school rules and bourgeois code of honorability, and, more importantly, by the impertinent challenge to his authority, Rath confiscates the postcard and vows to have a word after class with the perpetrator. At the same time, he closes the classroom window and blocks out the pleasurable sounds of schoolgirls singing, unconsciously affirming the volatile combination of the image of Lola and female voice/song. The combination of image and voice foreshadows his fall. By closing the window, he attempts to shut out the profane, to tame nature, to enforce rationality and paternal order. The scene evokes a modernist opposition between nature and knowledge, while betraying the fragile formations of subjectivity and desire. Indeed, what appears to be the simple pleasure of the disembodied female voice singing grows more threatening when matched with an eroticized body.

When two more postcards end up falling out of his star pupil's notebook after class, Angst, who has been framed, is summoned to Rath's

**Figure 2.2** Still from *Der blaue Engel*, 1930, directed by Josef von Sternberg.
Source: *Deutsche Kinemathek*.

office and dismissed, only after confessing to his classmates' nightly jaunts to The Blue Angel cabaret. Behind closed doors and hidden from the institutional gaze that is aware of the dangerous lure of the female body, illicit sexuality, and mass culture, Rath furtively inspects the images. Like his predecessor Schön, in G.W. Pabst's film *Pandora's Box*, who, according to Mary Ann Doane, "belongs to the premodern order where sexuality, riddled by contradictions, is nevertheless contained by the polarization of morality and secret desire," Rath falls prey, all the while fearful that the ubiquitous eye of the institution and its higher moral authority discover him.[13] Holding up the first image of Lola in unnatural proximity to his face and fixating on it, he then places the three images together, fanning them out like playing cards. The postcard images of Lola, delayed and then displayed in one of the film's few close-ups, inflame longing. Like his students, he gently blows on the feathered skirt of the cabaret singer to reveal Lola's thighs (see Figure 2.2).

In sharp contrast to the scene with the dead canary in Rath's room, the motif of feathers suggests a rebirth of sensuality in the figure of the Siren—often represented as a partial bird. The feathers on Lola's skirt turn the female body into an exotic, instinctual, and primitive object that arouses untoward fascination with the unknown. Thus, the female as nature and beauty is dangerously combined with the seductive voice and the image of Lola. Similarly, in her 1932 role as the *Blonde Venus*, Dietrich will slip out of an ape costume, thus consummating the association of woman with the primitive and nature. Lola's uninhibited sexuality bursts into Rath's classroom and his study, the two most intimate spheres of his identity. Rath succumbs to the advertisement that beguiles and intoxicates the viewer and unleashes erotic desire. The image sets in motion the spectator's fantasy and spuriously promises fulfillment. The encounter with the three images so charms Rath that he soon becomes star-struck. He is safe, however, until he steps over the threshold dividing his world from that of the imagined.

Yet, soon the image causes his simple, monotone, yet honorable lifestyle to unravel. It undermines his institutionalized masculine power and irrevocably unleashes a sexual awakening. That is to say, the image of the seductive female ruptures the traditional norms and values of bourgeois culture and the standards of the *Bildungsbürgertum* whose decline Rath represents. Linking Rath's gaze to the pubescent gaze of his students suggests a regression that classical cinema asserts in the subject's relationship to the image. Yet, Rath is more susceptible than the students, which lends the notion of the gaze a differentiated meaning.

Arguably, the generation of students is more familiar with the conventions of mass culture, which Rath "innocently" and awkwardly engages. Different from the adolescents whose transgressions are portrayed as harmless flirtations and appropriate within the purvey of their social standing, as seen in the myriad renditions of the prodigal son/husband in street films, Rath's desire for the sexualized spectacle scandalizes the established order—so much so that he is dismissed from the school, the seat of patriarchal logos and cultural validation.[14] Moreover, the boys subscribe to the traditions of masculinity and its accepted rites of passage even when they playfully tell Lola, "I love you." In contrast, Lola's presence, the assertion of her sexual agency, depletes Rath of masculine authority and feminizes him. On the one hand, the unsettling of masculine authority at the hands of the modern woman resonates with discourses of "masculinity in crisis" that characterize many texts of the Weimar Republic, ranging from the visual arts to film and to literature. On the other hand, Rath's transformation has much to do with the way he is positioned within the realm of mass culture whose staple was the modern woman. Since Lola's image as an entertainer depends on the gaze, her open invitation to look, as well as her visual accessibility, are misconstrued as physical/sexual promiscuity, if not prostitution, a deception on which the cult of distraction, or, as Miriam Hansen describes, "an openly commercial art," thrives.[15]

Not surprisingly, most readings of *The Blue Angel* within the last two decades have centered on the staging of gender and the gender-specific nature of the gaze, as opposed to earlier questions of literary adaptation. What follows is a brief discussion of these readings. In particular, Laura Mulvey's often-cited 1975 essay on visual pleasure laid the ground for early feminist film theory to explore the repertoire of images familiar to Western culture and to classical cinema, which established men as active lookers, thus as subjects or agents of the gaze, and women as its objects—that is, as bodies to be looked at. In keeping within a strictly heterosexual context, theorists like Mulvey attempted to make transparent the workings of dominant cultural regimes of looking and posited that men in classical cinema assume the role of the ideal spectator while women become the ideal spectacle.[16] For Mulvey, as for many early feminist film theorists who drew on psychoanalytical categories to examine social/cinematic repertoires of desire, cinema became the extension of a generic male psyche, the scene of working through anxieties of castration and lack. Consequently, the seductive female or vamp was viewed as the product of the male gaze and the image of woman actually representing her own exclusion and repression. An example of this visual dynamic in a later Dietrich film, and particularly of the female body cast as a projection of (male) desire, is her figure's response to a male suitor in the epigraph above, taken from Fritz Lang's 1952 film *Rancho Notorious*. Additionally, Dietrich's deference to von Sternberg in her memoirs and in numerous interviews exemplifies how deeply ingrained and accepted is the notion of male visual control and female acquiescence, despite Dietrich's own hand in her construction. It is a notion that the Weimar Republic's cultural theorists, such as Benjamin and Kracauer, developed in writings on mass culture, perception, and spectatorship, and that could be found in a number of literary texts.[17]

Influenced by Mulvey's insights, and in step with early feminist theory, Peter Baxter, in "On the Naked Thighs of Miss Dietrich," attributes the ongoing fascination with the image of Lola/Dietrich to the containment of male anxiety by providing men with the ultimate fetish, namely, her legs. The legs compensate for female lack in the psychoanalytical sense whereby the male fixates on an object that the female has in order to mask the absence of the phallus. Drawing on the Freudian model of the Oedipus complex, Baxter further asserts that Lola's stance "arrests the instant of fetishization, the instant before the child's glimpse of the female genital organ," or rather missing phallus, which arouses the fear of castration.[18] Lola's attire, which barely conceals her genitals, and the constant attention to her undergarments alludes to the repressed text of female sexuality and libidinal pleasure.[19] For Baxter, the key moment in the film is when Lola ascends the spiral staircase: Rath looks up and Lola drops her underwear on his shoulder. It ends up in his pocket and provides an excuse for returning to the nightclub. In 1930, the German Dadaist artist Hannah Höch pays tribute precisely to the fetishized object by placing Marlene's legs on a pedestal slightly crossed and upside down in high heels. Two men much like Rath's students are looking up, one has his hand cupped, suggesting that he is calling out to the legs. A woman's luscious lips appear in a knowing smile in the corner of a moon-shaped face delighted to see the effect of this body part on the male spectator.[20]

Since Mulvey's groundbreaking essay, feminist film criticism has called for a more differentiated understanding of the circulation of desire and more refined reading of spectatorship and gender, and the dynamic of looking and relationship to the image—distinctions that von Sternberg already recognized when developing the assorted characters in *The Blue Angel*. In her discussion of *The Blue Angel*, for instance, Elizabeth Bronfen shifts Mulvey's initial analysis of the gaze enough to disrupt the normative understanding of gender, while she reproduces the problematic aspects of Mulvey's work in universalizing the spectator. She posits a phenomenological understanding of the choreography of gazes in von Sternberg's film and a notion of gendered identity that challenge the alignment of male to spectator and female to spectacle.[21] Bronfen, along with Judith Mayne and other film and visual culture theorists, submits that women learn to watch themselves, which results in what she calls a "Selbstverdoppelung" (self-doubling) that locates women simultaneously within and outside of themselves. As a result, women never are at home in themselves—they are always conscious of their image and thus self-alienated. Put differently, women watch themselves being watched and consciously perform for the gaze à la Lola. According to Bronfen, women's self-alienation is most apparent in representations of the seductive female that performs for the male gaze.

Interested in the persistent attribution of women as "Fremdbestimmt" (defined by another), Bronfen also claims that masculinity and femininity are renegotiated in representations of the seductive female body.[22] As an obvious composite of male desire and female performance, the seductive female exposes the idea of control and calls into question the invulnerability of a male gaze, that is, the empowered male subject. Bronfen credits von Sternberg with a keen sense of the ontological instability of the male gaze and with showing how gendered arrangements, regimes of pleasure, submission, and control, vacillate, most obviously through Dietrich's cross-dressing, but also in the ways the gaze is choreographed. Von Sternberg so obviously stages the appropriating male gaze and shows how the female constructs herself for the gaze that his films actually end up exposing and even devaluing the very idea of a stable male gaze.[23] Accordingly, *The Blue Angel* makes visible the ambivalent interplay of gazes, and more significantly, "the bearer of the look and the one looked at uncannily alternate between a sadistic empowerment and a masochistic disempowerment."[24] By locating Rath and Lola within a sadomasochistic exchange with roles that oscillate between these two poles, Bronfen attempts to open up the rigidly coded positioning of male and female within regimes of sight, pleasure, and power, and to extend the range of spectatorial positions.

Yet, while Elisabeth Bronfen offers a compelling reading of the interplay of gazes to explain Lola's and Rath's ineluctable attachment, she retains paired-down notions of gender in the coupling of sadism and masochism that are bound to conventional heterosexuality even if the relay of power alternates. Her reading is predicated on Rath and Lola enjoying and relinquishing visual control alternately. In contrast to Bronfen, I argue that Rath never enjoys specular mastery in the realm of The Blue Angel club or in Lola's presence, but only within the classroom, and, even there, his authority slowly erodes after each encounter with Lola, until he is forced to leave the place that secured his specular privilege. His unskilled gaze fails to acquire mastery of the space of mass entertainment, not to mention of the new visual media, and by extension of cinema, or of modernity, which threatens his very cultural and psychic integrity. In my reading of *The Blue Angel*, Lola's gaze is flirtatious, bold, and unfettered; Rath generally appears timid and subdued in her presence. Lola is never the passive object of the controlling look, and contraindicative to Mulvey and Bronfen, her performance is intricately linked to commanding the gaze throughout. Even in the wedding scene—the initiation of the family romance—when she lovingly looks at Rath, he is timid and self-conscious. Lowering his eyes, he partakes in a discomforting duet of crowing and cooing. His cocky and "triumphant" rooster-like crowing in response to Lola's cooing, his high-pitched effusion of desire, undermines his dominant position, exposes his fragility and seals his displacement. Civilization and particularly modernity tip the fine balance of the natural world in which the rooster's position is secure. At the end of the film the cock's crow turns into unforgettable shrieks of despair. Dressed in a clown costume, Rath embodies the very role his displacement in the realm of the popular connotes, which consequently undermines any illusion of masculine authority. His inferior though at first inflated status as professor within the realm of the socially marginalized cabaret, and his lack of specular authority over the image and its incarnation, may account for Andrew Sarris's observation (see Chapter 1) that *The Blue Angel* is von Sternberg's most violent film.

Studlar's discussion of the masochistic aesthetic in von Sternberg's and Dietrich's Hollywood productions sheds light on the relationship between Rath and Lola, which goes beyond the conventional sadomasochistic pairing that Bronfen rehearses or beyond Baxter's deference to female lack. As Studlar explains, "Visual pleasure can be explained other than by a theory that focuses on sexual difference defined as castration threat," which would locate processes of looking in the Oedipal phase of psychic development.[25] Instead, Studlar situates visual pleasure in the pre-Oedipal, prelinguistic phase of child development, premiering the oral mother as the primary love object, and in memories of regressive archaic pleasures of the primal scene that approximates masochistic surrender. Significantly, pleasure does not derive from mastering or sequestering the threatening female but from submitting to her body and her gaze to attain symbiotic bliss. Striving for this blissful experience is paradoxical because fulfillment requires the dissolution of personal boundaries, which suggests extinguishing the subject (death). Bonding with the desired object must thus always be deferred; the object must remain unattainable. Studlar states accordingly: "The gaze determines but cannot control the object of desire. ...Within the masochistic scheme, the object of desire is as elusive as it is for the film spectator who glimpses the cinema's shadow representation of the absent object."[26] Central to the masochistic text is disavowal that derives from the renunciation of the mother's difference and the longing to meld with her. A function of the imagination, disavowal bears knowledge of what it is repressing but suspends it —just as the iconic (the image) cannot negate the indexical (what it refers to). Thus disavowal, suspension, fantasy, and fetishism form the substructure of the masochist's rejection of reality, which von Sternberg exploits in the iconicity of his texts and in "supersensual" displays. In their iconicity, his films approach *tableaux vivants* that suspend reality and affect a stasis that undermines classical narrative structures that rely on progress toward stability and the reestablishment of a traditional heterosexual order.

Referring to Dietrich and von Sternberg's Paramount films, yet applicable to *The Blue Angel*, Studlar asserts: "These films offer the perceptual play of a self-consciously performed spectacle that disrupts classical narrative flow and substitutes an excessive, regressive pre-Oedipal multiplicity of textual pleasures."[27] Through mood, texture and in hyper-exotic settings, such as in the cabaret, von Sternberg constructs an illusion that betrays itself in its blatant artificiality, despite the anti-illusionist exchange of sets. Chubby cherubs dot the stage, sending the spectator into a seventh heaven with the seductive Lola empowering the ascent. Moreover, von Sternberg uses artifice and other key characteristics of the masochistic text, such as repetition rather than progress, "the abrupt elision of decisive events," and an episodic structure.[28] For instance, the clock that chimes eight times to signal the beginning of class, that interrupts Rath's dream world and effects his frenzied departure after a night with Lola, does not mark the progression of time, but signifies his routine and alludes to his very existence. The clock in *The Blue Angel* seems to hold back time rather than reflect modernity's pulsating push toward the future, as can be seen in Fritz Lang's films. Furthermore, Rath repeatedly helps Lola with her stockings, which returns him each time to the site of his pleasure and pain. His submission to Lola renders the code of bourgeois conduct inoperative, and consequently frustrates the potential for a happy ending. The sexualized female, therefore, cannot be blamed for his demise.

The unguarded indulgence in the image begins with the postcards that tantalize Rath as described above. A dramatic disempowerment of his gaze, however, begins at the doorway of *The Blue Angel* when he strains to peer through the smeared windows, frenetically looking through each windowpane. Upon entering, he is ensnared, literally caught in a fishnet. Like a fish out of water, he also is caught in the spotlight that stands in for the entertainer's erotic gaze that blinds him, as Lola stands on stage duplicating the pose of the advertisement. When Rath lands in Lola's dressing room, he cannot keep his eyes off of Lola. Showcasing her legs through her movements and the cut of her costume, Lola consciously provokes desire. Yet, rather than exercise power and authority, his gaze remains furtive and timid and his fascination mingled with uncertainty. He is unable to enjoy her image privately and unscathed and visibly struggles with adhering to the code of respectability and allowing for the experience of surging erotic desire. "So you are the artist Lola Lola?" Rath asks. " I am Professor Dr. Immanuel Rath, a teacher at the local preparatory school." Sensing this inner turmoil, Lola playfully admonishes him: "That's why you should take your hat off in my dressing room!" As the performers try to pass through Lola's dressing room, they refer to Rath as a "Verkehrsstörung" (the cause of the stoppage of traffic). He obstructs the flow of traffic as someone whose desire and presence wreak havoc on the internal workings and the economy of the cabaret. At the same time, he becomes the potential casualty of the cabaret and its players; he is vulnerable to modernity's demands. It is no wonder that Lola later warns him before leaving for school after spending a night with her to watch out for the *Elektrische*, the streetcar, one of the motors and symbols of modernity and urban culture.

On his second visit to The Blue Angel, to return the undergarment that one of his students secretly slipped into his pocket and exchange it for his forgotten handkerchief, the symbol of his authority and civility, Rath passes by a number of posters of Lola. The reproduction of her image in posters, postcards, and mirrors heightens the awareness of Lola as projection and emphasizes the significance of the image in Rath's relationship to Lola. The posters suggest the primacy of the image and the power of representation, as well as reflect modernity's expanding range of visual culture, the increased specularization of everyday life, and the heightened visibility of the modern woman. Besides the posters, Lola's image appears threefold in three separate mirrors and then again in the three mirrors Lola uses to assemble herself for the stage, where she performs femininity.[29] Her image is arranged much like the three postcards Rath held in his hand, which further affixes his relationship to Lola to the realm of the imaginary. Lola embodies the complex relationship of specularized modern femininity that mass culture manufactured and which modern women used to constitute themselves within a more visually oriented social setting. By constituting herself as a spectacle, Lola asserts that she is not merely a modern subject, but a sexual subject as well.

Coyly seated next to her, Rath watches Lola, who looks at herself in the mirror, applying makeup to her eyes. She makes conscious the play of desire and appearance and of pleasure and the dependency of female performance on the male gaze, saying, "Nice eyes, huh?"[30] Without explicitly returning Rath's gaze, she undermines his attempts at voyeurism and disempowers his gaze by drawing attention to it. When he crawls under the table next to Lola's legs to retrieve the cigarettes that fell, she ribs, "When you are done send me a postcard." The continuous emphasis on visuality and desire heightens the dramaturgy of looking as well as reinforces Lola's erotic power over Rath. As he surfaces, Lola straightens his disheveled hair, bringing out the timid boy in the man, and thus blurs the tantalizing fascination with the sexualized woman with the all-powerful mother. Compromising his authority even further, Lola chides, "Your kids should see you now." Indeed, Rath is the one who is being seen when his students prop up the trapdoor of the basement where they are hiding and witness his deference to Lola. More injuriously, they watch as Lola blows on the compact of powder that Rath holds while she applies her makeup; its cloud obscures and even robs Rath of his vision, thereby undermining masculine visual authority, denying him the pleasures of watching, and unsettling his role as spectator. Later, Rath, the impotent child, will be cradled in the balcony and enveloped in Lola's song, believing that he is the sole recipient of her declaration of love.

**Figure 2.3** "Falling in Love Again." Still from *Der blaue Engel*, 1930, directed by Josef von Sternberg. Source: *Deutsche Kinemathek*.

Provocatively clasping one knee, wearing lace-frilled undergarments, garters, and a top hat, in one of the most famous shots in the film (an image that has become a trademark), Lola sings "Falling in Love Again." As a goddess on stage, she offers herself up to the desiring gaze. Yet, as the title of the song warns, a reenactment will take place and a return to the site of pleasure and pain. In this scene (see Figure 2.3), Rath becomes both audience and spectacle as he succumbs to the raptures of Lola and

**Figure 2.4** Rath holding Dietrich's Lenci African doll, which became her mascot and part of a larger collection of Lenci dolls. Still from *Der blaue Engel*, 1930, directed by Josef von Sternberg. Source: *Deutsche Kinemathek*.

the song's seduction. Yet, those who acquiesce to the masochistic scenario/text are expelled eventually, once the siren has lured them to embrace danger. Within the logic of the narrative, death becomes the ultimate fetish, and, as Studlar notes, "masochistic fatalism ensures the narrative closure of a perverse fantasy."[31]

Yet, until then the masochistic fantasy resumes its powerful hold. A night with Lola leaves Rath sitting in her bed with a black doll, an "exotic" totem of his transgression in the European vernacular. Rather than a scene of male conquest, Rath appears infantilized; the substitute love object is in his arms (see Figure 2.4). His experience with female sexuality, which Freud described as the "dark continent" (the figurative space of the unconscious and the erotic, the black doll), is an encounter with the oral, that is, the nurturing mother who both gives and withholds pleasure.[32]

When Rath emerges from Lola's bedroom to sit at the lavishly set breakfast table, Lola invokes the family romance, stating in Berlin dialect, "Ya see, you could have this every day" ("Na siehste, das könnste nun alle Tage haben!"), an admission that she too wishes to participate in such socially sanctioned institutions as marriage. Enunciating correctly in a formal High German, Rath replies: "There would be nothing that would stand in the way. I am after all not married" ("Dem stünde nichts im Wege—ich bin ja schliesslich unverheiratet"). While the patriarchal text of marriage shimmers through, the context and its asymmetrically situated participants undermine the plausibility of a successful middle-class, monogamous family romance.

In fact, nothing in the narrative suggests that these differences will be overcome. Moreover, the linguistic coloring of two very diverse class affiliations distends the scene of bourgeois bliss, already made artificial in a setting of sensual abundance. More tellingly, a poster of the magician and master of illusion Edmund Renk intrudes upon the scene and interrupts the quasi-harmonious space between Rath and Lola (see Figure 2.5). The image of Renk could be read as a *punctum*, in the sense that Roland Barthes has theorized, a detail in an image that "pricks" the observer.[33] Here is the other man (like the strongman Mazeppa who appears later), a more plausible match or suitor, if he has not already been one. The poster provides an image of an alternative masculinity that haunts the space between Lola and Rath, despite Lola's promise of bliss. It also refers to the illusion on which magic tricks count to fool the spectator. Rath falls for the illusion and later, at the hand of Kiepert, he will become a participant in the creation of illusions when on stage Kiepert pulls eggs out of his nose. The church bell's chimes cut short the idyllic promise of marital bliss. Harried and disoriented, Rath arrives in his classroom after eight o'clock, wearing a red carnation in his lapel, the symbol of both his displacement and his transgression. Rath is incapable of bridging two intrinsically incompatible spheres, which the film dangerously and improperly intermingles.

**Figure 2.5** "Ya see, you could have this every day." Still from *Der blaue Engel*, 1930, directed by Josef von Sternberg. Source: *Deutsche Kinemathek*.

That is not to say that the sexualized, carnivalesque sphere of the cabaret cannot coexist with middle-class morality. The school's headmaster understands Rath's moral indiscretion (Fehltritt), like in the bourgeois tragedy, yet warns him to keep his indiscretions closeted. The cabaret is a sphere that may be enjoyed but not seriously incorporated into middle-class life or legitimized. But Rath is smitten and defenseless. He valiantly steps in as the patriarch, as the father who wishes to impose order (which is denied him throughout the film) on his and Lola's relationship through marriage. His "proposal," however, occasions his dismissal. In his attempt to bring Lola into the bourgeois fold, a trope often rehearsed and rarely redeemed, he will join in the fate of other male protagonists during the Weimar Republic. Notably, Dr. Schön, a respectable banker in Pabst's *Pandora's Box*, meets his death after marrying the prostitute, Lulu (Louise Brooks), well aware that his transgression will cause his ruin. Indeed, when Rath proposes marriage, Lola, street-smart and modern, bursts into laughter; her response betrays their intrinsic incompatibility, in addition to alluding to the uncertain state of marriage during the 1920s—a topic I will explore in Chapter 3.

In many ways, Rath's proposal illustrates how von Sternberg's characters, whether in *The Blue Angel* or in his Hollywood films, "find justification for their masochistic behavior," as Studlar notes, "through plot predicaments that cannot mask the absurdity of their pursuit."[34] With the intensification of Rath's masochistic submission to the point of dissolution (death), the prospect of their liaison edges along an abyss. Before his death, he will experience a series of "petite morts," as when the postcards that kindled his lust spill out of Lola's suitcase onto the floor. The newly married Rath adamantly declares that he will guard his wife's image and integrity so long as he is financially solvent. Yet, financial need soon calls for him to relinquish his illusion of visual monogamy and sell the very photographs he once prized.

The transition from the once respected and groomed male to the disheveled itinerant sidekick reflects a downward trajectory linked to a profound misreading of his relationship to fantasy-induced desire and images. The illusions of the cabaret cannot be upheld indeterminately; once inside its machinery, and unaccustomed to its rules, Rath is sorely displaced in its sphere, which disables him both as husband and performer. His increasing impotence while Lola's career peaks jeopardizes the tenets of disavowal. Applying his clown makeup, a vacant stare and despondent image fills the very same mirror in which he once enjoyed the reflection of Lola. After constructing himself for the public gaze, he must perform on her same stage.

## Representation: "Caveat Emptor"

If the image of the female worker who imitates Lola's pose in the opening scenes of the film (see Figure 2.6) highlights the relationship of gender to the image, to mass entertainment and, more specifically, to the spectacle of cinema, then Rath's viewing of the postcards establishes a parallel, though vastly different relationship. The woman in the opening scene who has washed the window and then delights in the fantasy of becoming the sexualized female stages the internalization of the image and a wish for likeness.

Mary Ann Doane perceptively notes: "It is not accidental that the logic of consumerism and mechanical reproduction corresponds to logic of perception attributed to the female spectator whose nonfetishistized gaze maintains a dangerous intimacy with the image."[35] Doane points to a disabling closeness to the image that mimesis inspires when the viewer is of the same gender. In such cases, the image calls for an over identification and simulation of the image that, here, results in the imitation of the seductive female's pose. Comparing her pose to the poster-size image of Lola, however, stresses performativity and masquerade, which, in contrast to Doane's assessment, may actually enable female subjectivities through their performance of multiple roles. Proximity inspires a playfulness that empowers and expands the repertoire of individual female subjectivities.[36] The female worker strikes a momentary pose, which ends with her splashing a bucket of water on the display case in front of Lola's image—the fantasy is interrupted by the practical demands

**Figure 2.6** Still from *Der blaue Engel*, 1930, directed by Josef von Sternberg. Source: *Deutsche Kinemathek*.

of work. With this scene, von Sternberg alludes to the power of images and the *incorporation* of the image, for which the dream world of advertising aims. It could even be said that the female worker "inhabits" and makes the fantasy her own. Her submission to the image and to likeness that effects the apparent dissolution of the boundary between subject and object does not seem to threaten the female worker in the way that it endangers Rath. In showing the disparate responses to the image and its effect, *The Blue Angel* opens up questions of spectatorship that take into account gender, historical context, and the cultural spaces in which looking takes place. The disarming effect on Rath, as I have argued, has much to do with his social standing, his generation, and his "innocence," which makes him more susceptible to the illusion. Studlar's attempt to pitch cinematic viewing as a phenomenological experience that erases gendered distinctions and presumes similar pre-Oedipal pleasures in submission to the image subsequently addresses only one aspect of the viewing experience, albeit a central one to Rath's experience of mass culture. He abandons himself to regressive desires and to the deceptive promise of wholeness that the image and Lola's performance inspire. In part, he becomes the cinemagoer par excellence, except that Rath oversteps its boundaries and disregards its conventions.

**Figure 2.7** Otto Hunte's sketch of the entrance to The Blue Angel nightclub. Source: *Deutsches Filmmuseum*.

Rath's ultimate "perversion" is his disavowal of the boundaries between the real and the fantasy. His total absorption, in fact, feminizes him as a spectator.³⁷ Significantly, Rath's inability to discern representation from "reality," his "Pygmalionization" of Lola, his own vulnerabilities, and his lack of specular control, imperil the terms of his identity. In Studlar's words, "the film's overwhelming images invite a return to the states in which the ego dissolves."³⁸ By closing the gap between himself, the desiring subject, and the object, Rath violates the terms of the Oedipal trajectory whose fetishizing gaze maintains distance and heeds the threat of castration. Significantly, von Sternberg's pairing of Rath and Lola reenacts and languishes in the cinematic experience of pre-Oedipal pleasure that the "dream screen" evokes—with Rath as its unsuspecting attendant and pawn. Upon entering The Blue Angel, Rath passes over a threshold that blurs fantasy and "reality" and that vanquishes the difference between representation and actuality. Set designer Otto Hunte captures the significance of images and the imaginary in Rath's relationship to Lola in his sketch of the entrance of The Blue Angel nightclub through which Rath passes (see Figure 2.7).³⁹

The slippage between fiction and "reality" seems to be a commonplace as far as the representation of Dietrich is concerned. Her biographer,

Donald Spoto, writes, "Dietrich was von Sternberg's representation of an even more universal notion, however. With her we see just how deadly it is to pursue illusion. To believe that Lola-Lola can be a charming companion is to court disaster, as Jannings discovers."[40] The interchangeability between screen character and actor exemplifies the tenuous boundaries that lead even Dietrich's biographer to conflate the historical person and the image. Like Rath, Spoto seems caught up in Dietrich's allure, explaining her life through her fictional characters and her fictional characters through her life. Yet, as von Sternberg points out in his autobiography, even if he "had included *Caveat emptor* in the main title of *The Blue Angel*, no one would have paid heed anyway."[41] The fluidity of the boundary between image and actuality becomes dangerous once the spectator remains arrested.

The transition from the advertisement to the postcard to Lola, who "comes alive" after Rath blows on the skirt, thus breathing life into the image, emphasizes Lola's existence in the realm of fantasy.[42] The first time we see her, she replicates the pose on the poster. Her costumes, wigs, transparent dress allude to her as a figment of the imagination and transitory. Richard McCormick remarks on the self-reflexive tribute to cinema in this juxtaposition of still photograph and moving image, recalling the awakening of Caesare in Robert Wiene's 1919 expressionist film *The Cabinet of Dr. Caligari* that von Sternberg seems to cite in the architecture of the street that leads to The Blue Angel nightclub, or in the use of shadow when Angst is assaulted by his fellow students. More importantly, the transition from still to moving image underscores Rath's intimacy with the image and his investment of the object with libidinal fantasies of wholeness and omnipotence. A shot of Lola's legs follows, the synecdoche of female sexuality, isolated and unmotivated in terms of narrative, marking her as pure fetish. Rather than conceal female lack that must be fetishized to allay male fears of castration, Lola's legs "stand in" for wholeness and plentitude. They are the coveted objects of sexual awakening, which Rath has tucked under his arm in flight, in the drawing on the classroom chalkboard. It is interesting to note that this shot of Lola's legs is missing from the American film release.[43] Reading this omission in light of Paramount's delay of the US premiere of *The Blue Angel* until after the premier of *Morocco*, in order to trump its German rival, suggests continued rivalry.[44] Paramount figuratively attempted to amputate Ufa's success by withholding a moment of pure erotic pleasure.[45]

The cobblestone street that leads to The Blue Angel, a set designed by Otto Hunte that von Sternberg particularly admired, unbalances Rath's footing. Once in the realm of The Blue Angel and no longer on sure ground, Rath enters a world designed to arouse fantasies and release the bourgeois from his moral obligations. To emphasize this transition, von Sternberg creates an artificial world—a world that divorces the sign from its referent, disavows authenticity, and calls up the realm of exaggerated illusion. This could be called the von Sternberg "touch," since, as film theorist Peter Wollen notes, "Von Sternberg's cinema sought to sever the existential bond between the natural world and the film image, to emphasize the iconic aspect of the sign detached from the indexical in order to conjure up a world, comprehensible by virtue of resemblances to the natural world, yet other than it, a kind of dream world, a heterocosm."[46] I might add that the world of the cabaret, a real setting, intentionally reproduces the magic of dreams.

For both the initiated and the inexperienced viewer, the image of Lola is intended to fuel longing; she functions as a dream screen for the projection of desire and fantasy, as seen in the response of all her admirers. As a performer, Lola slips in and out of costumes, suggesting an elusive identity that exists to attract. One of the many costumes Lola wears, a replica of an eighteenth-century noblewoman's hoop dress that resembles a partial birdcage, is translucent and missing its back to reveal her undergarments and legs. The costume plays with the two-dimensionality of images and with surfaces, as well as with the game of revealing and concealing, and of the pleasure of seeing and the pain of separation essential to the masochistic text. In other words, in the world of The Blue Angel everything is deception, distraction, and appearance, that is, surface. It is no wonder that Rath passes through an expressionistically coded space (dark lighting and shadows) that leads him to an exotic, sensual world, a dream world that uses props, lights, costume, and spectacle to taunt and manipulate the spectator.

Still rooted in sentimentality and pathos characteristic of nineteenth-century subjectivities, and not in the modern "cynicism" that characterized a post-World War I generation that Patrice Petro describes as "knowing that everything is deception" but is still willing to be seduced, Rath is unprepared for the spectacle that inevitably burns him like a moth in his suicidal attraction to Lola's light. Implicit in this image is nature vanquished by modernity.[47] In Lola's presence, Rath is stupefied. His naïve relationship to the image recalls the anecdote with which Béla Balász begins his 1930 analysis of the cinematic aesthetic in *The Spirit of Film*. He recounts the tale of a Russian landowner and intellectual, who lives in the country removed from modernity's influences and consequently unfamiliar with the conventions of the cinema. Seeing a film for the first time in the company of children, and visibly as thrilled as they are by the barrage of images, the Russian is unable to decipher the story. To the bafflement of his companion, the Russian asks him what the film was about. Balász describes the Russian's experience as purely somatic; he was unable to create associations between images and assemble a meaningful story. Taking into account the relative newness of the medium, Balász concludes: "It was a new language, with which all city-dwellers were familiar, and which he, a highly educated intellectual, had not yet understood."[48] Like Rath, the Russian lacks exposure to the conventions of mass consumer culture and its distractions. The anecdote may shed light on Rath's uncensored childlike awe and submission to Lola's image and then to the performer, in contrast to his students. On the one hand, Rath arguably lacks visual literacy, which is needed to understand the conventions of visual culture. That is to say that Rath's ability to see and therefore know are impeded by the information (or lack thereof) he brings to the "text." Instructive here is Bourdieu's claim that the "capacity to see <voir> is a function of the knowledge <savoir>, or concept, that is, the words, that are available to name visible things, and which are, as it were, programmes for perception."[49] On the other hand, the drabness of Rath's world is so dramatically offset by the vibrancy of the cabaret and Lola's scintillating performance that the visual and its pleasures overwhelm and take hold of him. To compensate for what has been denied him in reality, he returns to Lola believing that he can possess her.

Rather than maintain the fetishizing distance to the image, he disavows the conventions that separate the real from fantasy and that are integral to the inner workings of cinema and fantasy constructions. When Rath visits Lola's dressing room for the first time, mass-produced posters of Lola, whose seductive image inspire visual consumption and erotic desire, envelop him.

In the arena of the cabaret/dressing room, Rath's identity is always configured in relation to the imaginary. Lola's reproduction, and even her mirror image, when she prepares for her performance, emphasize the process of image making and its deceptions. The multiple images of Lola, emphasized by the many poster images of her, explicitly locate her in the imaginary. Even the doubling of her name, Lola Lola, highlights her reproducibility. Furthermore, she is the site to which all of her admirers return, as she states when Rath makes his second entrance, this time unofficially: "They all come back." Consequently, Rath surrenders himself to the illusion that suspends the reality the image conceals.

Throughout the film, Lola Lola never really leaves the space of the cabaret. Her stage presence structures her existence. She is a product of that space, one of performance and make-believe, where fantasy and desire commune and the spectacle becomes the vehicle and vessel in the artificial world staged. It is no coincidence that Lola is so closely associated with the "Tingel Tangel," a word first coined in Berlin to describe a place of cheap musical entertainment and that stands in as a precursor to the cinema. As Jelavich describes:

> The official attitude toward such venues can be gleaned from the definition of the Tingeltangel established by a German court in 1904: "commercial presentations at a fixed place of operation, consisting of musical performances, especially vocal music, declamations, dances, shorter musicals and similar works, devoid of any higher artistic or scholarly interest, and which are capable, through either their content or their manner of presentation, of arousing the *lower instincts,* in particular the sexual lust of the audience." (emphasis mine).[50]

Film critics similarly believed that early cinema spoke to the so-called lower instincts; it stood in the tradition of familiar public diversions, like the variety, circus, and fairground. In fact, as mentioned in the previous chapter, the birthplace of cinema was "the Varieté in Berlin (vaudeville Theater in the United States, the Café-concert in Paris and the Music-Hall in London), which cinema soon came to replace."[51] Once established, its conventions became habit and spectators understood their role within and outside of the event and adjusted their expectations accordingly. Susan Buck-Morss comments on the viewing conventions that evolved with the establishment of mass entertainment: "At the fairs the crowd was conditioned to the principle of advertisements: 'Look, but don't touch,' and taught to derive pleasure from the spectacle alone."[52]

Some fifty-five years after the making of *The Blue Angel*, Woody Allen would take up the same theme of mistaking "film," and the tenuous separation of the "real" and "reel" world, in addition to the intense desire to overstep the boundary between fantasy and reality in his 1985 film *The Purple Rose of Cairo*. The relationship between the spectator (tellingly, a young woman), the glamorous world of images, and the projected desire onto an object is keenly represented when "Tom" steps out of the two-dimensional celluloid screen and into the "real" world to consummate the ideal love affair with the moviegoer Cecilia, a waitress. Allen addresses the complex operations of cinematic spectatorship, to which von Sternberg alludes, and that Kracauer succinctly addresses in 1927, in his influential essay, "The Little Shop Girls Go to the Movies" ("Die kleinen Ladenmädchen gehen ins Kino").[53] Here Kracauer describes girls of modest means who flocked to movie theaters in the 1920s, all hoping to be starlets one day, and who indulged in fantasies of falling in love with the "right" man who would afford them upward mobility. Fiction informs their fantasies and, in turn, the way in which they perceive the world or would like to experience it. Significantly, these film fantasies reveal the audiences' social reality as much as their dreams, or, as Kracauer posits: "The ridiculous and unreal film fantasies are the daydreams of society, in which its actual reality is brought to light and its repressed desires take shape."[54] Cecilia's longing for the image results in sheer submission to the world of fantasy in order to escape her difficult, lackluster life. Set in the 1930s Depression, around the time *The Blue Angel* was made, but located in New Jersey rather than in Berlin, Allen's film ends with Tom, the desiring and desired object, returning to the world of the imaginary, leaving the female viewer weeping and yearning for her absent lover.[55]

The movies provided outlets and experiences of pleasure and allayed fear as well as provided opportunities to dream. In keeping within a rigid paradigm of traditional gendered assumptions, Kracauer attributed subjective, emotional, and passive qualities to the female spectator, in contrast to the more "valuable" critical stance of male viewers, without exploring the possibility that spectatorship provided women a diversified repertoire of femininity and mobility. Yet, his attitude also makes Rath's position even more vulnerable—since his propensity for absorption feminizes his viewing activity. In looking beyond the facile binary oppositions of gendered viewing to which these early critics subscribed, the recognition of cinema's ability to mesmerize, of its affinity to dreaming, as Hofmannsthal suggests in the above epigraph, and the states of regression (absorption) it elicits, all speak to the psychological mechanisms of the cinematic apparatus that Studlar outlines (disavowal, fetishism, fantasy, scopophilia) that are closely linked to the structures of masochism.[56]

Indeed, the magic of the cinematic image that induces an auratic experience, in order to lose oneself and long for proximity, seems integral to cinematic spectatorship. That does not mean that all aspects of cinematic spectatorship comply with the structures of masochism, as diverse psychoanalytical treatments of cinema show. Von Sternberg's films powerfully produce masochistic narratives, with the masochistic script evolving more perilously for some of its figures.[57] In the example of the image of the female worker at the beginning of *The Blue Angel* and the representation of Woody Allen's female protagonist, it is undeniable that women are positioned differently than are men within the masochistic text. In fact, as I suggested earlier on, masochism is a requisite element of female subjectivity and considered normative. Thus, it is not surprising that Kracauer's worst fears are borne out in Rath's unequivocal submission to the image, which marks him as the susceptible subject of mass culture, a failed *Bildungsbürger*, and as an example of failed masculinity. Associated with passivity and a loss of agency and authority, he is ascribed a feminized role, thus confirming what was perceived as a crisis of male cultural authority during the interwar years.[58] The humiliated former high school teacher becomes the spectacle. The site of former pleasure eclipses into the site of his humiliation and symbolic death.

Consequently, the film does not recuperate the family romance, which would reinstate paternal authority. Quite the opposite: the final image of Lola undermines resolution and with it an Oedipal trajectory. Moreover, her image is hardly contained for the male gaze, as Judith Mayne contends. Lola'a audience disappears in the final shot of her. What is left is pure image and the cinemagoer's gaze that takes in the image and dreams on it. The image arouses fantasy and permits indulgence. The stage image is isolated, deterritorialized, with the gap between spectator and image closed to feature an icon that establishes an erotic rapport with the spectator and reflects back onto its viewers their own desire. Lola gains an ontological quality that transforms those she encounters.

To heighten the ethereal, star-like quality of the image of Lola in the last scene, von Sternberg uses a white voile curtain, against which the sequins in Lola's black outfit glitter. The white space, as the song "Falling in Love Again" tells us, is where moths collect and get burned by love. So remarkable is von Sternberg's use of light in this film, and particularly in this final scene of Lola, that Gilles Deleuze is prompted to exclaim of von Sternberg's films in general:

Everything happens between the light and the white. It is von Sternberg's genius to have brought to realization Goethe's splendid formula: "between transparency and white opacity there exists an infinite number of degrees of cloudiness <*trouble*> ... One could call white the fortuitously opaque flash of pure transparency." This is because the white, for von Sternberg, is primarily that which circumscribes a space corresponding to the luminous. And into this space is inserted a close-up face which reflects the light.[59]

Inserted to reflect the light, the female body in *The Blue Angel* is made for love.

Instead of a close-up, Lola, in the final scene of her, is presented singing in a full shot which arguably assumes the power of a close-up. It is what Deleuze calls an "affection-image"; it reflects the light and allows for contemplation, for dreaming on the image, for the undisturbed flow of desire, and the displacement of its potential power. Given Rath's tragic end, a close-up of Lola may have been too threatening and may have undermined the openness of the signifier. It might have reduced Lola to the role of the vamp—a popular 1920s figure of a woman who devoured her victims, which would blame Lola for Rath's downfall and undermine her survival. After all, the root of "affection image" is *affect*, whose double-edged meaning—to act upon or have an effect on someone, to move someone emotionally, or to infect or damage someone through disease—evokes a more ambivalent fascination with and fear of the image.[60] Furthermore, by privileging the full shot without depth, von Sternberg imparts flatness to the image that recalls the poster advertisement: the image as commodity, as a product for consumption that awakens and displaces desires and promises fulfillment. Closing the imaginary gap between image and spectator, the erotic image is generously offered up for visual pleasure; it is open and unimpeded.

At the end, Lola's image evokes desire that is far more ambiguous than that prescribed by heterosexual difference, and operations of mimicry and possession separate from each other as differentials of gender and sexual identities. Instead of order being restored, the final image suggests repetition. The next suitor will come, since she is made for love—and she will continue to sing her song to audiences worldwide. With this image, Dietrich will achieve international stardom and embody the glamorous spectacle for the rest of her career. Her life thereafter will be about cultivating and preserving the Dietrich image, even after she withdraws from public view to spend the last sixteen years of her life in a Parisian apartment behind closed curtains.[61] After making her films with von Sternberg, as her daughter Maria Riva writes, "Dietrich no longer recreated her image—simply perpetuated it—still requiring very hard work, just less inspiration."[62] Thus what begins with Lola seems to carry on throughout Dietrich's life. In a description of Dietrich, printed in a 1970 issue of *Vogue* that she edited, Kenneth Tynan notes, "She dedicates herself to looking, rather than to being sexy. The art is in the seeming."[63]

# Notes

1. Maria Riva, *Marlene Dietrich: By her Daughter* (New York: Alfred Knopf, 1993), 323.
2. Walter Benjamin, *Illuminations: Essays and Reflections*, translated by Harry Zohn (New York: Schocken Books, 1968). Benjamin strives to assert the "revolutionary demands in the politics of art," which can be used as a "weapon against fascism," by freeing art from such concepts as "creativity, genius, eternal value and mystery," which serve fascism but have also defined the creative process since Romanticism. Although his intent is historically specific, his model generally deals with the evolution of artistic practices and their relationship to the subject, i.e., the spectator.
3. Benjamin, 231.
4. Benjamin argues that film can never be subsumed by traditional notions of art, whose aura is produced by immediacy, as opposed to mediation through the camera. "This situation," Benjamin contends, "might also be characterized as follows: for the first time—and this is the effect of the film—man <sic> has to operate with his whole living person, yet foregoing its aura. For aura is tied to presence; there can be no replica of it" (233). With the introduction of technology, the way in which art is experienced naturally transforms the subject. Technical reproduction diminishes the distance between the object and its viewer, for it can bring the copy of the original into situations unattainable to the original itself. With his belief in the disappearance of the aura, Benjamin celebrates the new forms of experience that the cinematic apparatus makes available.
5. Benjamin, 227. Consequently, the further away the object moves from its original ritual function, the weaker the aura becomes. Its ritual value shifts to its "exhibition value," which for Benjamin gains political relevance because of its altered social function.
6. Benjamin, 227. Early film theory focused on the spectacle of the body and, as Sabine Hake notes, "many Weimar critics approached the body with almost religious reverence, claiming it as an object for metaphysical reflection" (*The Cinema's Third Machine*, 131).
7. Benjamin, 231.
8. As is true today, film stars' lives were public property much like the lives of theater actors, whose public and private personas were intimately intertwined. Moreover, actors' images are used to sell films as much as other products. The tobacco industry caught on to the marketability of their products through stars as early as the 1920s, and included the picture of a film star in its packs of cigarettes for consumers to collect. Once famous, Dietrich's image became a trademark for numerous products, among them the cigarette brand Lucky Strike.
9. Lotte Eisner, *The Haunted Screen* (Berkeley: University of California Press, 1972), 314.
10. Angelika Rauch, "The *Trauerspiel* of the Prostituted Body, or Woman as Allegory of Modernity," *Cultural Critique* (Fall 1988), 77.
11. See Rudolf Harms, *Philosophie des Films: Seine ästhetischen und metaphysischen Grundlagen* (Leipzig: Verlag von Felix Meiner, 1926), 15. Also, Fritz Lang's abstract suspension of the eyes in *Metropolis*, when the robot Maria casts a spell on her male audience, reveals eyes as powerful receptors of desire.
12. Pierre Bourdieu, "Distinction and the Aristocracy of Culture," *Cultural Theory and Popular Culture*, edited and introduced by John Storey (Athens: University of Georgia Press, 1998), 433.
13. Mary Ann Doane, "The Erotic Barter: *Pandora's Box*," *The Films of G.W. Pabst: An Extraterritorial Cinema*, edited by Eric Rentschler (New Brunswick, NJ: Rutgers University Press, 1990), 76.
14. Consider the many bourgeois sons who were encouraged to gain sexual experience with prostitutes and female servants, as in Marieluise Fleisser's portrayal of the servant in her 1929 play *Pioniere in Ingolstadt*.
15. Miriam Hansen, "Early Silent Cinema: Whose Public Sphere?" *New German Critique* 29 (Spring/Summer 1983), 174.

16. See Laura Mulvey, "Visual Pleasure and Narrative Cinema," *Feminism and Film Theory*, edited by Constance Penley (New York: Routledge, 1988): 57–68. Since Mulvey's groundbreaking study, its shortcomings have been discussed widely. Mainly, she compounds the vernacular of dominant culture by leaving unacknowledged such significant defining factors of identity as class, ethnicity, race, and sexual preference.
17. These theories and representations of male visual control, when carefully read, reveal inconsistencies. For example, many accounts underscore Dietrich's contributions to her construction. Her meticulous control of the lighting and camera angles when shooting her, or of her costuming, not to mention her detached style of acting that attracted von Sternberg and the film's critics in the first place, loosen the grip of traditional understandings of gender and power. It could also be said that von Sternberg's anguished relationship to Dietrich, which various biographers describe, suggests a shared vulnerability with Rath—a vulnerability that expresses itself in the encounter with the sexualized and all-powerful female and that undermines notions of male sovereignty.
18. Peter Baxter, "On the Naked Thighs of Miss Dietrich," *Movies and Methods II*, edited by Bill Nichols (Berkeley: University of California Press, 1985), 564.
19. Josef von Sternberg, "The von Sternberg Principle," *Sternberg*, edited by Peter Baxter (London: British Film Institute, 1980), 52–53. One need not look far to find how such notions of the primacy of the (anxiety-ridden) male gaze find resonance in an assortment of cultural formulations. On various occasions, using as his inspiration Flaubert's dictum, "Bovary, *c'est moi*," von Sternberg proclaimed "Dietrich, *c'est moi*." He recounts in his memoir *Fun in a Chinese Laundry*: "I recall Marlene's complaints, while she submitted to fitting into my vision of her, that for nothing in the world would she care to undergo such torment as she thought was being inflicted on her. She did not object to the transformation, but neither did she relish it. Of course, in her case the glamour had to be maintained in motion, not on being made to appear ravishing in a few posed photographs" (224).
20. I am indebted to Patrice Petro's *Aftershocks of the New: Feminism and Film History* (New Brunswick, NJ: Rutgers University Press), 121, for drawing my attention to this image of Dietrich's legs in Hannah Höch's *Marlene* (1930).
21. Elizabeth Bronfen, "Vertreibung aus dem vertrauten Heim: *Der blaue Engel* (Josef von Sternberg)," *Heimweh: Illusionsspiel in Hollywood* (Berlin: Verlag Volk & Welt, 1999), 97–142. In her essay, Bronfen addresses Dietrich's rise to stardom and departure from Berlin. In the film, Rath experiences a homecoming. Jannings does too: *The Blue Angel* is the first film in which Jannings performed after returning to Germany from Hollywood.
22. These representations subsequently contain subversive moments since women's self-alienation (*Selbstentfremdung*) and distortion (*Entstellung*) are inscribed in the image of the seductive woman.
23. In a similar vein, Bronfen states that if the male subject needs the privileged object of his gaze to secure his own identity, this dependency reveals a profound insecurity. Thus, the male gaze, according to Bronfen, is also *Selbstentfremdet* (self-alienated).
24. Bronfen, 124 (my translation). "Der Blickende wie die Angeblickte auf unheimliche Weise zwischen einer sadistisch ermächtigenden und einer masochistisch entmächtigenden Haltung changieren."
25. Gaylyn Studlar, *In the Realm of Pleasure: Von Sternberg, Dietrich, and the Masochistic Aesthetic* (New York: Columbia University Press, 1992), 29.
26. Studlar, 66.
27. Studlar, 108.
28. Studlar, 110.
29. Interesting in this context is what Maria Riva, Dietrich's daughter, wrote of her mother in *Marlene*: "By 1922, Marlene could sprint across the length and breadth of Berlin, appear as any woman called for … The first time Lena went on an "extra" casting call, she wore a pirate's hat, a pheasant's tail feather stuck through its crown, a panne velvet coat, complete with dangling four-legged fur piece of a very long-dead red fox, and, stuck in her eye, her father's monocle" (43).

30. In Irmgard Keun's *The Artificial Silk Girl*, the protagonist Doris describes the circularity of the gaze and desire. When walking in the streets of Berlin, she spots her image in a display window and is pleased with what she sees and what men will see.
31. Studlar, 123.
32. Erica Carter reads the black doll as another indication of the multiple identities that Dietrich represented. She writes: "Traditionally, the doll is for girls and women a powerful figure of identification; thus Dietrich's capacity to put herself in the place of the black other is already suggested in the black playmate that is an apparently incidental element in the mise-en-scène in *The Blue Angel*. The suggestion here of mobile ethnicity is reinforced in Dietrich's later films." Erica Carter, "Marlene Dietrich—the Prodigal Daughter," *The German Cinema Book*, edited by Tim Bergfelder et al. (London: British Film Institute, 2002), 75.
33. Roland Barthes, *Camera Lucida: Reflections on Photography*, translated by Richard Howard (New York: Noonday Press, 1981), 43–45.
34. Studlar, 117.
35. Mary Ann Doane, *The Desire to Desire: The Woman's Film of the 1940s* (Bloomington: Indiana University Press, 1987), 32. See Miriam Hansen's analysis of Adorno's writing on mass culture. Here she notes: "Simulating immediacy, individuality, and intimacy, the 'characters' of mass culture spell out norms of social behavior—ways of being, smiling, and mating. Regardless of the explicit messages touted via dialogue and plot, the viewer is ceaselessly asked to transcode image into script, to read the individual appearance of a star as an imperative of identity—'to be like her'—and to articulate the most subtle nuances in terms of the binary logic of 'do and don't.'" Miriam Bratu Hansen, "Mass Culture as Hieroglyphic Writing: Adorno, Derrida, Kracauer," *The Actuality of Adorno*, edited by Max Pensky (Albany, NY: State University of New York Press, 1997), 88–89.
36. Weimar culture may have had an even more nuanced understanding of the significance of the display window as a space that transforms or reveals identity. In "Die Frau vor dem Schaufenster" (The Woman in Front of the Display Window), *Frankfurter Hausfrau* (February 20, 1924), the author introduces the display window as the window to women's souls and advises prenuptial men to take their possible wives for a stroll through the streets and secretly observe their reaction to the various display windows that decorate the streets of the metropolis—in this case Frankfurt. The suitor will learn that the features of a once-innocent "Backfisch" (teenager) become "ugly, greedy and envious" ("hässlichen, habsüchtigen, neidischen Züge") and a "childishly demanding spite ("kindisch verlangender Trotz") manifests itself. The author portrays various types of women in relation to the display window and does a symptomatic reading of their character and suitability for marriage. The author particularly warns against those types of women who are drawn to chocolate displays or those who visit bookstores. Those who frequent flower shops are the most eligible spouses and make the best future mothers. See also Dirk Reinhardt, *Von der Reklame zum Marketing: Geschichte der Wirtschaftswerbung in Deutschland* (Berlin: Akademie-Verlag, 1993); Janet Ward, *Weimar Surfaces: Urban Visual Culture in 1920s Germany* (Berkeley: University of California Press, 2001).
37. During the Weimar Republic, women were often discussed as being more susceptible to images or less guarded, owing to what was described as their inability to discern fiction from reality. See Frank Kessler and Eva Warth, "Early Cinema and its Audiences," in *The German Cinema Book*, edited by Tim Bergfelder et al. (London: British Film Institute, 2002), 121–29.
38. Studlar, 179.
39. See www.filmportal.de
40. Donald Spoto, *Falling in Love Again: Marlene Dietrich* (Boston: Little, Brown, 1985), 27.
41. Josef von Sternberg, *Fun in a Chinese Laundry* (New York: Macmillan, 1965), 227.
42. Bronfen writes: "Dass es zuerst das Bild der Verführerin Lola ist, also die Repräsentation und nicht der konkrete Leib, das zwischen und in den drei zentralen Räumen der Erzählhandlung—dem Heim des Professors, dem seiner Herrschaft unterworfenen

Klassenzimmer und dem ihm völlig fremden Kabarett 'Der blaue Engel'—zirkuliert, bevor es dann an Lolas bzw. Marlene Dietrichs Gestalt festgemacht wird" (120).
43. See Thomas Doherty, "*The Blue Angel*," *Cineaste* 27 (Spring 2002), 44; Ernst Marshall, "Notes of London Screen," *New York Times* (July 20, 1930), X4: "Some of the scenes in the Ufa production in which she <Marlene Dietrich> exercises her allurements are described as transgressing the bounds of what the censors in Hollywood would consider to be at all proper."
44. Stefanie Wehnert and Nathalie Bielfeldt, eds., *Mein Kopf und die Beine von Marlene Dietrich. Heinrich Manns Professor Unrat und Der blaue Engel* (Lübeck: Buddenbrookhaus, 1996), 101.
45. In 1956, Paramount attempted a remake of *The Blue Angel*, directed by Edward Dmytryk and starring May Britt as Lola and Curt Jurgens as Rath. This remake is a sanitized version of von Sternberg's film. Rather than rely on images, dialog drives the narrative. Most notably, Rath is "saved" at the end by the principal of the school. After his humiliating performance and breakdown, the principal and loyal friend leads him out of The Blue Angel and down the right path to a rehabilitation center, as is suggested in the final shot of him and Rath walking down the street that marked their daily routines.
46. Andrea Slane, *A Not So Foreign Affair: Fascism, Sexuality, and the Cultural Rhetoric of American Democracy* (Durham: Duke University Press, 2001), 224.
47. Petro, *Aftershocks of the New*, 109.
48. Béla Balász, 10 (my translation). "*Die Handlung*, der Kinder mühelos folgen konnten, hatte er nicht erfasst. Denn es war eine neue Sprache gewesen, die allen Städtern geläufig war und die er, der hochgebildete Intellektuelle, noch nicht verstanden hatte."
49. Bourdieu, 432.
50. Peter Jelavich, *Berlin Cabaret* (Cambridge, MA: Harvard University Press, 1993), 21.
51. Joachim Paech, *Literatur und Film* (Stuttgart: Metzler, 1997), 1. Also see, Horst Claus, "Varieté—Operette—Film: Berührungspunkte und Konkurrenzkampf aus der Sicht des Fachblattes 'Der Artist,'" *Musik Spektakel Film: Musiktheater und Tanzkultur im deutschen Film, 1922–1937* (Frankfurt am Main: Edition Text und Kritik, 1998), 67–84. Claus writes: "In April 1913, the journal *Artist* ascertained: 'The chanson quarter is dying out. In a whole row of chanson bars, where the spotlight once shined on the skimpy fanciful costume of more or less good soubrettes, the projector now casts its magical rays of the wonders of cinematography on the walls'" (71, my translation).
52. Susan Buck-Morss, "Dream World of Mass Culture: Walter Benjamin's Theory of Modernity and the Dialectics of Seeing," *Modernity and the Hegemony of Vision* (Cambridge: MIT, 1991).
53. Siegfried Kracauer, "Die kleinen Ladenmädchen gehen ins Kino," *Der verbotene Blick* (Leipzig: Reclam, 1992), 156–60. "Die blödsinnigen und irrealen Filmfantasien sind die Tagträume der Gesellschaft, in denen ihre eigentliche Realität zum Vorschein kommt, ihre sonst unterdrückten Wünsche sich gestalten."
54. Kracauer, 158.
55. Emilie Altenloh, *Zur Soziologie des Kinos* (Leipzig: Spamersche Buchdruckerei, 1914). A few years earlier than Kracauer but echoing his observation, Emilie Altenloh commented in her 1914 study that female moviegoers responded more strongly than male moviegoers to the aesthetic components of film and allowed themselves to be totally absorbed.
56. Miriam Hansen, in "Benjamin, Cinema and Experience: 'The Blue Flower in the Land of Technology,'" *New German Critique* 40 (1987), 212, challenges the notion of the incompatibility of cinema and auratic experience. Interestingly, she asserts that the cinema is not divested of the aura: "The discontinuous return of an auratic mode of experience through the backdoor of the 'optical unconscious' allows us to reconsider the concept of aura itself and perhaps to demystify some of its implications."
57. In von Sternberg's autobiography, *Fun in a Chinese Laundry*, he discusses his own take on masochism and film, focusing on the experience of the actor: "Masochism is a curious form of pleasure induced by an initial submission to abuse or some form of degradation.

Were it to be examined in relation to the actor's need for applause, this being the apex of pleasure, it must be obvious that if he should not be applauded after enduring what he may consider abuse, repercussions must be expected. His anguish will remain until it is released in one form or another, the easiest discharge being the venting of his fury and displeasure at anyone who indulges in incomplete methods of exciting him" (120)."

58. See Judith Mayne, "Marlene Dietrich, *The Blue Angel*, and Female Performance," *Seduction and Theory: Readings of Gender, Representation and Rhetoric*, edited by Diane Hunter (Champagne-Urbana: University of Illinois Press, 1989), 28—46, and Elizabeth Bronfen, "Heimweh: Illusionsspiele in Hollywood." Both Judith Mayne and Elizabeth Bronfen argue that paternal authority is reinstated at the end of *The Blue Angel*, suggesting a resolution and the end of crisis. For one, Bronfen explores the tension between the imaginary and the symbolic, situating Rath in the realm of the symbolic, that is language, and Lola in the imaginary. She contends that Rath's scopophilia betrays the paternal laws he represents. The symbolic accedes to the imaginary and is destroyed by its powers, as witnessed in the last scene in which Rath's dead body, according to Bronfen, participates in the imaginary. The dead male body conceals the fragility of the symbolic represented by Rath's inability to resist the seductive woman. He returns to the site of the symbolic, i.e. the school, but only as its fetish, thus suspending the "deadly difference between these two realms." At the same time, Lola, that is Dietrich, enters into the realm of international stardom and the symbolic order of the Hollywood film industry, so that Bronfen sees a more complicated attribution of gender in this elision. Judith Mayne's reading differs largely in the way she represents Rath within the narrative structure. In her estimation, he regains narrative authority and order triumphs over the carnivalesque atmosphere of The Blue Angel nightclub, which characterizes the space only at the beginning of the film. According to Mayne, Rath's character not only changes the nightclub but his needs define the progression of the narrative; it is "the activation of his desires <that> provides the necessary complications and oppositions to make a story" (36).
59. Gilles Deleuze, *Cinema 1: The Movement-Image*, translated by Hugh Tomlinson and Barbara Habberjam (Minneapolis: University of Minnesota Press, 1986), 93.
60. Louis Audibert writes of *The Blue Angel* that "the film abounds in medium shots and medium long shots, indices of consolidation; compared with full shots, which instill or maintain distance and order, they permit displacements, mutations which inwardly transform themselves, they change proximity into promiscuity; mixture and confusion usher in perversion and ruin. Even certain long shots (such as the audience in the cabaret) are treated as an overlapping of medium shots and medium long shots; zones of light and shade slice across bodies, while a proliferation of objects cuts up the space, refusing it any depth, thus mingling the protagonists in a common destiny" (in "The Flash of the Look," *Sternberg*, edited by Peter Baxter, 97). Compared to his use of the close-up in other films, von Sternberg uses it sparingly in *The Blue Angel* (ten shots in all).
61. At a screening of *Her Own Song* in Tucson, Arizona (2004), Dietrich's grandson, David Riva, spoke of her seclusion at the end of her life as a means of preserving her image.
62. Maria Riva, 34.
63. Patrick O'Connor, *The Amazing Blonde Woman: Dietrich's Own Style* (London: Bloomsbury, 1991), 18.

*Chapter 3*

# DISILLUSIONMENT AND ESPRIT: WEIMAR'S MODERN WOMAN

> Beautiful woman of Berlin! During the day you are working, and in the evenings ready to dance. You have an athletically steeled body and beautiful skin that cosmetics just brighten up. With the same speed that your musty provincial town blossomed into a metropolis, you conscientiously obtained beautiful legs and the necessary mixture of reliability and carelessness (frivolity), of vagueness and definition, of goodness and coolness.
> **Franz Hessel, 1922 in** *Vogue*

> The women in Berlin are beautiful and well groomed and in debt.
> **Irmgard Keun,** *The Artificial Silk Girl*

To read *The Blue Angel* in terms of a masochistic aesthetic lends vast insight into the internal psychodynamic of character and reflects on attributes of cinema and spectatorship as early as the 1920s. Yet, if the text is looked at as a cultural artifact, then it is also necessary to expand the textual workings beyond the film aesthetic and take into account the historical context and its imprint on the image. In doing so, representation achieves a depth that goes beyond the surface. As I have shown in Chapter 1, the complex cultural wars discursively waged during the Weimar Republic resonate with the encounter between Rath and Lola and the spheres they represent. Chapter 2 explores Rath's relationship to Lola as cinematic image and product of fantasy and historicizes the encounter with visual culture. In this chapter, Lola is viewed through the lens of gender as it was newly sketched and debated during the Weimar Republic, and intricately linked to discussions of modernity and mass culture. Thus viewed within the context of the Weimar Republic, her figure opens itself up to a complex of narratives on the modern woman that commanded the 1920s, and to assorted discourses that contributed to defining her appearance as historical figure and product of visual culture. Despite von Sternberg's seeming guard against the incursions of the patriarchal text, that is, history, in his composition of a masochistic aesthetic, history invariably resides as a powerful peripheral text within the narrative and strips on occasion the masochistic aesthetic of disavowal. Marriage and female employment take front seat in *The Blue Angel*, two topics that either have been fully neglected in most readings of *The Blue Angel*, or only cursorily mentioned. So contrary to Kracauer's critique of the film as pure ornament, the historical discourses invariably puncture the aesthetic surface of *The Blue Angel* to betray contours of the social realities of the Weimar Republic.

The scenes in which the social reality starkly asserts itself are hardly as alluring or intoxicating as those scenes that emphasize surface and performance, as when Lola is on stage, or even backstage, self-consciously constructing herself for the public gaze and the seductions of popular culture. Even her participation in constructing herself for the gaze can be read historically as a sign of the progressive visibility of the modern woman in the public arena and as indicative of a heightened self-awareness in attracting the anonymous gaze. Thus what follows is the way in which discourses on the modern woman, the crisis in marriage and the state of female employment converge and both explicitly and implicitly inform *The Blue Angel*.

Most narratives of the modern woman begin with an account of the unprecedented opportunities that were available to women during the Weimar Republic, many of which were unthinkable in previous decades. Owing her existence largely to social changes brought on by World War I, by technological developments and economic necessity, by the proliferation of visual media, and by the development of commodity culture with its increased strategies of display, the modern woman entered public space, particularly that of the metropolis. Narratives of the modern woman include the many professions that were open to women for the first time and feature especially a new class of clerical workers, a population that became a part of the burgeoning cityscape. The plethora of leisure activities women engaged in that ranged from movies to shopping in department stores, to meeting in cafés, to participating in sports, in addition to changes in sexual practices, relationships, attitudes, and lifestyles, and even in hairstyles (the page or bob) and attire (short dresses and pants for the more daring) defined her representation and existence.[1] As a momentous social actor in cities, dynamic and youthful, and cast as employee, shopper, pleasure-seeker, and as a prime subject of visual culture and the literary imagination (her image was literally everywhere), the modern woman became an emblem of the Weimar Republic and its diverse obsessions. In many ways, Dietrich serves as a symbol of the modern woman in its more extravagant and extroverted version. Her biography while growing up and living in Berlin is representative of the changes that tested normative notions of gender. From the way she managed her career, appearing on many stages and in films throughout the 1920s, to the way she managed her marriage (both Dietrich and her husband had lovers and maintained a marriage in appearance), she played in modernity's laboratory and enjoyed the free spirit and opportunities of the age.

The challenges to traditional notions of gender that the new woman posed thus resulted in her becoming the foil against which the culture of modernity was read. As is expected, she became the focal point of debates that pitted modernity's enthusiasts against its despondent detractors, resonating with the politically polarized debates throughout the 1920s about the state or "health" of the nation. These debates addressed every aspect of modern life ranging from femininity, family, sexuality, marriage, fashion, and mass culture and oftentimes betrayed a sense of disorientation and anxiety over the loss of control that characterized the age. Depending on political orientation, the modern woman, much like mass culture, was either celebrated as the icon of modernity and progress or blamed for cultural decline. On one hand, she embodied social changes, freedom from restrictive social norms, liberalism, and the seductive promises of the new age and progress. On the other hand, she was perceived as an aberration of nature, lacking motherliness and therefore representing an affront to family values and the clear, traditional division of gendered spheres, and the respective roles men and women were to play in those spheres. In their critique of young women's lifestyles, cultural conservatives were spurred particularly by declining birth rates and the gender imbalance effected by World War I.[2] The uncertainty that the modern woman produced stemmed largely from the interwar generation's refusal to subscribe to an understanding of femininity foisted upon them by the pre-World War I generation. These conflicting and competing attitudes toward femininity (and masculinity) attempted to define, and thereby employ for their own purposes, the phenomenon of the modern woman whose development and historical significance, as Stefan Zweig boldly noted, had a greater impact on the early twentieth century than did World War I.[3]

Given her powerful symbolic presence during the Weimar Republic, it is vital to analyze Lola as the modern woman that stepped onto the historical stage during the interwar years, and to see her within the contradictions and tensions that defined the rapidly changing era. These contradictions are expressed often in the characterization of Lola as both whore (Magdalena) and mother (Maria), which reflects more on women's precarious social position during Germany's interwar years, and the anxieties that the image of the cool, independent woman aroused, than on women's actual experience. The composite of Christian names portrays the outer reaches of the pendulum that swung between women's uncertain reception in the public sphere, equating her "publicness" with promiscuity, and the pressure to maintain the traditional values of the private sphere, where women performed and were defined as wives and mothers.[4] Fritz Lang exploited this polarized iconography in 1927 in his representation of the technological robot Maria and her nurturing, maternal alter ego in *Metropolis*. These binary oppositions, as Anton Kaes observes, literally comprise Dietrich's name, Maria Magdalena, before she abbreviated it to Marlene. However pervasive and entrenched this polarized understanding of femininity may have been (and still is), this view of Lola associates her primarily with sexuality, as a function either of pleasure or economic gain, that is, prostitution or reproduction. It awkwardly equates her stage presence and "visibility" with promiscuity and her support of Rath as maternal. Eloquently fleshing out the tensions that defined the experience of the modern woman at the twilight of the 1920s, Kaes further sharpens the contours of Lola: "The ambivalence that characterized the modern woman in the later part of the Weimar Republic shimmers through in Lola's role play: self-supporting through employment and having become independent of a man, sovereign, cold and unsympathetic (from the male perspective)—and then again pressed into the traditional role of mother and wife."[5]

This insistence on the historical specificity of Lola raises questions about such figurative designations of Lola as "the eternal feminine" or femme fatale, a turn-of-the-twentieth-century fantasy, which Bram Dijkstra analyzes as "a cultural war on women," and even problematizes them. He continues: "born out of an age of extreme sexual repression that turned women into raw nature, the femme fatale threatened masculine superiority and prowess, undermining his place in the Darwinian battle of the fittest."[6] Associating Lola with this image makes short shrift of the impact of her doubled role as image and as modern woman and forces her into paradigms with which modernity broke. More significantly, to dehistoricize her appearance and function in such a way unwittingly suggests that femininity is resistant to history. In 1930, Elsa Hermann perceptively recognized the need to read gender historically, presumably in response to the dramatic changes femininity experienced and the deficiency of language to characterize these changes. She astutely maintains, "That is why the concept of femininity, which was right for the past, must not be applied to the present, since femininity," as Hermann reminds her readers, "is a cultural factor in its various appearances."[7] Hermann's call to consider the historical context in order to understand the dynamic processes of femininity, or for that matter of gender, is crucial not only because it insists on women as an effect of and participant in history, but it allows for a more nuanced understanding of how gender is variously formulated and performed.

Thus seen through the liberal lens of the Weimar Republic, Lola comes into view not as prostitute, vamp, or fallen angel but as the modern woman whose alleged liberation depended on a paycheck. Her sexuality was considered ambiguous and her body a challenge to bourgeois norms precisely because such age-old dichotomies as mother/whore had exhausted themselves in the more complex definitions of femininity in the interwar period with women enjoying mobility and a wider range of life choices. In addition to the radical social changes the 1920s underwent, film and other forms of visual culture, such as advertising and fashion magazines, projected varied versions of the new woman, which significantly contributed to expanding the repertoire of gendered identities, offering her more capacious forms of identity than in previous eras.[8] Compared to the image of femininity before World War I, Mathilde Vaerting claims in 1932, "Femininity has become more differentiated. The uniformity of women has diminished, the differences among women has increased. The new femininity has produced new ways and forms of being that were unknown before."[9] Hannah Höch's photomontages *Da-Dandy* (1919), *The Beautiful Girl* (1920), *Dada Ernst* (1920), and *German Girl* (1930), while critical of capitalism's rationalization and commodification of the new woman, also draw attention to femininity as a multifaceted and complex synthesis of technology and culture.[10] Perhaps not surprisingly, the collage or montage, forms familiar to avant-garde art of the 1920s and illustrated women's magazines, appears to be the most adequate means of capturing the panoply of simultaneous yet divergent tendencies that contributed to composing the new woman. Tellingly, in his review of *The Blue Angel* and description of Lola, Fritz Olimsky deviates from clichéd dualities and bows to her indeterminacy: "Despite all of her cheekiness, she is not directly vulgar and even allows for a bit of soul to peek through at times. A wonderful mixture, one might even say, a symbol of the inscrutable complexity of women."[11]

As can be seen from the many "takes" of the modern woman, the various roles and appearances she took on even called for a new lexicon of gender that complicated yesteryear's facile polarizations. Lynne Frame identifies three types of women that biomedical and popular discourses described as the "Gretchen, Girl and Garçonne" who were rated predominantly in terms of "marriageability" and their conformity to or deviation from traditional notions of femininity.[12] It is interesting to note that French and English are used to describe these typologies (except for Gretchen), suggesting their "foreignness" (a foreign body) in the German context. Perhaps to this list should be added the *Junggesellin* or bachelorette frequently addressed in journals and newspapers.[13] The Gretchen-type, a country bumpkin, was cast in tradition, as a 1931 cartoon in *Uhu* of Dietrich attending a spinning wheel like Rapunzel, with her dress hiked up over her thighs to show a garter belt, suggests (see Figure 3.1).[14]

Alternatively, the Girl was seen as urban, attractive, athletic, young, and outfitted with directness and openness, which had critics decrying the loss of mystery and eroticism in the new generation of women. She mostly was found in the ranks of the newly emerging class of clerical workers. This type also was known for her "sex appeal," a term that migrated from the United States and entered the German vernacular

**Figure 3.1** "Marlene Dietrich plays Gretchen," *Uhu* (October 1931). Source: *Ullstein Verlag*.

without translation.¹⁵ Sex appeal described that "certain something," a magic that transcends beauty, and that Lola sings about in "Beware of Blonde Women"/"Nimm dich in acht vor blonden Frauen."¹⁶ Dietrich's often-alluded-to sex appeal was attributed to her glamour and flirtatiousness, and more famously to her legs.¹⁷

Though hardly a "girl," Dietrich fashioned herself more according to the provocative Garçonne, another type of modern woman. The figure of the Garçonne, a fashionably "masculinized" woman with short cropped hair and known for sporting pants, could be seen modeled in the cabaret performer Claire Waldoff, one of Dietrich's many lovers, whose style Dietrich was said to emulate. Waldoff was known for her brash, androgynous caricature.[18] The popularity of the Garçonne style also can be gleaned from films and magazines that featured modern, independent and fashion-conscious women. Gabriele Tergit, a journalist of the time, comments on the general confusion discerning young women from young men, which increasingly challenged gender boundaries: "The girl looks like a man that looks like a girl, called a Garçonne, that consciously renounced the feminine form in the 1920s."[19] In *The Blue Angel*, this crossing is symbolized by the top hat that lends Lola an air of transgression and accentuates her sexual ambiguity and an inassimilable power. Backstage in Lola's dressing room, her top hat hangs next to Rath's, marking a potential egalitarian distribution of power, except that "his" signifies tradition and his place in bourgeois culture, while "hers" represents an upheaval of traditionally gendered spaces and roles and deposes the familiar fixtures of culture, wreaking havoc. More than Lola, Dietrich took full advantage of the expanded repertoire of female representation (and contributed to it) and of its expression in women's fashion in the 1920s, which included cross-dressing.[20] Taking on the role of the Garçonne, she wore pants and a monocle, smoked cigarettes, and adopted a boyish style when she cruised through Berlin's nightclub scene,

**Figure 3.2** The calendar serves as a temporal referent. Still from *Der blaue Engel*, 1930, directed by Josef von Sternberg. Source: *Friedrich-Wilhelm-Murnau-Stiftung*.

or otherwise dressed extravagantly to attract attention. Her path to such haunts as the Eldorado Club or The White Rose or Le Silhouette could most probably be found in Curt Moreck's alternative guide to Berlin, *Führer durch das 'lasterhafte' Berlin*.[21] Dietrich's daughter writes that for *The Blue Angel* her mother got the idea for her white satin top hat and ruffled panties from a Berlin transvestite. According to Maria Riva, "She <Marlene> insisted that only *they* knew how to wear the obligatory garter belt with style."[22] All in all, these *types* of women indisputably crossed gendered boundaries in appearance, attitude, and lifestyle and took advantage of their newly acquired opportunities, while grappling with the challenges of modernity.

That history informs and haunts a number of images in *The Blue Angel* is indicated by the explicit inclusion of temporal markers. In one of the few close-ups the film offers, the singed calendar pages designate the years 1925–1929, thereby establishing the years of Lola's and Rath's union, and Rath's decline (see Figure 3.2).

These years coincide with a period of unbridled enthusiasm for American culture, that is, mass culture, among cultural liberals and the general public of the Weimar Republic, with modernity in full swing. It was a time of economic prosperity accompanied by the introduction of Fordism and Taylorism, by urban development, and by the emergence of a population that sought entertainment. In addition to the years superimposed on the screen, specific dates are highlighted. November 24 is prominently displayed, a month after the crash of the New York stock exchange, which sent shockwaves through Europe and gradually led to an economic depression in Germany. The introduction of these dates insists on the historical framework as an organizing principle integral to the narrative, and accordingly, provides a foil against which the images must be read. The sale of the postcards of Lola, the icon Rath cherished, which she shrewdly kept for tougher times, subtly signals the profound volatility of the era, in addition to Rath's misjudgment. Fanning out the postcards on a small tray, Rath sits next to a partial poster of Lola—with only the view of her legs in the frame. He is no longer audience to Lola's performance of "Beware of Blonde Women," laid over the image. Instead he becomes an icon of the unspoken consequence of living out desire and betraying class boundaries. When he berates the audience, Lola challenges his arrogance and soberly counters, "In fact we live off them." Kiepert chimes in and criticizes Rath for his slovenliness. Near to breakdown, Rath exits the dressing room, vowing to leave—a drama that Lola seems resigned to by now—but then returns to submissively help slip on her stockings and curl her hair. Indeed, Rath's economic dependence on Lola is contrasted sharply with her sustained success.

When Kiepert announces the upcoming show as a great chance for Rath to succeed and an opportunity finally to earn his own keep and restore his masculinity, Rath refuses to perform in his hometown. Kiepert

**Figure 3.3** "You have allowed this woman to support you for five years." Still from *Der blaue Engel*, 1930, directed by Josef von Sternberg. Source: *Friedrich-Wilhelm-Murnau-Stiftung*.

appeals to Rath's sense of manliness and admonishes him: "You have allowed this woman to support you for five years. We are leaving tomorrow morning! End of story!" Thoroughly domesticated in this one scene only, Lola stands behind Rath, wearing an apron and washing her stockings, and watches the interaction between Kiepert and Rath (see Figure 3.3). Eyeing the new contract, she defends Rath and admonishes Kiepert not to make fun of the old man. In a gesture of sympathy, she takes Rath's hand to console him. These scenes of the social reality and of Rath's progressive disintegration are evidence of the inability to sustain the masochistic enterprise. When tested against the harsh historical realities that unwittingly infuse the text, the illusion of bliss cannot be upheld. The iconic gives way to the indexical in the attribution of the cabaret performer as wife and breadwinner. In other words, these images, far removed from the arresting displays of the "staged" female body, bear the burden of realism. Later on, Rath will step onto the stage at the urging of Lola, whose contemptuous stare further degrades the cuckold husband. While Rath's "cultural" impoverishment speaks to anxieties over the severe erosion of class attributions, and with it that of "German" identity brought on by mass culture, Lola's financial support of her husband magnifies women's economic empowerment as well as

Weimar's economic turmoil and again squarely identifies her as one of Weimar's modern working women. The calendar date reads 1929, and marks the transition to Rath sitting vacantly before a mirror and applying clown makeup.

The image of Lola as breadwinner juxtaposed with Rath's failed masculinity potentially speaks to the anxieties that the modern woman aroused in the German middle class, owing to her new economic power and independence—an anxiety that found expression in numerous venues ranging from politics to psychoanalysis to art. Besides being a path filled with obstacles, as many women writers have described, the modern woman's struggle for independence, not to mention financial security, was often blamed on her "boundless egotism" and even defined in terms of pathology, owing to the betrayal of her natural vocation and biological destiny—something the Nazis would attend to in 1933. The prominence of women in the workforce challenged traditional social structures and ignited debates that became even more volatile during the years of economic instability.

In an effort to preserve traditional notions of femininity in the workforce, while conceding to the economic and historical demands placed on women that necessitated their working, Gertrud Bäumer, an early pioneer of the women's movement, found ways to rhetorically reconcile women's "natural calling" with their need to work in "Die Frau in der Krise der Kultur" (Women in the crisis of culture, 1930). She called on women to infuse the workspace with spirituality and to act as moral beacons, deeming this task their raison d'etre and thus their national duty. Yet, with increased economic uncertainty, it became more difficult to legitimize women's presence among the ranks of the employed. The growing debate toward the end of the 1920s over women working complicates the juxtaposition of the image of Lola as "working gal" and the scarred masculinity of Rath. For modernity's disaffected, the creeping threat of unemployment proved even more that female employment was the root of social mayhem. The many calls for women to return to the private sphere and free up jobs for men were answered by defenders of women's right to work, who additionally refused to accept marriage and work as mutually exclusive life choices. In "Die berufstätige Frau in der Ehe" (The gainfully employed woman in marriage, 1930), Gerda Torenburg argued that female employment no longer should be viewed as a holding tank for prenuptials, especially in regard to professional women. She notes: "The active woman often suffers from a lack of productivity in marriage, especially if she is independent by nature and had a stimulating and interesting career before marriage. A profession should no longer be thought of as a means to compensate for a woman's drive toward marriage and motherhood. That applies particularly to women who work in the sciences or the arts, or who held responsible posts, in which they became accustomed to calling the shots."[23] Similarly, in "Twilight for Women?" Hilde Walter warns against the growing resentment in 1930 coming from all political quadrants toward female employment. "Women have become unpopular," she writes. "That is not good news because it touches on things that cannot be explained by reason alone. An uncomfortable atmosphere is gathering around all employed women. A possibly unorganized, but nevertheless, very powerful countermovement is targeting all of them; individual women will be feeling its effects sooner or later."[24]

In contrast to representations of female employment after World War I and during a period of economic prosperity in Germany from 1925 to 1929—when women's work was heralded for its significant contribution to the economy, despite inequitable wages—the new pressure to expel women from the workforce, Walter observes, results from wanting to forestall the specter of mass unemployment. Opponents to women's participation in the labor force sought grounds to dismiss them, citing women's ineffectiveness and their emotionalism, which allegedly distracted them from their work and disrupted an otherwise smooth-running office—a blame, Walter interjects, that data does not support. In response, she calls for an objective presentation of facts, and, more profoundly, for unearthing the underlying motives behind targeting women: "Psychologists," she states, "must uncover the sources from which this male emotional disturbance is constantly renewed. They could perhaps investigate the extent to which an unknown sexual fear prevents the majority of men from seeing economic facts objectively and clearly."[25] Besides challenging the argument of "men's right to work," Walter perceptively addresses the prejudices women faced, holding them responsible for modernity's social chaos and men's economic impotence and vulnerability.

The crisis of male subjectivity insinuated in Walter's assessment conjures up a similar prognosis of masculinity at the dawn of the Weimar Republic that casts a long shadow over the jubilant heyday of economic prosperity and performance and that continued on in many social and cultural practices. In *Lustmord,* Maria Tatar unearths precisely the fears that Walter addresses and detects in the excessive representations of sexual murder in Weimar works (for example, in the works of Dix, Grosz, Döblin, and Lang), the need for its executors (artists, writers, and filmmakers) to symbolically punish their own vulnerability, their experience of emasculation, and to quell fears that are affixed to the female body. In the many portraits of mutilated female bodies, Tatar concludes that the male artist rages against the feminine in order to reconstitute masculinity and reclaim the ability to create. Louise Brooks, after working with Pabst on various films, tellingly concluded: "He was conducting an investigation into his relations with women, with the object of conquering any passion that interfered with his work."[26] In Pabst's *Pandora's Box* (1929), the character Jack the Ripper accordingly murders Lulu (played by Brooks) after she has escaped legal prosecution for the murder of her newly wed husband.[27] In contrast, Lola thrives on her allure and is spared punishment, while Rath pays for his attraction to Lola with his life.

In addition to Lola's role as breadwinner and the complex narrative of female employment that surrounds her figure, her portrayal as detached and cold, and her casual indifference (which became Dietrich's trademark), resonates with behavior shared by characters in assorted popular fictions during the Weimar Republic. In fact, the fascination with Dietrich, according to Garber, "lay in the entire ensemble: aloof, indifferent, unapproachable, self-knowing, not a sex object but a sexual and sexualised subject, the narrative and enigma of sex itself."[28] These qualities informed her performance of Lola, which Herbert Ihering also noted in his review of *The Blue Angel*: "But this sensual lack of emotion is stimulating. She's vulgar without acting."[29]

The "coldness" described here typifies a generation that was suspicious of sentimentality, and as Max Brod explains, "as a result of the war, the younger generation justifiably learned to mistrust everything that partook of passions of the heart. ... Accordingly, irony becomes the single artistic tool of the younger generation. In writing as in music ..."[30] The irony Brod speaks of is most apparent in Lola's acknowledgment of being made for love in the title song, "Falling in Love Again," and in the deceptive status of her image.[31] The "coldness" ascribed to the mid-1920s was summarized as a trend described as the *Neue Sachlichkeit* (new objectivity), which took its name from a 1925 art exhibit in Mannheim. Considered as an antidote to romanticism, to the pathos of expressionism with its grave suspicion of technology, and as an effect of the experience of war, "coldness" characterized the pervasive disposition of the time, manifesting itself in painting, photography, and design (most prominently in Bauhaus), and generally becoming a way of life.

Known for its sobriety, objectivity, and distance, the Neue Sachlichkeit found expression in archetypes such as those portrayed in August Sander's photography (for example, the secretary, the baker, the bricklayers), or the girl and garçonne mentioned earlier. In photography, as in literature and painting, the Neue Sachlichkeit aimed at recording objectively the wide range of experiences that made up daily life in the metropolis. In contrast to expressionism, it was influenced by a profound affirmation of modernity, technological progress, and Americanism. Technology was viewed as a means to improve the standard of living—allowing for full participation in the nation's economic boom—and to stand in the service of life, rather than destruction. Henry Ford's autobiography, *My Life and Work* (1923), became a bestseller in Germany, and, with it, rationalized labor, Fordism and Taylorism, and rationalization, in general, as a means to reorganize people's lives, from the office to the household and to interpersonal relationships, became synonymous with democracy. The modern woman, the elevator, jazz, film, the department store, glass, and the radio tower became its symbols. As opposed to the concept of "culture" (*Kultur*), civilization (*Zivilization*) was lauded as an expression and celebration of modernity. The merger of art and consumerism and the increasing pleasures of leisure and consumption were lauded. The so-called functionalization of art, at the same time, profoundly unsettled the boundary between art and commercialism.

The "coldness" or sobriety of the interwar years bore yet another side that characterized the general disposition of the new generation. In *Verhaltenslehren der Kälte* (Cool conduct), Helmut Lethen provides a symptomatic reading of the predominant disposition that the clean, functional, and economic (rather than ornate) lines of modern design replicated. He describes the modern temperament as removed, reserved, unsentimental, de-eroticized, and candid, and ascribes these modalities of being to the extreme sense of disorientation and uncertainty that succeeded the war.[32] Being cold or "sachlich" was viewed as the most efficient way to manage personal relationships; it was a tool for social engineering and indicative of a structure of feeling associated with modernity. "Es liegt in der Luft," Marcellus Schiffer's chanson sung by his wife Margo Lion, best expresses the prevailing mood, while mocking its callousness:

| | |
|---|---|
| Früher, das war' einmal Zeiten, | Those were the days, |
| Der Satz ist nicht zu bestreiten, | The sentence cannot be disproved. |
| Man bestand von früh bis spat | One was from early till late |
| Nur noch aus Nervosität! | Just a bundle of nerves! |
| Starb ein Vögelchen dem Bauer, | If the farmer's bird died, |
| Trug gleich die Familie Trauer. | The whole family mourned immediately. |
| Heut ist eine andere Zeit. | Times are different today. |
| Triffst zum Beispiel du Herrn Koch, | For example, if you run into Mr. Koch, |
| Fragst du ihn voll Sachlichkeit: | You inquire soberly, |
| Was, Herr Koch? Sie leben noch? ... | What, Mr. Koch? You're still alive. |
| Es liegt in der Luft eine Sachlichkeit. | A sense of sobriety is in the air. |
| Es liegt in der Luft eine Stachlichkeit | A sense of prickliness is in the air.[33] |

To a great extent, the detachment and coolness that characterized a lifestyle as well as Lola's performance, and that defined human relations, is said to have developed as a means to survive a densely populated urban setting that excited, agitated, and potentially overtaxed the nervous system. As the population of Berlin grew from 2 to 4.5 million between 1910 and 1925, it required a new set of skills to navigate the metropolis. Living in the metropolis had a stage-like quality that required its inhabitants (at times) to learn what Lethen calls, "strategic self-stylization." "The aim," according to Lethen, "is to train a functional 'I.'"[34] What Lethen describes in his caricature of the "cold persona" (the urbanite) is the evolution of a sophisticated self-reflexivity that also resulted from the increased specularization of daily life in the fast-paced metropolis. The term *Selbstinzenierung* (performance) implies a theoretically complex relationship between subjectivity and appearance. It suggests performativity—a form of self-invention and masquerade, and calls for a reconceptualization of the subject in the twentieth century. Vastly different from the fixed, unified subject of the nineteenth century, twentieth-century subjectivities became more varied and malleable—particularly regarding the many new registers of femininity. Film and advertisements, alongside the plethora of popular fictions in print media, essays, and manuals provided abundant examples of how to dress and "act." When the protagonist Doris, in Irmgard Keun's highly praised novel *The Artificial Silk Girl* (1932), tries to con her employer into forgiving her many typographical errors, she deliberately adopts a role: "So I put on my Marlene Dietrich face as I go into his office, like I'm making those big eyes at him, like I can't wait to jump into bed with him."[35] As this, and the opening scene in *The Blue Angel* of the female worker striking a pose of Lola show, self-stylization takes on a variety of forms that are emphatically gendered, a fact that Lethen leaves undifferentiated.

Refining Lethen's argument by taking into account gender, Patrice Petro provocatively characterizes the prevailing appearance of coolness, specifically in reference to women's experience of modernity, as an expression of boredom. In spite of the novelty and dynamism of the age, little in fact had changed for women. According to Petro, Dietrich's stage appearance in *The Blue Angel* reflects this state of boredom, especially during Lola's final performance: "Lola's blasé sexuality—her seeming lack of affect, often described as coldness, but perhaps better understood as boredom—suggests that sex, as much as modernity, promises nothing to the woman; or, if it does, that *this* promise is always already broken."[36] Surely, the modern woman faced many hurdles that made difficult her full participation in society. The question, however, is whether these promises were already broken before they ever were made.

As Petro has noted on numerous other occasions, the 1920s brought on dramatic transformations of subjectivity, with concepts of femininity, particularly, stretched beyond the previous generations' wildest dreams. The heightened specularization of the modern woman, especially in the urban environment, prompted an awareness of appearance and affect that has been thought unprecedented. Liz Conor concurs: "For perhaps the first time in the West, modern women understood self-display to be part of the quest for mobility, self-determination, and sexual identity."[37] As mentioned elsewhere, the proliferation of identities through performance and play, the dream worlds that visual culture conjured up, and the many different versions of the new woman that emerged all contributed to complicating the performance of gender within the arena of daily life. In addition to the multiple images of Lola, the copious reproduction of female images is emphasized briefly when Rath bursts into the troupe's dressing room behind Lola's, on his first visit to The Blue Angel nightclub. In addition to the female performers who stare out at Rath, myriad images of women line a pillar (see Figure 3.4). The proliferation of images of women in various guises thus unequivocally contributed to redefining notions of gender and subjectivity in the same way that display windows transformed the experience of the street and its female public.[38]

Breaking down the subject/object relation of being seen and seeing, the female subject participated in (and commanded?) her own presentation. As the mirror and display window reflected her image back to her, she could improve, amend, transform, in short, practice self-fashioning, however tentative. The impact of self-conscious constructions of femininity translated into self-assertive "displays" of female subjectivities. "This dramatic shift from inciting modesty to inciting display, from self-effacement to self-articulation," Liz Conor continues, " is the point where feminine visibility began to be productive of women's modern subjectivities."[39] Once again Irmgard Keun's protagonist Doris serves to exemplify the circuit of gazes as she walks the streets of Berlin and admires her own reflection. "I see myself—mirrored in windows and when I do, I like the way I look and then I look at men that look back at me."[40] Lola deliberately primps herself, tugging at her stockings or her

**Figure 3.4** Rath slipping deeper into forbidden realms. Still from *Der blaue Engel*, 1930, directed by Josef von Sternberg. Source: *Friedrich-Wilhelm-Murnau-Stiftung*.

underwear or applying her lip liner, all too aware of the effect she has. The mirrors in *The Blue Angel* thus emphasize the significance of appearance and the consciousness that belongs to staging femininity.

Yet, the modern woman was much more that what she *appeared* to be. As a composite of tendencies that converged and competed, she embodied modernity's unique superimposition of the same, the new, and the projected. Lola is self-stylized, hopeful of both tradition's and modernity's promises, and bored all at once. She performs for the gaze, endearing herself to Rath while playing with his "innocence;" yet rolls her eyes to demonstrate her ennui with Guste's sentimental outburst at Lola's wedding. Lola also flirts with Rath and the idea that their quaint breakfast, which she prepares after their first night together, could become routine. Indeed, Lola's contradictory behavior reflects the difficult transition into modernity not only in terms of crossing congested streets, but, more treacherously, in terms of negotiating and interpreting gender relations.

The complexity of maneuvering uncharted territory and the fine balancing act required to negotiate new turf are evidenced in the plethora of articles and manuals addressing modern life and lifestyles. Film and fiction often served as guideposts. Women's growing visibility in the public sphere called for new modes of behavior, which often were slow in keeping apace with modern necessities, as can be gleaned from reactions to women's new roles and the conundrums both men and women faced.[41] Many works by women writers addressed the problem of male employers expecting additional "services" from female employees as a condition of their employment.[42] Similarly, since the public sphere traditionally fell into the male domain, as many essays on the *flâneur* illustrate, it was not unusual for women who moved through urban spaces, many of whom belonged to the new class of female clerical workers, to be mistaken for prostitutes.[43] The pervasive misapprehension of women on the streets as streetwalkers sexualized the urban environment, particularly for men, as many expressionist paintings or "street films" show—in which the street leads to a bar, a carnival, a bordello where bourgeois men sought escape. Revealing the continued preoccupation with the "problem," but from a different vantage point, a 1932 essay by the commissioner of police, "Is One Allowed to Speak to Girls on the Street?," rejoins tongue-in-cheek: it all depends on the man. In Georg Grosz's accompanying sketch illustrating dissonant expectations of an older man addressing a young "Girl," the girl responds, "You bore me, mister!"[44] Another take on women's presence in the streets is Marcellus Schiffer's composition "My Best Girlfriend" ("Meine beste Freundin"), which Dietrich and Margo Lion provocatively sung in a duet in 1928, prompting rave reviews. Jelavich writes that the song "ostensibly described two women on a shopping excursion. It made clear, however, that they were dissatisfied with their husbands and had a very intimate relationship with each other. The song became an unofficial anthem for German lesbians in the late twenties."[45]

| | |
|---|---|
| Wenn die beste Freundin | When a best girlfriend |
| Mit der besten Freundin, | With a best girlfriend, |
| Um was einzukaufen, | In order to buy something, |
| Um was einzukaufen, | In order to buy something, |
| Um sich auszulaufen | In order to go out |
| Durch die Strassen latschen, | Walk through the streets, |
| Um sich auszuquatschen, | In order to talk, |
| Spricht die beste Freundin | The best girlfriend says |
| Zu der besten Freundin: | To the best girlfriend |
| Meine beste Freundin! | You are my best girlfriend! |

The redefinition of the public sphere during the Weimar Republic—envisioned somewhat as an extension of the private sphere (for example, the use of glass in architecture "privatized" public exteriors)—resulted also in the transformation of the private sphere, with such institutions as marriage and family responding to the needs of the era and thus coming under intense scrutiny. During the Weimar period, the open discussion of sexuality, birth rates, abortion, birth control, and the differences in male and female sexual conduct suggests the rapid erosion of the traditional boundaries between private and public life. The dramatic shift away from the Wilhelminian conservatism of the nineteenth century and its restriction on public discourses on sexuality, which earlier generations shunned, was reflected especially in the open and widespread discussions on marriage and sexuality.[46] Indeed, the numerous commentaries on women's right to sexual gratification, female sexuality and eroticism, and abortion and motherhood significantly reveal that women's bodies were prominently featured in Weimar discourses, and that the female body even became a focal point in sorting out the new age.

Throughout the 1920s, marriage, interestingly, ranked among the topics that were as hotly debated as the modern woman, with recommendations spanning the political and professional spectrum on how to best manage and consummate intimate relationships. Information manuals and other publications such as *Lehrbuch der Liebe und Ehe* (1928, The handbook of love and marriage) or *Die Erotik in der Ehe* (1928, Eroticism in marriage) sought to redefine heterosexual liaisons. What becomes clear when analyzing the plethora of essays on marriage is that the "emancipation of women" catalyzed a dramatic transformation since the gains women made strained normative definitions of masculinity and femininity. Gina Kaus notes in 1930: "The job-related independence of woman and her demand for equal rights in marriage are intricately connected."[47] Employment, consequently, changed the ways women perceived themselves and their relationships.

Even before the Weimar Republic, champions of women's rights and sex reformers such as Helene Stöcker, who lived in a "free marriage," questioned the validity of the bourgeois institution of marriage that installed women in the private sphere and prescribed their duties. Putting the final nail in the coffin of marriage, sexologist Magnus Hirschfeld more pointedly declared, "The war was the beginning of the end of the old patriarchal marriage."[48] New forms of marriage were proposed such as *Kameradschaftsehe* (marriage of camaraderie), which implied equality and emphasized the partnership in marriage, or "eroticized marriage," in answer to the perceived crisis in marriage.[49] A 1930 edition of *Die Literarische Welt* devoted to "Contemporary Erotic Questions" ("Erotische Fragen der Gegenwart") featured commentaries on the front page juxtaposing "The Christian Marriage," which advocated for the sanctity of traditional marriage with an emphasis on marriage as a long-term commitment, and "The End of Marriage" ("Untergang der Ehe"), which was penned by the leftist social critic Alice Rühle-Gerstel. Rühle attributes the "draft" in marriage to the change in female subjectivities, which she assesses as still evolving: "The male has long been thoroughly individualized. But women are still on the path to developing a personality."[50] In an effort to resuscitate the perceived ailing institution of marriage in "Ehekrise—Liebesnot?" ("Marriage Crisis—Need for Love," 1930), Erna Grautoff ascribes the increased failure of marriages in the 1920s to the higher expectations placed on spouses than in earlier times, when gender roles were more narrowly scripted, and when women were more willing to adapt to the needs of their partners because of financial dependency. Grautoff targets radio and film as powerful influences on (misleading) expectations with their vast surplus of "blissful images of idealized lovers and spouses, leading young people to believe that they can emulate the images and even have a right to the same experiences."[51] Significantly, she faults the Neue Sachlichkeit as an expression of "deceit or boredom." In her estimation, this sensibility calls for "freedom of morality," which ends up robbing the new generation of moral judgment, and of an understanding of the deeper meaning of love. She proposes educating people about love and marriage in order to prepare them for this type of "human community." Her call to educate resounds in a number of essays that additionally promote sex education and, in fact, promote a rational approach to the problem of the crisis in marriage.

Given the precarious ground on which marriage stood, it is interesting that it plays such a central role in *The Blue Angel*, and that it is assured failure from the outset because of the intrinsic incompatibility of Rath and Lola. In this context, Andrew Sarris's astute assessment of critics' superficial and prim reception of this topic deserves mention. He notes: "If 'serious' criticism of the cinema were not as puritanical as it is, the experiences of Lola and the professor would seem more pertinent to the hidden world of domestic sexuality than is now the case."[52] The more "domestic" scenes—those that critics often elide presumably because they are more fleeting than the captivating images of Lola's performance, which the camera unabashedly romances—speak to the tensions and frailties of the Weimar years. They provide complex visual and narrative commentary on the state of marriage and the economy, and on generational and class differences, made obvious in Rath's and Lola's divergent modes of behavior, on the status of the modern woman, and on the extreme vulnerability of masculinity, especially toward the end of Weimar's golden years. In the breakfast scene, discussed in the previous chapter, Lola plants the seed of marriage, though never expecting it to materialize. The "proposal scene," nonetheless, soon follows, after Rath, reprimanded for his indiscretion, warns the headmaster of his school against maligning the reputation of his future wife.

The "proposal scene" begins with the cabaret troupe packing up for its next destination. Time is of the essence, and the ringmaster, Kiepert, scolds his wife Guste for idly sitting on a suitcase and smoking a cigarette: "Why did I marry you anyway," he rhetorically asks, to which she replies without affect: "I've wondered that many times myself." Their interaction anticipates the theme of marriage and sets the stage for Rath's entry in formal attire. He is carrying a bouquet of flowers with the intention of proposing to Lola. Directing Rath upstairs, Kiepert compromises Rath's reputation by reminding him that he already knows the way.

Kneeling on the bed and busily packing her suitcase with her back to Rath (allowing both Rath and moviegoer an unimpeded view of her legs),

**Figure 3.5** Lola on stage even while she is packing up her belongings. Still from *Der blaue Engel*, 1930, directed by Josef von Sternberg. *Friedrich-Wilhelm-Murnau-Stiftung.*

**Figure 3.6** "You want to marry me!" Still from *Der blaue Engel*, 1930, directed by Josef von Sternberg. *Friedrich-Wilhelm-Murnau-Stiftung.*

Lola, constantly on stage, is framed by curtains and a large poster of a clown's face on one side that looks directly into the camera (catching the viewer and Rath looking) with a "knowing" smile. The juxtaposition of disregard and regard and then the alignment of Lola's and the clown's face emphasize Lola's self-conscious performance of the part she plays (see Figure 3.5). At the same time, their "doubled gaze" positions Rath as both fool and foolhardy. In the countershot, Rath is seen framed in reference to the poster of Lola that serves as a visual leitmotif. In this scene, however, Lola is dressed in the signature clothes of the new woman, a suit (jacket and skirt) with a bowed tie and bowler hat. Accepting the flowers Rath hands her, she considers them farewell presents and cavalierly throws them on the bed, only to realize that she has offended him. Flirtatiously consoling him (the image of Lola framed by curtains is like a portrait), she assures Rath of her return next year. Not yet finished, Rath presents her with a ring and then formally asks for her hand in marriage. She seems stunned (see Figure 3.6). Taken aback at first, Lola's recovers from the surprise and laughs in disbelief: "You want to marry me!" Rath gently admonishes her to fully appreciate the "seriousness of the moment, my child," which ironically seems to be exactly what her response implies. Her laughter comments on the impracticality of their alliance in particular, and on marriage in general. It expresses an unguarded, and a profoundly self-reflexive, comprehension of their misalliance and of Rath's disavowal, a condition for masochistic pleasure, as discussed in Chapter 2. Her laughter therefore bursts the romantic illusion that love conquers all differences, an illusion that pulp fiction fueled and that von Sternberg cynically dispels. For Rath, the modern woman is an unintelligible cipher that he misunderstands.

In sharp contrast to the representation of marriage in classical narratives, in which marriage serves to reestablish the status quo, and, more significantly, to bring wayward women back into the societal fold by making them respectable, patriarchy falters bitterly in their union. Lola's laughter pierces any hope of marriage recuperating traditional gendered relationships and sheds all pretense of establishing stability. The rituals of marriage in *The Blue Angel* are even parodied during the wedding celebration when Rath and Lola imitate the mating ritual of fowl. After Kiepert, the magician, pulls eggs out of Rath's nose, Lola rests her head on Rath's shoulder and begins to coo. He responds by crowing. Later, Rath struts about their common apartment like a rooster. The idyllic nuptial nest is compromised in these displays of inflated masculinity, which within the next two scenes is rapidly stripped of authority and sovereignty.

While Rath's desire for Lola is portrayed unambiguously in scenes of seduction and submission, the narrative less transparently offers an explanation for Lola's attraction to Rath. Might it be that Rath is the "real man" that Lola captures in her spotlight at the beginning of the film? Is he someone who treats her with respect and who promises protection—a feeling in which Lola basks, especially when Rath stands up for her to Kiepert and the merchant marine, who offers money for her company? His mannerism and sensibilities are much different than what Lola is accustomed to in the milieu of the cabaret. More meaningfully, Rath represents a means of upward mobility and, with it, the chance to experience the respect that his standing promises. Even Guste, Kiepert's wife, imagines a better life with a "real man" like Rath. At the wedding celebration, she wistfully laments that had she been younger, she might have had a chance to become the wife of a "Professor," indeed a distinguished title in German culture at the time. Her comment sheds light on the underlying motive for Lola's marriage to Rath. As the modern woman, her aspiration is no different than those featured in scores of popular magazines, movies and novels, in which young working women of modest means yearned to meet men who would afford them security and a chance to improve their economic standing. Marriage signified a means to achieve upward mobility and leave the workforce. Thus Lola's "attraction" to Rath may be understood as the promise of a better life, of entry into the more respected social spheres, of her *embourgoisement* along with the ennoblement of her art, and the fulfillment of a dream articulated in her pronouncement, "I am an artist."

As the modern woman, Lola is more than image. Indeed, the one-dimensional, slick surface and poster-image takes on a new meaning when measured against the historical reality that contributed to shaping her. On closer investigation, Lola evokes Weimar culture's complex and contested array of psychological, social economic conditions, each compelling in their own way, and embodies a convergence of discourses that are decidedly at odds with each other. Sexually charged and innocent, callous, cold, good-willed and caring, accepting and protective of Rath, and perhaps bored and bitterly disillusioned with all of the dashed hopes of the age, Lola continues her performance.

After making *The Blue Angel,* Patrick O'Connor writes, "Dietrich complained that she would never again be able to show her face in Berlin, so lewd and shocking were the things she had to do."[53] Despite Dietrich's dislike of the film because of its earthiness, and despite her objections, she later admitted in her autobiography, "The costumes that I wear in *The Blue Angel* have become a symbol of my person and for the decade that influenced the film."[54] Her objections to the film are less convincing when read against Dietrich's lifestyle, demeanor, and her ambiguous sexual identity that invariably crossed over into her films, beginning with *The Blue Angel.* She embodied the modern woman of the Weimar Republic and became a projection, as did Lola, of its surface and depth.

## Notes

1. See Sabine Hake, "In the Mirror of Fashion," *Women in the Metropolis: Gender, Modernity in Weimar Culture,* edited by Katharina von Ankum (Berkeley: University of California Press, 1997), 185–201.
2. "In 1925 there were 32.2 million women to 30.2 million men, or 1,072 women to 1,000 men, a differential that, it was hoped, would be reduced by the time of the next census (1933)," write Renate Bridenthal and Claudia Koonz in "Beyond *Kinder, Küche, Kirche*: Weimar Women in Politics and Work," *When Biology Became Destiny: Women in Weimar and Nazi Germany,* edited by Renate Bridenthal et al. (New York: Monthly Review Press, 1984), 45.
3. The poem that appeared in *Die Dame* (1925) takes stock of the modern woman's many attributes depending on the perspective and interests of the beholder. Most revealing is that everyone seems to have an opinion of her:
   What is the modern woman?
   A charming *Bubikopf*—says the hairdresser
   A model of depravity—says Aunt Klotilde
   A complex of sexual problems—says the psychoanalyst
   Comrade and soul friend—says the youth
   Miserable housewife—says the reactionary
   Expensive—says the bachelor
   The best costumer—says the stocking dealer
   An unhappiness for my son—says the mother
   The center of the sanatorium—says the doctor
   The same, since the dawn of history—says the wise man.
4. See Anke Gleber, *The Art of Taking a Walk: Flanerie, Literature and Film in Weimar Culture* (Princeton, NJ: Princeton University Press, 1999); Katharina von Ankum, "Gendered

Spaces in Irmgard Keun's *Das kunstseidene Mädchen*," *Women in the Metropolis: Gender and Modernity in Weimar Culture*, edited by Katharina von Ankum (Berkeley: University of California Press, 1997), 162–84.

5. Anton Kaes, "Film in der Weimarer Republik: Motor der Moderne," *Geschichte des Deutschen Films*, edited by Wolfgang Jacobsen, Anton Kaes, and Hans Helmut Prinzler (Stuttgart: Metzler, 1993), 94 (my translation). ("Gleichzeitig schimmert die Ambivalenz in Lolas Rollenspiel durch, die in der späten Weimarer Republik die moderne Frau charakteriziert; durch Berufstätigkeit selbstständig und unabhängig vom Mann geworden, souverän, kalt, mitleidlos (aus männlicher Perspektive) und doch auch wieder in die traditionelle Rolle als Mutter und Ehefrau gepresst.")

6. Bram Dijkstra, *Idols of Perversity: Fantasies of Feminine Evil in Fin-de-Siècle Culture* (New York and Oxford: Oxford University Press, 1986), 4.

7. Elsa Hermann, "Weiblichkeit-ein Kulturproblem?" *Das Heft* 2 (October 10, 1930), 6–7 (my translation). ("Deshalb darf auch der Begriff 'weiblich', wie er für die Vergangenheit richtig war, nicht auf die Gegenwart übertragen werden. Denn Weiblichkeit ist ein Kulturfaktor in seinen verschiedenen Erscheinungsformen.")

8. See Barbara Kosta, "Cigarettes, Advertising, and the Weimar Republic's Modern Woman," *The Text as Spectacle: Visual Culture in Twentieth-Century Germany*, edited by Gail Finney (Bloomington: Indiana University Press, 2006), 134–53.

9. Mathilde Vaerting, "Die heutige Rolle der Virginität im Seelenleben des jungen Mädchens," *Der Querschnitt* 12, 4 (April 1932), 246 (my translation). In this article, Vaerting describes the unique "emotional <mental> state" of the modern woman, which finds an outlet in claiming a "right to one's own love life." She diagnoses a variety of new symptoms such as marriage addiction (*Ehesucht*), addiction to erotic experimentation (*erotische Experimentiersucht*), and sees a trend in women who prize their profession, and are mindful of marriage compromising their careers. See also "Die Ehe und die junge Generation: Realpolitische Überlegungen zu einem unpolitischen Thema," *Frau und Gegenwart: Zeitschrift zur die gesamten Fraueninteressen* 31 (July 31, 1928).

10. See Maria Makela, "The Misogynist Machine: Images of Technology in the Work of Hannah Höch," *Women in the Metropolis: Gender and Modernity in Weimar Culture*, edited by Katharina von Ankum (Berkeley: University of California Press, 1997), 106–27.

11. Fritz Olimsky, "Der blaue Engel," *Berliner Illustrierte* (March 23, 1930), 40. ("Aber bei aller Frechheit ist sie nicht direct ordinär und lässt hier und da sogar beinahe so etwas wie Seele durchblicken. Eine wunderbare Mischung, fast möchte man sagen ein Symbol für die unergründliche Kompliziertheit der Frau.")

12. See Lynne Frame, "Gretchen, Girl, Garçonne: Weimar Science and Popular Culture in Search of the Ideal New Woman," *Women in the Metropolis: Gender and Modernity in Weimar Culture*, edited by Katharina von Ankum (Berkeley: University of California Press, 1997), 12–40. I use the term differently from Frame, whose example of the Girl comes from an article in the *8-Uhr-Abendblatt*.

13. The etymology of *Junggeselle* starts in the fifteenth century to describe an apprentice in a guild. The notion of bachelor came later. A woman, in contrast, was referred to as a virgin or *Jungfrau* (literally, young woman). The word *Junggesellin* was often used in the 1920s in reference to single working women. Many articles that address the more practical aspects of single life, such as housing, cooking, and time management, use this term. See, for example, Edith Berger, "Die Junggesellenwohnung," *Das Heft* 2 (November 1929), 9–10; Elisabet Neff, *Die Schnellküche der Junggesellin* (Stuttgart: Francksche Verlagshandlung, 1926). On the front cover, Neff writes: "70 recipes, the best of the best, none of them take more than 20 minutes." The book is written with the fast pace of life in mind, and for bachelorettes, who are often overworked and tired of waiting to be served in restaurants, and who want to withdraw and recuperate in the privacy of their rooms.

14. The image is taken from Christian Ferber, ed., *Uhu: Das Monats-Magazin, 1924–1933* (Berlin: Ullstein Verlag, 1979), 219.

15. Anita, "Sex Appeal: Ein Schlagwort für eine alte Sache," *Uhu* 5 (October 1928), 72–77. This term joins other loan words frequently used in the 1920s that were taken from English, such as "five o'clock tea," "flirt," "dancing," and "cocktail." Together they reflect the social changes that came to Germany via America or England, with which the German language could hardly keep up.
16. Being blonde places her in a long line of mythic blondes like Aphrodite or Venus, the goddess of love, or Helen of Troy, a symbol of classical beauty. Both figures will be associated with Dietrich in von Sternberg's *The Blonde Venus*, where she plays Helen Faraday, a composite of mother and alluring entertainer.
17. Yvonne, "Zeigen Sie mal Ihre Beine, gnädige Frau," *Das Magazin* 38 (October 1927), 1495–1501. Dietrich's legs were not the only legs on display in Berlin. Raised hemlines—the fashion of the time—exposed women's legs, allowing for visual access and intimating "knowability;" sheer stockings also allowed for transparency. For instance, a 1925 issue of *Das Magazin* boldly calls for women to show their legs and features dancers, actresses, and other prominent women.
18. Kristine von Soden and Maruta Schmidt, eds., *Neue Frauen: Die zwanziger Jahre* (Berlin: Elefanten Press, 1988), 159 ("boxt und foxt und golft und steppt / und unter uns gesagt auch neppt"). She was known to "box, fox, golf, step / and, between us, also nip."
19. In her court reports, *Blüten der Zwanziger Jahre: Gerichtsreportagen und Feuilletons, 1923–1933*, edited by Jens Brüning (Berlin: Rotation, 1984), Gabriele Tergit describes a young couple to illustrate the blurred gender boundaries during the Weimar Republic: "Sometimes now couples can be seen in parkas, and one has to look twice to discern which one is the male because the girls have a boyish boldness in their faces and hair and their clothing is no different from that of her companion. Only one thing has remained the same. The young man informs the girl of the goings-on and not the other way around" (67, my translation). See also Erika Thiel, *Geschichte des Kostüms: Die europäische Mode von den Anfängen bis zur Gegenwart* (Amsterdam: Heinrichshofen, 1980); Vera Steinhart, "Vom Geltungskampf der Frau: Die Nachahmungspsychose bei der modernen Frau," *Die Neue Generation* 3 (March 1929), 121.
20. See Marjorie Garber, "From Dietrich to Madonna: Cross-Gender Icons," *Women and Film: Sight and Sound Reader*, edited by Pam Cook and Philip Dodd (London: Scarlet Press, 1993), 16–20. Garber lists a number of films in which Dietrich cross-dresses, and discusses the many imitations of Dietrich. Among the many allusions to Dietrich's performance of Lola, Garber notes in particular Liza Minelli in *Cabaret*, Lucchino Visconti's *The Damned*, and Madonna.
21. Curt Moreck, *Führer durch das lasterhafte Berlin* (Leipzig: Verlag moderner Stadtführer, 1930).
22. Maria Riva, *Marlene Dietrich: By Her Daughter* (New York: Knopf, 1993), 46.
23. Gerda Torenburg, "Die berufstätige Frau in der Ehe," *Das Heft* 19, 2 (September 12, 1930), 4. ("Die aktive Frau leidet in der Ehe nicht selten unter ihrer Unproduktivität. Besonders dann, wenn sie eine im Grunde selbständige Natur ist und vor ihrer Ehe in einem anregenden und interessanten Beruf gestanden hat, der ja heute längst nicht mehr lediglich eine Sublimierung ihres Triebs zu Ehe und Mutterschaft darstellt. Das gilt vor allem für die Frau, die künstlerisch oder wissenschaftlich arbeitet oder aber auf verantwortlichem Posten gestanden hat, wo sie selbstständig zu disponieren gewöhnt war.") See also Elsa Hermann, "Bedeutet Frauenarbeit 'schädliche Konkurrenz?'" *Das Heft* 15, 2 (July 18, 1930), 4–5.
24. Hilde Walter, "Twilight for Women?," *Weimar Republic Sourcebook* 210.
25. Ibid. Despite the new alternatives and open avenues that women enjoyed during this period, such as the right to vote and to employment as well as to higher educational opportunities, many women were ill equipped for the challenges of the "new" era. Their conditioning was still the result of "older" values, making the passage into the modern era more difficult. In 1933, Fleisser retrospectively describes the atmosphere of the 1920s. She states: "Von der Stellung der Frau werde ich des langen und breiten sprechen. Stellt euch vor, … werde ich sagen, in was für eine Zwickmühle sich damals die Frauen

befanden." (I will be speaking in depth and breadth about the status of women ... Just imagine, I'll say, the quandary women faced then.) Günther Rühle, ed., *Materialien zum Leben und Schreiben der Marieluise Fleisser* (Frankfurt am Main: Suhrkamp, 1972), 176.
26. Quoted in Heide Schlüpmann, "The Brothel as an Arcadian Space? *Diary of a Lost Girl* (1929)," *The Films of G.W. Pabst: An Extraterritorial Cinema*, edited by Eric Rentschler (New Brunswick, NJ: Rutgers University Press, 1990), 82.
27. Mary Ann Doane, "The Erotic Barter: *Pandora's Box*," *The Films of G.W. Pabst*, 76. But while Lulu's "allure is a function of the illicit, unbounded nature of her sexuality," as the modern girl, she is punished for perverting the institution of marriage and for the irresistibility of her image.
28. Garber, 16.
29. Herbert Ihering, "*The Blue Angel* and *An American Tragedy*," *Sternberg*, edited by Peter Baxter, translated by Nick Greenland (London: BFI Publishing, 1980), 25.
30. Max Brod, "Women and the New Objectivity," *The Weimar Republic Sourcebook*, edited by Anton Kaes, Martin Jay, and Edward Dimenberg (Berkeley: University of California Press, 1994), 205.
31. Tellingly, Hanna Vollmer-Heitmann plays off the song's title for her book on the 1920s and the modern woman. See *Wir sind von Kopf bis Fuss auf Liebe eingestellt* (Hamburg: Kabel, 1993). See also, Birgit Haustedt, *Die wilden Jahre in Berlin: Eine Klatsch und Kulturgeschichte der Frauen* (Berlin: Berliner Taschenbuch Verlag, 2002).
32. Helmut Lethen, *Verhaltenslehren der Kälte: Lebensversuch zwischen den Kriegen* (Frankfurt am Main: Suhrkamp, 1994).
33. *Uhu: Das Magazin der 20er Jahre (Berlin: Oktober 1924 bis Oktober 1934)*, edited by Christian Ferber (Berlin: Ullstein Verlag, 1979), 198. See also Erna Grautoff, "Ehekrise—Liebesnot?" *Das Heft* 4, 2 (February 14, 1930), 2. See also Kristine von Soden, *Die Sexualberatungsstellen der Weimarer Republik 1919–1933* (Berlin: Druckhaus Hentrich, 1988).
34. Lethen, 64 and 36 respectively. "Verhaltenslehren üben strategisch angelegte Selbstinszenierung ein; ihr Ziel ist das Training eines funktionalen Ichs."
35. Irmgard Keun, *The Artificial Silk Girl*, translated by Katie von Ankum (New York: Other Press, 2002), 16. See Peter Panther, "Die Dame im Vorzimmer: Die Privatsekretärin als Gouvernante, Bollwerk und Amme," *Uhu: Das Monats-Magazin, 1924–1933*, edited by Christian Ferber (Berlin: Ullstein Verlag, 1979), 181–83.
36. Patrice Petro, *Aftershocks of the New: Feminism and Film History* (New Brunswick, NJ: Rutgers University Press, 2003), 122.
37. Liz Conor, *The Spectacular Modern Woman: Feminine Visibility in the 1920s* (Bloomington: Indiana University Press, 2004), 29.
38. Janet Ward Lungstrum, "The Display Window: Designs of Desires of Weimar Consumerism," *New German Critique* 76 (Winter 1999), 115–60.
39. Conor, 29.
40. Keun, 88.
41. Mathilde Vaerting describes an experiment that a friend undertook to investigate attitudes toward women's independence. He asked what people thought about women going by themselves to cafés and found that, regardless of age or social background, those who lived in the country rejected the idea, while respondents in the city found the question absurd. "Die heutige Rolle der Virginität im Seelenleben des jungen Mädchens," *Der Querschnitt* 12, 4 (April 1932), 249.
42. See Christa Anita Brück, *Schicksale hinter Schreibmaschinnen* (Berlin: Sieben Stäbe Verlag, 1930) or Grete von Urbanitzky, *Sekräterin Vera* (Hannover: Adolf Sponholz Verlag, 1930).
43. Keun, 1. As late as 1932 in *The Artificial Silk Girl*, the protagonist Doris encounters men on the streets of Berlin who assume her availability. Recalling her friend's advice, Doris reflects: "You don't get anything out of letting yourself be talked to on the street. You owe yourself some self-respect, after all."
44. Polizeikommandeur Heimannsberg, "Darf man junge Mädchen auf der Strasse ansprechen?," *Der Querschnitt* 12. 4. (April 1932), 253.

45. Peter Jelavich, *Berlin Cabaret* (Cambridge, Mass.: Harvard University Press, 1993), 193.
46. See Gina Kaus, "Von der Ehe," *Das Heft* 13, 2 (June 20, 1930), 4.
47. Ibid., 4.
48. Magnus Hirschfeld, *Sittengeschichte der Nachkriegszeit* (Leipzig: Verlag für Sexualwissenschaft, 1930), 284.
49. Margarete Weinberg, "Zur Problematik der Ehe," *Die Neue Generation* 7–8 (July–August 1930), 183–87. See Vibeke Rützou Petersen, *Women and Modernity in Weimar Germany: Reality and Representation in Popular Fiction* (New York: Berghahn Books, 2001).
50. Alice Rühle-Gerstel, "Der Untergang der Ehe," *Die Literarische Welt* 24, 6 (1930), 1. ("Der Mann ist längst durchindividualisiert. Aber die Frau ist noch auf dem Marsch zur Persönlichkeit.") Rühle calls for changes in marriage and family law, equal competence in childrearing, and for the right for women to keep their names and citizenship. See also Edith Jacoby-Oste, "Die Ehe und die junge Generation," *Frau und Gegenwart* (1928), 3–4. The author pleads for understanding the new generation. Discussions of sexuality and eroticism are more urgent. For every 116 men to 100 women, only 56 men are marrying. Lack of interest in marriage has a number of reasons, she speculates, among them the possibility of multiple relationships, the housing shortage, low wages, the view of marriage as posing more hardships and less security.
51. Grautoff, "Ehekrise—Liebesnot?," 2.
52. Quoted in Patrick O'Conner, *The Amazing Blonde Woman: Dietrich's Own Style* (London: Bloomsbury, 1991), 21.
53. O'Conner, 21.
54. Marlene Dietrich, *Marlene Dietrich: Ich bin, Gott sei Dank, Berlinerin,* translated by Nicola Volland (Berlin: Ullstein Verlag, 2000), 85.

*Chapter 4*

# THE SEDUCTIONS OF SOUND

> Contrary to what one would be inclined to think, music is not intended to restore mute spectacles to full reality by adding sound to them. Exactly the reverse holds true: it is added to draw the spectator into the very center of the silent images and have him experience their photographic life.
> **Siegfried Kracauer, *Theory of Film***

> If she had nothing more than her voice, she could break your heart with it. But she has that beautiful body and the timeless loveliness of her face. It makes no difference how she breaks your heart if she is there to mend it.
> **Ernest Hemingway**

*The Blue Angel* owes its "life" to the emergence of sound. Because of its importance as one of Germany's first sound films, it participates in a wider discursive field that addresses the uneven transition from silent to sound film in Germany, the newly discovered power of sound, and its effect on audiences. Toeplitz refers to *The Blue Angel* as a "signpost film," and as a conversion-era film, it tests the conventions of silent film and daringly plots its own acoustic principles.[1] Ironically, in the early stages of sound cinema, debates on its aesthetic value echoed those that accompanied the emergence of cinema outlined in Chapter 1, that assigned an inferior status to the alliance of music and mass culture because of the reliance of mass culture on the mechanical means of reproduction. Leftist critic Willy Haas mordantly observed, "The so-called 'front against sound film' is the usual intellectual nonsense. In part, they are exactly the same gentlemen who before 1921 talked about the movies like they would speak about a whorehouse for sailors, and to deal with it seriously was much beneath their literary dignity."[2] Like early cinema, sound upset finely tuned definitions of culture, testing again the relationship between mass culture and art, and, with it, definitions of (a very vulnerable) German national identity. Moreover, the advent of sound complicated even more the theoretical relationship between art and film because of the new reliance on dialogue, bringing cinema into closer proximity to theater, thereby again questioning the lines of aesthetic demarcation. On a more practical level, directors who had theater experience were thought more qualified to direct sound films, since the transition from theater to sound film was perceived as more fluid.

Given the volatility of the cultural wars during the late 1920s, this chapter focuses on the ways in which *The Blue Angel* enlists sound, and especially music, to amplify and conceal the tensions among notions of national culture, art, and mass culture. It explores how the notion of German cultural identity in crisis at the end of the Weimar Republic is played out in the conversion from silent to sound film and in the aesthetic and narrative construction of *The Blue Angel*. Additionally, the chapter explores the relationship of sound, image, and spectator. If sound bestows on the image a heightened sense of reality and feeds into the illusion of presence, proximity, and plentitude in the psychoanalytical sense described in Chapter 2, then how does Lola's song conceal the deprivations of the image and further facilitate the disavowal of cinema's lack? Put differently, how does sound effect the seduction of Rath?

## The New Technology

Before embarking on a discussion of the dramaturgy of sound in *The Blue Angel*, let us consider the complex reception of sound in the late 1920s to contextualize better the difficulties, both technical and cultural, that von Sternberg faced. Indeed, the history of the beginnings of sound cinema in Germany is a complex and scattered narrative of inventions, experiments, patents, business consolidations and syndications, international financing and finessing.[3] This history is far too complex to tell here, except to say that German studios, despite attempts to introduce sound to film throughout the 1920s, lagged far behind US studios in sound production.[4] Reasons for the cautious adoption of sound include the number of patents held in different hands and the number of failed sound film experiments in the mid-1920s, which curtailed the enthusiasm of stockholders, studio executives, and producers. Reluctance translated into modest allocations of money for further experimentation, despite groundbreaking technological developments in Germany throughout the 1920s. The lack of standardized equipment in addition to the anticipated cost of transitioning into sound both for production studios (sound films costing 30 to 50 percent more per film) and theater owners also dampened the initial eagerness to convert to sound.[5] Furthermore, the increased number of moviegoers between 1927 and 1928 made sound conversion appear less urgent. The fear of losing an international market, since the exaggerated mimicry of silent films easily overcame linguistic barriers, further explains the caution with which studios proceeded.[6] The image of the tower of Babel was evoked regularly as a metaphor of the potential pitfalls of sound—an image that Fritz Lang anticipated in his film *Metropolis*.[7] Among the prodigious advocates of sound who presciently urged German studios to embrace technological progress was Erich Pommer.[8] Yet Ufa remained conservative in its early endeavors, designating only 5 percent of its productions for sound.[9] What the German film industry did not fully accept at first was the opportunity to establish a national cinema and increase the number of moviegoers that sound would promote. These benefits were acknowledged retrospectively after yielding to pressures to produce sound films in order to remain competitive.[10]

Given the enormous rivalry between German and Hollywood studios, it comes as no surprise that the debates on sound were tainted with a deep-seated resentment toward Hollywood in particular and the USA in general. Some German critics disparaged sound films as a symptom of an American cultural malaise that sound would serve to drown out. The "talkies" were perceived as an added capitulation to cultural capitalism and to baser forms of entertainment that undermined the establishment of an art film culture. Countering the cultural pessimists, but nevertheless sharing their concerns with the new technology, critics like Willy Haas and Kurt Pinthus acknowledged the inherent potential of sound film and its power over audiences, but insisted that German filmmakers maintain standards of high quality and avoid replicating the inferior mass-produced products of its foremost competitor. Danish-born Asta Nielsen, who rose to fame as a silent film star in Germany, spoke for many whose skepticism of the new media was mixed with a nostalgia for silent cinema and its inevitable death: "Sound films are still so primitive that their technical quality is not worth discussing. But once they become technically perfected, it will mean the death of film art, the death of the true essence of film."[11] In fact, initial criticism of sound had much to do with the inferior quality of early sound technology, rather than a philosophically principled resistance to the new medium. Theater and film critic (and enduring skeptic) Herbert Ihering, for instance, expressed his apprehension toward the new technology in "Beware of Sound Film Politics" ("Vorsichtig Tonfilmpolitik"). Here he reports on audience responses to a silent and a sound version of Alfred Hitchcock's British thriller *Blackmail*. The overwhelming majority surveyed preferred the silent version, leaving Ihering to conclude, "We will be able to accept talkies only when they have achieved the same quality of movement, contrasts and exchanges as in silent films. Editing functions to accent not prolong. Lengthy dialogs—atrocious. Worse than in the theater!"[12]

For many people employed in the film industry, sound technology was a bittersweet newcomer that either offered exciting opportunities or threatened livelihoods, already made precarious because of Germany's economic uncertainty.[13] The broad spectrum of arguments for or against sound among directors, actors, film-studio moguls, and staff are well known by now, but it is worth reviewing them nevertheless, in order to provide a fuller cultural context for Lola's song. To begin with, directors expressed initial reservations (and even hostility) toward sound, believing that sound might compromise the "artistic" value of the visual medium and enervate the technological and artistic accomplishments of the silent era, throwing it back to its status as lowbrow entertainment. Many in the film industry predicted that sound would set aesthetic limits, and would only occasion redundancies, rather than add to the image.[14]

What is more, justifiable existential concerns spawned early opposition to sound: musicians who accompanied silent films as part of an orchestra or as soloists risked unemployment, as did silent film stars whose voices or acting styles failed the test of the new medium.[15] With the advent of the "talkies" in 1929 in Germany, the careers of many silent film stars declined rapidly, except for those who, like Emil Jannings, were quick to accept the inevitability of the coming of sound and thus worked to secure a place in the new medium.[16] Because sound was still in its embryonic stage in Germany in 1929, Jannings expressed great confidence in the advancement of sound technology, all the while shamelessly promoting himself as a stage actor who was more likely to master the new medium because of the inherent kinship between the "talkies" and theater. Referring to the difficult transition for many silent-film actors without theatrical training, Jannings opportunistically offered: "All these worries do not apply to actresses and actors who come from the theater. For us, sound film opens up new and great artistic possibilities, which we seize all the more willingly since the silent film has acquired a certain monotony ... From an artistic point of view, Germany has work cut out for itself. We most probably have the best material in actors."[17] (Ironically, reviews of *The Blue Angel* often criticized Jannings for being too theatrical.) While duplicitously acknowledging its shortcomings, particularly in conveying the "finer nuances of language," he reminded his readers that "millions of people" had a difficult time understanding radio voices because of the lesser sound quality in its early stages.[18]

Not until the 1929 premiere of Lloyd Bacon's *The Singing Fool* (1927) did the fervor for sound peak in Germany. According to Thomas Saunders, Bacon's American film "marked the breakthrough of talking film on the German market, and after the Ufa sent a team to the United States to study sound production, launched a wave of 'talkies' that same year."[19] As a result, German studios aggressively established themselves in the national market in order to marginalize American productions. The Ufa expeditiously signed contracts with Tobis and Klangfilm to provide the necessary sound system and recording equipment for its venture into sound after letting contracts lapse. Walter Ruttmann's film *Melodie der Welt* (1928–29) was the first sound feature film. Funded by the large ship company Hapag, the fictional story of a sailor, who returns to Hamburg to his sweetheart, frames the travelogue of documentary images that dominate the film. Wolfgang Zeller's musical score and a pallet of sounds were added to silent images to create a partial sound film.[20] Other early attempts at sound included Max Reichmann's *Der Günstling von Schönbrunn*, with sound spliced into sequences, and Rudolf Walther-Fein's full talkie, *Dich hab' ich geliebt*, a 1929 Aafa-Film production. These films were followed by Carl Froelich's 1929 film *Die Nacht gehört uns* (The night belongs to us) and Hanns Schwarz's 1929 operetta *Melodie des Herzens* (Melody of the heart), filmed in four languages, and marking Ufa's breakthrough into sound, followed by *The Blue Angel*. Those, like *The Blue Angel*, filmed in multiple languages exemplified how sound film could cross national borders and secure national and international markets.[21]

Despite the expense and the considerable problems such multilingual practices initially posed, two versions of *The Blue Angel* were filmed simultaneously: one in German and the other in English.[22] Before dubbing or subtitles became standard practice, film studios resorted to filming "multiple versions" in order to secure multilingual markets, often having a different cast step onto the same sets, or having different versions filmed consecutively. In *The Blue Angel*, the cast remained the same with adjustments made to the script depending on the German actor's English fluency.[23] In the English-speaking version, which cost the studio 2.4 million marks to produce, and which Carl Winston supervised, Professor Rath is transformed into an English teacher who forbids his pupils to speak German. Despite targeting the English-speaking market, this version kept much of the sparse dialog in German, which garnered mixed reviews abroad.[24] Similar to the way in which Rath drilled his students to perfect their English pronunciation, von Sternberg coached German actors in their English lines, speaking each sentence for them and synchronizing some dialog after the fact. Many of the actors, such as Hans Albers, spoke an incomprehensible English.[25] Dietrich effectively spoke her own lines in both versions of the film, even though von Sternberg's wife offered to provide the English text.[26]

As for Jannings, who was well aware of the professional stakes (and whose flawed English accounted for his decision to leave Hollywood), *The Blue Angel* served as a litmus test of his ability to transition into sound film and perform as a *Sprechschauspieler* (talking actor). This explains why contemporaneous reviews focused specifically on the quality of his voice in his debut talkie. The British newspaper *The Commonwealth* (1930) reported, "It is good to know that he <Jannings> can now be numbered among the few great artists of the talking screen."[27] The *New York Times* dispatch of the premiere of *The Blue Angel* in Berlin summed up German reviews, saying, "Jannings's voice was good and Fräulein Dietrich's voice was described as marvelous. The manner in which tone and picture were balanced, supporting each other, was particularly praised."[28] Reflecting on the distortion particularly of women's voices in early sound films, Herbert

Ihering emphasized the success of Dietrich's voice: "For the first time in sound film does a woman's voice have timbre, coloring and expression."[29]

Taking into account the poor state of sound technology in Germany at the time (with the exception of the bunker-like *Tonkreuz*, a sound-proof building that Ufa quickly constructed), it is remarkable, as Saunders notes, that *The Blue Angel* "demonstrated German technical quality and proved that sound was not the source of artistic inhibition indicated by the early musicals."[30] Essentially, von Sternberg overcame many technical obstacles by relying on ingenuity and resourcefulness to compensate for what the German studio system sorely lacked. In his own words: "The Germans had neither the proper equipment nor the experience to make a film with sound, and able as my cameramen, Rittau and Schneeberger, were, and eager as the capable set designer, Otto Hunte, proved to be, the indoctrination process was no easy matter."[31] In order to eliminate the sound of the camera, von Sternberg used multiple cameras and had soundproof booths built large enough to fit him and his cameramen and allow them to move from one crate to another to insure the continuity of sound.[32] The camera was subordinated to the needs of sound, as in most early sound films. Echoing the frustrations of many filmmakers during the conversion era, who considered sound films a recording medium rather than an art form, von Sternberg, recalling his early work, went so far as to identify sound as the camera's enemy: "It was for the time being a reproductive instrument, as the microphone is to this day; and to reproduce is not to create."[33] To compensate for the loss of mobility, von Sternberg employed four cameras simultaneously; a silent camera was used for the clock tower and the street scene—the only scenes in which the camera was entirely mobile. The severe restrictions placed on camera movement meant increased shot lengths and less editing. Editing was restricted primarily to scene changes and actors had to remain in the vicinity of microphones.

While production problems, for the most part, were solved creatively with techniques established in Hollywood studios, *The Blue Angel*, like many other first "talkies," faced challenges that extended beyond production to reception. Owing to the novelty of the medium and in the absence of conventions to produce sound films, much less to view them, laughter or applause often interfered with the acoustic reception of dialog. After the premiere of *The Blue Angel*, the *Filmkurier* reported: "The talkie commands a heightened attentiveness of the ear from beginning to end. If you miss a few lines of dialog, it is difficult to get reoriented. It was evidenced in the far too short applause pauses that were scripted into particularly good scenes, as the film silently rolled on. The applause thundered on into the next scene and abruptly ceased because of the need to hear."[34] Besides reflecting the immense success of the film, the enthusiastic applause intimates that the film audience behaved as a theater audience might, expecting actors to gauge their delivery and wait for the audience to settle back into the performance. More interesting in terms of reception is that sound reportedly had a spellbinding effect on the audience in ways never experienced before. Perhaps it was much like the experience of Professor Rath on first encountering the siren Lola. The awe-inspiring effect of sound titillated the senses and offered modern sensibilities yet another means of intoxication.

For the film's music, von Sternberg retained Friedrich Hollaender to work on the musical score and lyrics, as well as Robert Liebmann. Hollaender was well known in cabaret circles in Berlin as composer, musician and as author of some of Berlin's finest revues. In *The Blue Angel*, he appears in the wedding scene playing Mendelssohn's "The Wedding March" on piano, followed by the celebratory "Hoch sollen sie leben." He also appears as one of the musicians in the orchestra pit of The Blue Angel nightclub with the Weintraub Syncopators led by Mischa Spoliansky, one of Berlin's most innovative and talented jazz bands. The actress Lucie Mannheim, Jannings's choice for the part of Lola, brought Hollaender to accompany her on the piano for her screen test. For a while, it was thought that he also accompanied Dietrich when she showed up without music and unprepared for her audition. In the meantime, it is believed that Peter Kreuder provided musical accompaniment for Dietrich and prepared with her the sketch for the screen test.[35] It was the interplay between Dietrich's nonchalant, yet feisty style that convinced von Sternberg of her potential as Lola.

As evidenced by the number of operettas in this early phase of conversion, music played a central role in the shift from silent to sound filmmaking. So important was music, as Hollaender writes in a 1930 essay in the *Reichsfilmblatt*, that his compositions affected the conceptualization of *The Blue Angel*: "The director, von Sternberg, wanted to get to know my compositions before beginning his studio work. He expected the music to inspire his own work." The popular hit, "Ich bin von Kopf bis Fuss auf Liebe eingestellt" ("Falling in Love Again"), Hollaender claims, "gave such sharp contours to the role of Marlene Dietrich as the seductive cabaret singer that it naturally determined the plot. This song immediately created the atmosphere that the material powerfully demanded."[36] Indeed, music figures as a powerful narrative device and vehicle for dramatic effect in *The Blue Angel*. It announces and underscores the conflict, defines characters and their cultural contexts, and lends a historically unprecedented depth to the image. By the same token, sound heightens the visual tension, elaborates on thematic undertones, and intensifies the dramatic trajectory. It thus plays a crucial role in both narrative and thematic development.

## Von Sternberg's Use of Sound

In *The Blue Angel*, sound and image combine to create a volatile potion. Witnessing one of Germany's first sound films, reviewers of *The Blue Angel* marveled at the acoustic texture of the film. Kurt Pinthus expressed in superlatives his enthusiasm for *The Blue Angel*: "This Ufa sound film, up until now the most expensive, is without a doubt the most artistically valuable and promising film ever made in Germany."[37] He continued: "One could never before see so clearly how sound film could develop into its own genre, in part through combining and contrasting the stuff of theater and film, beyond theater and film."[38] Pinthus cites a number of scenes (the seduction of Rath and the marriage scene) as examples of how von Sternberg powerfully engaged the potential of sound to produce dramatic effect. Similarly, Herbert Ihering applauded the director's masterful implementation of sound: "Sound for him is not imitation of reality, but a dramaturgical, formal, stylistic principle."[39] Indeed, in his first sound film, *Thunderbolt* (1929), von Sternberg met the challenge of making the new technology work in favor of the images. In *The Blue Angel*, however, he understood even better its power. Here sound elaborates on the image and draws the audience deeper into the illusion, making the boundary between fantasy and reality more tenuous. At the same time, music becomes complicit in operations of gender and class; it is thus both socially and culturally inflected, demarcating two distinct spheres that are worlds apart.

In *The Blue Angel*, von Sternberg provides a self-reflexive tribute to the new technology on numerous levels. For one, sound represents life, as the chirping bird in Lola's apartment, a symbol of vitality and sensuality, suggests, in contrast to the dead parakeet in the mute and stark living quarters of Rath. Second, the artful choreography of the absence and presence of sound draws attention to sound as an integral part of the narrative. When Rath, for instance, closes the window of his classroom to shut out the schoolgirls' melodic performance of the folksong "Ännchen von Tharau" in a neighboring school, the scene foreshadows the seductive power of the female voice and song. In this scene, sound bridges two distinctly gendered spaces. Because the folksong is disembodied, it gains an ethereal, transcendental quality that rings of romantic purity and innocence, in contrast to the intrepid embodied music of the cabaret singer. In effect, the scene announces the struggle between profane pleasure and the romantic ideal of love, its promise of wholeness, and the nostalgic emotional states it evokes, while intimating the forbidden passions underlying the ideal. Sternberg also plays with the absence and presence of sound to acoustically link the cabaret stage to the backstage dressing room. By means of sound, the filmic space extends beyond the limits of the frame. Sound references a space outside the frame that exists conterminously with the image. Here, the stage continues to define Lola long after the door that separates these spaces has been shut to block out the performance of snake-charming music, a dancing bear, and the sounds of the Varieté.

The mute clown, played by Reinhold Bernt, often initiates the transition from sound to silence by opening and closing the dressing room door. One of the more elusive figures in *The Blue Angel*, he serves as a remnant of the silent era when cinema focused on the body, and when pantomime was identified as its closest relative—he invites a reading of the pure image and reminds the viewer of cinema's roots in the carnivalesque. Sabine Hake claims: "As the first silent art, its proponents argued, pantomime had actually prepared the ground for the cinema and should therefore serve as the model for all future developments. Giving the cinema a premodernist identity allowed writers to assess its social and cultural functions while ignoring its actual challenges to bourgeois culture."[40] Kracauer refers to the clown as the "mute observer" who follows the development of the relationship between Rath and Lola, interrupting the relay of their gazes as in the famous scene of Rath's visual and acoustic seduction. Once Rath surrenders to the sensuous arena of the cabaret, the clown is banished from the text only to be replaced by Rath.[41] His prescient gaze, however, exposes the professor, also a vestige of premodern sensibilities, and suggests that the modern siren will dash him.

Among cinema's early directors of talkies, von Sternberg claimed to have created a sound style that bears his signature.[42] In his memoir written years after directing *The Blue Angel*, he evokes the musical term "counterpoint," a compositional technique that describes the simultaneous combination of two equally significant but contrasting parts. It is a technique, as Caryl Flinn notes, "that ascribed to sound the power of penetrating the surface and lending the image depth."[43] In von Sternberg's own words, "Sound had to bring to the image a quality other than what the lens included, a quality out of the range of the image. Sound had to counterpoint the image, add to it—not subtract from it. ... Sound was realistic, the camera was not."[44] While the image could be manipulated, sound promised veracity. Sound breaks through the surface of the image, lends to it a complexity that silent film only rarely could match. As one of the pioneers of sound film, von Sternberg not only developed a personal style, but also contributed to developing a whole new cinematic vocabulary, in which he set leitmotifs against one another and against the image. The confluence of sound and image thus produce a sense of both unity and fragmentation; sound evokes various registers of meaning, comments on the image, and provides sharper contours.

To produce his distinct "sound style," von Sternberg drew foremost upon Wagner's aesthetic enterprise, upon the "romantic and Wagnerian ideal of the total work of art as nearly as possible," as Prawer maintains in his eloquent study of music in *The Blue Angel*.[45] The link to Wagner adds an interesting dimension in terms of cinema's execution of Wagner's aspiration of a *Gesamtkunstwerk*, that is, the synthesis of all the arts, which sound technology facilitated. Besides masterfully combining camerawork, lighting, *mise en scène*, and editing, von Sternberg enlisted musicians and sound technicians to produce a synthetic aural collage, a wide-ranging sound palette that consisted of opera, art songs, folksongs, and popular chansons, in addition to, as Prawer notes, a spectrum of "animal noises, different timbres of the human voice, gradations of speech from the pedantically distinct to muttered complaints, whistling, song, instrumental music including ensemble playing as well as solo piano and clarinet, bells, glockenspiel, music box effects coming out of a black doll, sirens."[46]

The tribute to Wagner tangibly surfaces in the opening, in the overture of the film, in the seamless interweaving and juxtaposition of contrasting themes that anticipate and generate its overall meaning and internal conflicts.[47] The "themes" are made up of well-known verses and newly composed film music; they contrast genres of music, those that represent high art and those that are associated with mass culture. Chiming the well-known verses of Ludwig Hölty's moralizing poem "Üb immer Treu und Redlichkeit" (Practice loyalty and honesty forever), the music from the church bells is interlaced with Lola's signature chanson "Ich bin von Kopf bis Fuss auf Liebe eingestellt." The melody of the slow waltz softens, and complicates the austere, measured melody of Hölty's composition on virtue. The choice of a waltz gains added meaning in this context, since it is a ballroom dance that during the 1800s represented "the abstract values of the new era, the ideals of freedom, character, passion, and expressiveness" that at first shocked polite society.[48] The overture concludes with Lola's song overpowering and then drowning out altogether the music that will be descriptive of Rath. These two contrasting musical themes allude to the dramatic encounter of divergent worlds, those of the pedant Rath and of the sumptuous cabaret performer Lola Lola. They hint at the dramatic conflict of sacred—that is, romantic—and profane love, more specifically, of the struggle between duty and sensual desire, between self-discipline and abandon.[49] Finally, the cinematic overture of Hollaender's finely intoned compilation of music emerges from a black screen. The absence of the image emphasizes sound as a new filmic code and a new structure of meaning.

The credits accompanied by the overture transition into the establishing shot of a small town. Chickens are heard squawking—an additional acoustic leitmotif that threads its way both visually and aurally through the narrative—as the poster announcing Lola's arrival comes into view. The squawking ominously sets the stage for Rath's self-depreciative crowing on the stage of The Blue Angel nightclub back in his hometown. Capitalizing on the potential of sound to strengthen the dramatic effect, von Sternberg uses Rath's tortured, heartwrenching crowing on stage to intensify and exteriorize his emotional breakdown and dissolution.

Like cinema, Lola's songs belong to the realm of "Kleinkunst" (trivial art), whereas the music associated with Rath falls into the domain of "serious art," tended by a cultural elite to reinforce traditional assumptions of power and privilege and the dominant social order, which von Sternberg exposes in all of its fragility in the wake of modernity—that is to say, Lola is represented by chansons and by a repertoire of popular hits, while Rath is associated with art songs, instrumental music, and what pervasively is perceived as an authentic German heritage rooted in notions of *Bildung*.[50] In contrast to art songs, Lola's songs are products of the culture industry that are designed for commercial mass consumption and expected to appeal to "lowbrow" tastes. By tapping into these divergent musical traditions, the image and narrative function of Lola and Rath gain social and historical depth.[51] The astute, strategic interplay of two divergent musical "catalogs," one that draws from high and the other from mass culture, underscores the drama of a contested cultural identity in *The Blue Angel*. Thus the musical score comments on and reinforces the cultural wars that shaped the Weimar Republic.

To return then to the cinematic exploration of the counterpoint tradition and use of leitmotifs, it could be argued that the aural structure of *The Blue Angel* simultaneously produces and dispels illusions of unity and harmony and lends to sound the ambiguous task of communicating crisis and redemption. Indeed, the film's hybrid aural structure bears out the fracturing of cultural authority that some saw as a necessary means of energizing Germany's fragile democracy, and that others viewed as a symptom of the destabilization of national integrity. The heterogeneous style of the musical soundtrack conveys what Ernst Bloch coined as "the asynchronous synchronicity" or "synchronicity of the non-synchronous" (*Gleichzeitigkeit des Ungleichzeitigen*) to describe Germany's fraught modernity. That is to say, the assemblage of musical snippets replicates the fragmentation and tensions that typified modernity and modern life and that reflected cinema's basic heterogeneity. The dramatic oppositions expressed in the soundtrack therefore are weighted. They bear the specter of national, cultural, class, and gender biases and expectations that are often at variance with each other.

## Rath

If music adds depth to the image rather than "subtracts from it," as von Sternberg maintains, and if it heightens presence, then the association of Rath with eighteenth- and nineteenth-century musical traditions greatly extends his meaning beyond the corporeal image to a time before modernity, as understood in association with the Weimar Republic. In other words, like von Sternberg's implementation of sound to expand the dramatic space of the cabaret, the brief musical fragments affixed to Rath clearly anchor him in eighteenth- and nineteenth-century classical musical traditions and allude to his sensibilities and training. The repertoire of music that identifies Rath is Franz Schubert's "Die schöne Müllerin" ("The Fair Maid of the Mill"), which sounds from the black doll Rath cradles in Lola's bed; Friedrich Silcher's "Ännchen von Tharau," a love song that the schoolgirls sing; Friedrich Kuecken's nineteenth-century "Ach, wie ist's möglich denn, dass ich dich verlassen kann," a folksong that Rath whistles to his parakeet prior to discovering it dead; "Oh, du lieber Augustin," heard when the door opens during one of Rath's first visits to Lola's dressing room, which forecasts loss; and Ludwig Christoph Hölty's "Üb immer Treu und Redlichkeit," a tune that calls for moral integrity. These folksongs and canonical art songs, sublime in their instrumentality, are synonymous with a German aesthetic culture that enjoys an elevated status in Western art music considered "serious." More specifically, Rath is configured within the highly prized musical traditions of German Romanticism, whose guiding principles are based on discourses of authenticity, essence, interiority, individualism and, above all, notions of idealized love. The romantic scores acknowledge emotion over reason, irrational sentimentality over rationality, and infinite longing. For the most part, these songs herald unwavering devotion and surrender to an idealized passion; they also profoundly betray an anxiety of loss.

A close look at the art songs and folksongs that characterize Rath reveal an idealized notion of romantic love. The lyrics express a subliminal yearning and willing abandon that prefigure his susceptibility to Lola's song. The folksong "Ännchen von Tharau," originally a marriage song written in 1637 by Simon Dach and translated into High German by Johann Gottfried Herder, with Friedrich Silcher composing the melody in 1827, describes a symbiotic union with the desired love object and the dissolution of individual boundaries to intensify the experience of the self. The "speaker" is willing to give up both his material wealth as well as his soul for his beloved and engage in a secular *unio mystica*. "Ännchen," the diminutive of Anne, emphasizes her youth, her purity, and her innocence and renders her harmless. The simply measured tune restrains and distills the intensity of the passion expressed in the declaration of total surrender.[52] Instead, surrender is sanctioned as a noble sentiment and an ideal to which a couple should aspire, as is suggested in the performance of the song by the schoolgirls. The sweet, sentimental romanticism is provincial and safe:

> Ännchen von Tharau ist's, die mir gefällt. Sie ist mein Leben, mein Gut und mein Geld. Ännchen von Tharau hat wieder ihr Herz auf mich gerichtet in Lieb' und in Schmerz. Ännchen von Tharau, mein Reichthum, mein Gut. Du meine Seele, mein Fleisch und mein Blut!
>
> <Ännchen von Tharau is the one I love. She is my life, my estate and my wealth. Ännchen von Tharau has her heart set on me once again in love and pain. Ännchen von Tharau, my wealth, my estate. You are my soul, my body and my blood.>

In the nineteenth century, such folksongs were made popular through the efforts of the late romantics, like Achim von Arnim and Clemens Brentano, whose particular interest in folk traditions (folk ballads, folklore, fairytales) led them to collect, rewrite, and publish folksongs in *Des Knaben Wunderhorn* (1808). Folk traditions, according to the Romantics, represented a means to explore the historical and cultural heritage of the nation. They were perceived as unadulterated expressions of the "German soul," of its essence. As an integral expression of nature, these traditions harbored the national spirit and expressed an authentic national origin, and genius that artists could tap.

In addition to mining folk traditions as a source of national identity, the Romantics looked to the Middle Ages for inspiration, and displaced their utopian longing onto bygone eras, thereby fetishizing a phantasmagorical space to compensate for the sense of perpetual loss. The musical repertoire associated with Rath thus plays with sentimentality and nostalgia for plentitude and with an understanding of high culture as a foundational text of Germanness that in the absence of German nationhood in the early nineteenth century was essential to German bourgeois identity. In other words, the music related to Rath significantly constitutes Germany's classical heritage and aligns him with traditional, albeit conflicted notions of German national identity during the Weimar Republic. By contrasting this musical tradition with contemporaneous popular music and cabaret, Hollaender undoubtedly drew on this knowledge to intensify the dramatic cultural and social conflict of the film and provoke the timbres of romantic illusion. Since, as Kathryn Kalinak perceptively notes, "musical conventions, which become ingrained and universal in a culture as a type of collective experience, activate particular and specific responses," Hollaender arguably selected these well-known pieces.[53]

As Rath is on his way to The Blue Angel nightclub for the first time, the song "Es war einmal ein Liebespaar" (Once upon a time there were two lovers) accompanies him. This song further evokes the trope of a utopian love relationship in its recitation of a fairytale-like love affair between a hussar and a girl that yields a formulaic happy ending. The melody of the song, transcribed in 1825, wafts out of a house in the seedy seaside district:

| Es war einmal ein treuer Hussar, | Once upon a time there was a loyal hussar, |
|---|---|
| Der liebt sein Mädel ein ganzes Jahr, | Who loved his girl a whole year, |
| Ein ganzes Jahr und noch viel mehr, | A whole year and much more, |
| Die Liebe nahm kein Ende mehr. | Love was everlasting. |

Cast as a soldier and wanderer, a common romantic trope, Rath enters the unknown, treacherous sphere of the lower class and of mass culture. The combination of the *mise en scène* and the displacement of a romantic love song into the backstreets of a harbor suggest a more ominous outcome. The song ironically foreshadows his upcoming encounter with Lola and begs the question of the durability of their liaison. The theme of "true" love serves as a counterpoint to the destructive love relation that awaits him. The musical fragment serves as a warning against deviation and as an expression of a yearning for romantic love with its undercurrent of sensual desire. Indeed, the notion of romantic love, spoken from a male perspective, dominates the musical commentaries of Rath, whose universe may be far removed from the tawdry side of town, but still is filled with the fantasies and latent desires articulated in romantic folk and love songs.

Franz Schubert's composition "Die schöne Müllerin" ("The Fair Maid of the Mill," 1823), whose *Lieder* date mostly from the 1820s, exemplifies intimate expressions of intense emotional desire and the themes of the Romantic period. It sounds from the black doll Rath cradles after awakening in Lola's bed.[54] The song stands for Rath's venture into sensuality, the taboo experience of femininity and the exotic. Among the twenty songs from this Schubert cycle (based on poems by Wilhelm Müller), von Sternberg evocatively chose "Wohin?" The question word "Where to?" inspires ideas of fate, adventure, and hopelessness. It is emblematic of the solitary wanderer in romantic songs who is intrinsically connected to nature. Irresistibly drawn to the sound of a brook ("Du hast mit deinem Rauschen, Mir ganz berauscht den Sinn" / Your bubbling has intoxicated me), an apprentice miller follows its course only to realize that the sound emerging from the brook is the song of water nymphs. They promise that the stream will lead him to a mill and, by implication, to the miller's daughter and happiness. The erotic undertones in the many images of water speak to the desire for absorption, for engulfment, for the dissolution of personal boundaries, and a nostalgic pursuit of wholeness and unity in the symbiosis of two hearts.[55]

But like most romantic poems, eternal love cannot be consummated or reciprocated. It remains an unrequited ideal that never can be fulfilled, despite the life-threatening longing it arouses. Consumed by the notion of love and drawn heartbroken into the depths of the brook, the rejected apprentice dies after his rival, the hunter, intrudes on his love life and takes his sweetheart. The huntsman, like the strong man Mazzepa in *The Blue Angel*, inspires a confident masculinity against which the apprentice cannot compete. Indeed, "Die schöne Müllerin," a drama of love, jealousy, and death, forecasts Rath's fate. In the juxtaposition of the music and the black doll, longing is mixed with the exotic and the appropriation of the unknown. While his pedantic lifestyle frowns on indulgence in excess, the black doll stands in for the repressed and for libidinal desire that the classical music tradition allegedly refines. Music in this form is a vehicle for containing desire and channeling it into a reserved, educated appreciation that transcends (represses) the body.

The nod to romantic traditions continues in the theme of birds that serves as a prominent leitmotif, most blatantly developed in the wedding scene. Birds symbolize the rituals of love, tamed nature, and the wish to bridge the distance between lovers. Distance in this context denotes physical distance, not social or class differences. In "Ännchen von Tharau" the lines include "Du bist mein Täubchen" (You are my dove); in "Wär' ich ein Vögelein" (If only I were a bird), the protagonist expresses his exclusive love and the fear of separation—yet, if he were a bird, he soon would be close to his lover. The deliberate play with these romantic themes and motifs in *The Blue Angel* effect a kind of romantic irony in the tradition of a counterpoint that emerges from the space between music and image.

Yet, romantic sentimentality elucidates only partially the contours of Rath's emotional life and cultural moorings. Religion as a defining text of German middle-class values and lifestyle complicates longing and desire. The moral imperative "Tue Recht und Scheue Niemand" (Do right and fear no one), engraved in a plaque in Rath's bedroom, in addition to the directive in "Üb immer Treu und Redlichkeit" that chimes as a leitmotif from the church tower, governs his life.[56] This theme song continuously alerts Rath to remain on the path of virtue, which his social milieu and calling demand. It can be heard in the overture of the film mentioned earlier, as well as in the breakfast scene with Lola, and in the final scene of Rath's death. The message of the poem (Hölty was the son of a Lutheran preacher), loosely translated as, "Be loyal and honest until your dying day, and do not stray an inch from God's path," lives in tension with the welling desire expressed in Romantic music.

Capitalizing on this tension, and undermining the imperative of staying the moral course, Mozart ironically poached the melody of Hölty's poem to compose Papageno's aria in *The Magic Flute*, in which he pines for a wife. Thus Papageno, a bird catcher, journeys through the countryside in search of "a soft little dove." This borrowing leads Luise Dirscherl and Gunther Nickel fittingly to wonder, "While Hölty's poem was being copied into family albums and autograph albums, did no one in the nineteenth century notice the ironic underpinning awarded it with Mozart's music."[57] Needless to say, Hollaender noticed it, and even built on the ironic tension of the double-edged meaning of the melody "Üb' immer Treu und Redlichkeit," showing, as Prawer writes, that "the erotic lurks within the straitlaced injunction."[58] The musical score associated with Rath thus masterfully locates him within the tensions of law and desire, the potential defining elements of melodrama.

In the final scene, Rath flees the cabaret, the space of his subjective disintegration, and steals through the dark streets to return to his former classroom, where he dies. Music once again arrests him in a time and space both outside of modernity and as its casualty. As the night watchman hobbles up the stairs to find Rath, the light from the flashlight bounces to the rhythm of Hollaender's menacing composition, which bears traces of *The Magic Flute*. It reminds the listener of ideals and passions gone afoul and of the spotlight Lola used to capture her real man. The music dramatically mounts, developing into a melody, and then transitions into a serene orchestral rendition of Rath's signature song, "Üb immer Treu und Redlichkeit." The combination of the two scores remind the spectator of Rath's transgression and simultaneously signals his possible redemption, a redemption that the visuals deny him. Returned to his rightful place, to the site of his forsaken identity, Rath becomes one of the many prodigal sons of German cinema. Yet, even though the music suggests his personal redemption, the camera slowly abandons him as a ruin of masculinity and bourgeois cultural authority. The screen fades to black again, as in the beginning of the film, and only the sound of the church bell fills the void, tolling the end of Rath's existence and the cultural values he embodied.[59]

Except for the sparse, yet calculated use of music, a predominant muteness, that is, lifelessness, characterizes the spaces that Rath inhabits. In his sphere, words often erupt into commands; language conveys authority and ostensible cultural superiority. In contrast, Lola is associated with the realm of sensual aural pleasure conveyed in the performance of her songs, the musical doll, and the chirping bird. Rath's flaw is bringing intangible romantic longing for the Blue Flower, a symbol of desire for an infinite sacred love that transcends temporal earthliness, to the feminized, eroticized space of The Blue Angel cabaret, where the laws of mass culture reign.

## Lola

In contrast to the musical bits that define Rath, Lola's songs are central to the film. She poses as a siren (deviant by their very nature, the sirens appeared in art first as birds with the heads of women, and then later as women, sometimes with the wings and legs of birds), whose "nature" is to beckon audiences to experience somatically the melodious lyrics of love that Hollaender and Liebmann composed especially for the film. As a siren who invites transgression, her voice is nature, pleasure, and temptation, all of which threaten the quotidian male. Timid yet enthralled, Rath is shown to be a failed Odysseus as he sits in the balcony, for he does not tie himself to the mast in order to resist Lola, but allows himself to be entranced and absorbed by her. Instead of withstanding the aural (now directly perceived by the cinema audience through sound technology) and visual temptations, and preserving both his privileged view of the stage and pleasurable detachment, Rath succumbs to Lola's image and song of love, loses his bourgeois bearings and shipwrecks. In other words, distracted from the inevitable outcome that the classical text foretells, he accedes to the popular.

In an analysis of Adorno and Horkheimer's Odysseus allegory, Rebecca Comay writes, "the ear is in fact the essential organ of equilibrium."[60] Yet the balance is fragile, as we know from the precautions Odysseus took when he requested his crew to leave him tied to the mast regardless of his pleas to be released. Lola's song destabilizes Rath, pulls him out of his staid life, and allows him to escape, so that he needs to be deceived by the promises of her song and her presence. Wearing a top hat and garter, her hands drawing up her knee, Lola sits on a barrel and leans back; she serenades Rath, who is perched in the balcony of the cabaret, basking in her delivery and her captivating song "Ich bin von Kopf bis Fuss auf Liebe eingestellt," the film's theme song. It is no wonder that this image sells the film time again.

In this scene of seduction, both Rath and Lola are on display. Elizabeth Bronfen argues that they alternately pose as object and agent of the gaze. Lola applauds Rath, who bashfully accepts the audience's acknowledgment of his social position and status as special guest, while he indulges in the spectacle of Lola and is beguiled.[61] Yet, even when the music stops so that the magician Kiepert can introduce Professor Rath to the audience, the reminder of his social role neither interrupts the dream world nor rescues him from immersion in Lola's performance. Nor do the lifesavers that ironically decorate the balcony and remain fastened save its occupant from drowning in Lola's presence, reinforced and secured through sound. Instead of the wished-for reciprocal staging of Lola and Rath that Bronfen asserts, Lola maintains visual and acoustic authority throughout the performance. She never relinquishes her power; she controls the performance and hardly "fortifies the male spectator against his own losses," which Kaja Silverman identifies as the underlying structure of classic cinema.[62]

In effect, Rath relinquishes the boundaries of his identity and falls for the promise of love and sensual pleasure—even though the promise all along is a deceit.[63] The deception occurs first by means of sound, and the ways in which it lends "realness" to the image. That is to say, sound provides the image (a simulacrum) with substance and masks its absence. Second, sound suggests that Lola's song and performance (her masquerade) are descriptive of her essence, of her motives and mystery. To that end, her voice allows for the disavowal of absence, promises immediacy, and sustains fantasy. The power of cinematic sound and, even more compelling, voice lies in its authenticity and in its capability, according to Kaja Silverman, of "restoring all phenomenon of loss" that the image bears. In other words, it compensates for the absence of the image.

In her performance of "Ich bin von Kopf bis Fuss," the synchronicity of female voice and image creates emotional excess with which Lola baits her audience. She unabashedly declares her promiscuity, her excessive desire, and she confesses over and over again to an addiction to love and its pleasures. In fact, she loves the game of love, which she plays with anyone within acoustic range. It is her nature and thus unalterable. Rath's timid and enchanted look reveals his vulnerability as Lola lulls him with her offering. Her voice opens up an emotional space and fuels Rath's dreams and longing. It is no wonder that von Sternberg's films with Dietrich as his vehicle are associated with dreams. Marcel Oms contends, "for him <von Sternberg> the discovery and the practice of sound will only amplify this filmic vocation for liberating the powers of the dream. ... Thus obliging the spectator to participate in the film, urged by all its senses to the illusion of living."[64] Significantly, pleasure does not derive from containing or controlling the threatening female but from submitting to her image, her gaze, and more importantly, to her voice, which assures symbiotic bliss. Rath abandons himself to regressive desires and to the illusory promise of wholeness that Lola's image and voice inspire.

During the time of the performance reality is suspended and the narrative arrested and the audience is invited to linger and merge with the image that Lola determines. Thus, classical narrative structures that rely on progress toward stability and on the reestablishment of patriarchal order are undermined in the performance, and Rath with them. Indeed, the combination of the image and music lower Rath's guard and encourage him to dream. In psychoanalytical terms, Lola's song evokes an "oceanic feeling," immersing its auditor in a pre-Oedipal state in which the boundary between the self and other is obscured. Speaking of the power of music on the human psyche, Claudia Gorbman finds that "as early as 1917, Frieda Teller writes that for the adult listener, music 'causes the censor to weaken' ... it causes a temporary, benign regression, transporting the subject to the pleasurable realm of early phantasies."[65] The principal sound in constituting the aural imaginary is the voice of the mother, so that seduction takes place through the sound of the female voice. The next morning, Rath awakens in Lola's bed. He appears in the time between sleeping and waking, in a liminal state of bliss, and remains in the fantasy world of Lola's backstage bedroom until the church bells interrupt it later during their breakfast, and call him back to his duties. Yet, Lola's music has unleashed memories of regressive archaic pleasures, of the primal scene that approximates masochistic surrender to an indeterminable power beyond rational control. Neither Rath nor Lola can help it.

Aware of the effect of song, Lola also warns her audience, as Circe warns Odysseus of the irresistible power of the sirens' song, in her performance of "Nimm dich in acht vor blonden Frau'n" (Beware of Blonde Women) on the stage of the Blue Angel. The reference to blonde evokes the image of Aphrodite, the goddess of love, whose first depictions were as a blonde and who, according to Joanna Pitman, represented "the world's original model of sexual fantasy."[66] In the German popular imagination, blonde is a powerful signifier associated with the fabled Lorelei, a preeminent Romantic image of a siren who sits on a cliff along the Rhine River and combs her golden hair. In Heinrich Heine's 1844 poetic tribute to this legend, the Lorelei's song diverts sailors' attention, causing them to shipwreck and be swallowed up by the river. The clichés associated with blonde also circulated widely in the popular press of the Weimar Republic. For instance, "Warum werden Blondinen bevorzugt?" (Why are blondes preferred?), a 1928 satirical essay in *Uhu*, sketches blondes as unfaithful women who readily overlook their partner's moral indiscretions because their next admirers are waiting in the wings.[67] Lola describes blondes as perilously mysterious, charming, and "captivating." Above all, she alludes to the difference between "sein" and "schein," between essence and surface appearance that baffles the spectator.

According to Greek mythology, the alternative for Rath would be to plug his ears with wax like the boatmen in Homer's epic and deny himself the pleasure of the seductive melodies. Or, as in the presence of high art, and particularly the art song, Rath would have to become the bourgeois concertgoer, who maintains distance and contemplates the sublime with aesthetic detachment, aware of the conventions that the performance of art songs demand, its elicitation of emotional rapture that serves to expand the depth of individualism and indulge in longing while calling for self-reflection. Comay describes the posture of the "bourgeois as modern concertgoer as taking cautious pleasure in "art" as an idle luxury to be enjoyed at safe remove."[68] Consumption ideally takes place outside of commercial venues, which were seen as catering only to the nervous, distracted sensibilities of the time. In the realm of the popular, Rath, too, would have to grasp the nature of the cabaret performance, the convention of direct address, the "art" of commercialism and advertising, and understand the pleasure of consuming the product for momentary satisfaction. Instead, Rath, as humanist educator, invests in the exclusive and intimate declaration of romantic love and unwittingly translates longing into gratification even though it takes place on a stage before an audience of rowdy seafarers and longshoremen. Unlike them, Rath forgets the boundaries between self and the performer and merges with a world that robs him of agency and effects his dissolution. He is seduced by the magic of the cabaret performance, enchanted by Lola's voice. Her association with the magician Kiepert is no accident. They both produce and sell illusions.[69] In a 1920 cabaret program Hollaender proposed that if cabaret does not move an audience to think, it should at least capture it.[70] Indeed, the spectacle and music bowl over the archaic, humanist subject, subverting the ideals that have become threadbare in the tumultuous years of the Weimar Republic.

Like other fictional mariners, and unlike the merchant marine who is willing to pay for Lola's favors, Rath too is swept away, enveloped in Lola's voice. As the scene of him hawking the very postcards he once refused to sell suggests, he pays dearly. A poster of Lola on the wall behind the fallen professor, the same one that initially announced Lola's show, hovers over him, displaying her from the waist down. Her legs (a symbol of her sexuality) literally tower over him as a fetish that no longer can supplant his castration or feed the illusion of disavowal (see Figure 4.1). Moreover, her song "Nimm dich in acht vor blonden Frau'n" fills the frame; the voice-over poignantly comments on the reckless pursuit of

**Figure 4.1** "Beware of Blonde Women." Still from *Der blaue Engel*, 1930, directed by Josef von Sternberg. Source: *Deutsche Kinemathek*.

desire, the ravaging effect of falling for all that Lola embodies, and the failure to heed the warning. Once the source of endless pleasure, the female voice has stripped Rath of masculine authority, effected its crisis, and uprooted him from his class. Unshaven, unkempt, and dressed in tattered clothes, misplaced and displaced in the cabaret milieu, he is the tragic shadow of his former self. Significantly, the scene powerfully returns the disheveled Rath to the site of his disempowerment (the legs) and conveys the bitter consequence of the search for bliss in complete masochistic surrender to the conventions of the popular. In *The Blue Angel*, the siren is neither domesticated nor does she die, but rather she continues visually and aurally to undermine patriarchal order by evoking the memory of ecstasy and inducing forgetting in order to allow for dreams. She is the place to which all return.

While Lola's voice and song mask absence and evoke the phantasm of wholeness, her self-reflective and self-conscious performance, the artifice of the *mise en scène*, and the candidly sexualized lyrics complicate the promises of realism and mock the illusion she simultaneously produces. In other words, her self-assured performance problematizes sound in relation to the assurances of realism and to the illusionary "nature" of cinema and performance. The artificiality of setting, coupled with Lola's overt sexual performance and the sobriety of the lyrics, dislodge any possibility of "honesty" or "sincerity"— Rath's leitmotif—or of romantic love. Love lasts for the duration of the performance. By its very "nature," the songs Lola sings belong to the realm of the popular, which means they are time-bound, immediate, and ephemeral, and will be replaced by the next "Schlager" (popular hit). Even before the premiere of *The Blue Angel*, Lola's theme song was heard on the radio and the record could be purchased. Music served as a powerful advertisement for both the film and Marlene Dietrich. Indeed, "Ich bin von Kopf bis Fuss auf Liebe eingestellt" later became her signature song.[71] In addition to the explicit address of serial love, Dietrich's delivery creates a dissonance between melody and words that undermines any possibility of sincerity—a trope misplaced in the halls of the cabaret and Weimar culture. Patrick O'Connor claims: "One hears immediately that the art of the Berlin *diseuse* was a recognizable tradition from which Dietrich took her method; speaking the words slightly against the music, only singing on the note when it was exactly within her limited range."[72] Lotte Eisner appropriately describes Lola's songs as "loaded, ambiguous songs," and she too remarks the underlying irony.[73]

Lola's performance thus resonates with the "intention" of the liberal cabaret during the Weimar Republic to criticize and mock middle-class lifestyles. Cabaret songs were famous as anti-bourgeois parodies of romantic love—a sentiment that aroused suspicion among the modern, interwar generation disillusioned by the carnage of World War I. Rich in double entendre, the cabaret repertoire reflected a deliberate gesture toward anti-romanticism, a loathing for pretense and sentimentality, and an overall cynicism or skepticism of the age expressed, as mentioned above, in the Neue Sachlichkeit. Peter Jelavich writes that cabaret artists "mocked the kitschy romanticism of much popular entertainment; they satirized conservative moralists who denounced the loosening of sexual mores, and made fun, in turn, of those liberalized sexual manners. Cabaret was something of a tease; it satirized and sustained simultaneously the erotic energy of the day."[74] In other words, with the liberalization of sexual mores during the 1920s, cabaret performers lampooned traditional values and gender norms with ribald songs and comically overstated enunciation, taking on middle-class values and sensibilities. Performers taunted an all-knowing audience whose catcalls and interjections, as during Lola's performance, demonstrated their participation in the game of deception unfolding on stage. For the most part, the audience remained distracted and disengaged.

By the mid-1920s, female cabaret entertainers such as Claire Waldoff, a longtime friend of Dietrich who influenced her style, openly invited male audiences to join in, much like Lola does in *The Blue Angel*. Lola singles out Rath and assigns him the role of the "real man" in the song: "Kinder, heut' abend da such ich mir was aus, einen Mann, einen richtigen Mann

(Children, this evening I gotta get a man, just a man, a real man). In a bold reversal of gender roles, Lola espies her "real man" and captures him in her spotlight when he ventures for the first time into The Blue Angel nightclub. As in the performance of her other songs, Lola is the agent of her desire. This "hunt" for love is reminiscent of Papageno's search for a wife in *The Magic Flute*. Further spoofing the romantic symbolism of art songs in this song, the more common sparrow "heralds spring," as Prawer notes, in contrast to the unique melodious song of the nightingale, which evolved into a literary symbol of romance.[75] "Frühling kommt, der Sperling piept duft aus Blütenkelchen" (Spring has come, the sparrow sings, all is bright and cheerful): the evocation of the sparrow makes banal the traditional idealization of love in literature and music. Thus, the song and the constellation of Lola on stage and Rath below in pursuit of his students ends up poking fun at the male subject and by extension at the institutions he represents, along with the sensibilities of utopian love expressed in romantic songs. The song predicts the inability of Rath to perform in the unfamiliar space of show business, dangerously removed from the spotlight of bourgeois culture.

Indeed, the synchronization of the image and sound in *The Blue Angel* makes the sexualized female more alluring and more treacherous, as Eisner's use of the word "loaded" additionally implies. In her performance "Ich bin die fesche Lola" (They call me naughty Lola), Lola pans the audience with her hands on her hips and sings provocatively, "Ich hab ein Pianola zu Haus in mein'm Salon. / Ich bin die fesche Lola, mich liebt ein jeder Mann, doch an mein Pianola, da lass ich keinen ran" (At home my pianola, it works for all its worth. The boys all love my music, I can't keep them away. So my little pianola keeps working night and day.) The lyrics by Robert Liebmann, which Hollaender set to a foxtrot, liken sexuality to an instrument and alternate suggestively between vulgarity, morality, and invitation, while holding the listener at bay.

Lola's aggressive sexualized stage presence marks a clear shift in performance styles of earlier 1920s cabaret. In a 1930 issue of *Uhu*, music theorist H.H. Stuckenschmidt claims that in earlier cabarets "bourgeois solidity was the dream of all chanson singers, the latent refrain of their songs. Highly moral concepts like love, desire, homeland, and marriage provided the foundation from which the most lascivious texts were constructed. The blue flower blooms forever in the background."[76] Toward the end of the Weimar Republic, cabaret abandoned conventions of morality and the piquant evocation of its erotic underbelly, thereby forfeiting nuance. Instead, cabaret produced candid sexualized performances that destroyed all illusion and challenged traditional concepts of morality and its accompanying sensibilities. For Stuckenschmidt, Dietrich's brazen delivery of the film songs, even more blatantly sexually nuanced on the album that Electrola issued, reflect the shamelessness of the times. He contends: "Any and all aesthetic and moral standards fail when confronted with the sexual undertone. The unquestioned cult-like emphasis and glorification of sexuality definitively cancels out and suppresses the concept of 'the beautiful.' Whether we condone or disapprove of it is a private matter. But we cannot and should not avoid it, since it reflects the time in which we live."[77] Bourgeois eroticism conveyed through suggestion is abandoned for directness. Indeed, the audience is left without illusions. Gone too are the aesthetic principles that Stuckenschmidt evokes as the foundation of high culture. The general tone of his essay is that of loss, of nostalgia for an irretrievable past that was ruled by a moral code and decorum, rooted in middle-class values that distinguished private from public sphere and professed the control of sensation and instinct.

Lola's success represents the assertion of mass culture in the age of mechanical reproduction, the breakthrough of sound film, as well as a shift in social mores. In his 1941 essay "On Popular Music," cultural theorist Theodor Adorno, who criticized the film's adaptation of Mann's novel for its capitulation to the laws of mass culture, addresses the standardizing effect of popular music that undermines the humanistic notion of the individual and reinforces capitalism's mandate. Somewhat ironically, even the "presence" of serious music in cinema, according to Adorno, whose essay on music further polarizes mass culture and high art, lends it a precarious status. The marketplace arguably standardizes and robs high art of its singularity. In an effort to create consumers, popular music relies on passive and regressive listening and is guided by the principle of return.[78] Both Lola's song and image speak to the law of returning both commercially and psychoanalytically in terms of regression and pleasure.

Indeed, Lola, that is, Dietrich, continued to mesmerize international audiences with her repertoire of songs. And after leaving behind her film career, she continued to perform her songs until 1975. She sang for audiences around the world, beginning as film star, as USO performer during World War II, and then ending with concert tours that drew thousands of fans worldwide.[79] Her success was measured by the applause she enjoyed and archived. Adolf Heinzlmeier reports, "Among the objects she left behind is a recorded collection of applauses from various concerts."[80]

Soon after the premieres of *The Blue Angel* and *Morocco*, Dietrich's image served as a vehicle to sell sound technology.[81] An advertisement for "Electrola" in the Berlin magazine *Uhu* shows Dietrich with Gary Cooper and features a recording of Dietrich's songs, "Leben ohne Liebe kannst Du nicht" (Life without love) and "Wenn ich mir was wünschen dürfte, käm ich in Verlegenheit" (Were I able to make a wish, I would feel ashamed).[82] The recording represents pure sound, dislocating voice from image. Ironically, when Dietrich withdrew from the public eye in 1979, after twice having fallen off the stage and injuring herself, she returned only through sound. In Maximilian Schell's 1984 documentary *Marlene*, she refused to lend her image to the film. In spite of Schell's cajoling to film her, he was left only with their recorded conversations and earlier film clips and photographs, in order to sketch Dietrich's rich and turbulent life. In place of her immediate image, Schell edited reams of archival material, including films scenes, and photographs on which she commented. *Marlene* premiered at the Berlin Film Festival and went on to win numerous awards.

Beginning in 1979, Dietrich's ear and voice became her primary means of accessing the world outside of her Paris apartment on the Avenue Montaigne. Considered a notorious, late-night caller, a "phonaholic" with nine phones in her Paris apartment, her disembodied voice continued to connect her to family, friends, and admirers.[83] For Ernest Hemingway and many others, her voice was enough to conjure up the image of Hollywood's film goddess and lose oneself in fantasies. Her voice became synonymous with the "talkies," and her repertoire of songs with desire. For Rath, these songs represented his absolute surrender and demise.

## Notes

1. Jerzy Toeplitz, *Geschichte des Films* (Berlin: Henschel, 1972), 2: 31.
2. Wolfgang Jacobsen et al., eds., *Willy Haas: Der Kritiker als Mitproduzent* (Berlin: Edition Hentrich, 1991), 219. ("Die sogenannte 'Front gegen den Tonfilm' ist der übliche Literaten-Unsinn. Es sind z.T. genau dieselben Herren, die vor 1921 über das Kino wie über einen Matrosenpuff gesprochen haben, mit dem sich ernsthaft zu beschäftigen, tief unter ihrer literarischen Würde war.")
3. For an extensive discussion of advancements in sound technology in the first half of the twentieth century, see Wolfgang Mühl-Benninghaus *Das Ringen um den Tonfilm: Strategien der Elektro- und der Filmindustrie* (Düsseldorf: Droste, 1999). The year 1925 saw the founding of Deutscher Tonfilm. In 1928, the Ton-Bild Syndikats (TOBIS) was founded as a way to consolidate the numerous companies (Küchenmeister, Tri-Ergon, Petersen-Poulson and Lignon Systems), which ended the "Tonfilm-Krieg" (sound-film war) (109). By 1930, Ufa had nine sound-film ateliers. For discussion of the Paris Treaty, which effected a standardization of equipment internationally, see Charles O'Brien, *Cinema Conversion to Sound: Technology and Film Style in France and the U.S.* (Bloomington: University of Indiana Press, 2005), 17.
4. According to Mühl-Benninghaus, Germany led other nations in sound experimentation with the invention of the "Tonfilm" and many other technologies. The "Tonfilm" relied on the gramophone to accompany images. In other words, sound was synchronized with the images. Otto Messter was one of the pioneers of this technology, with Guido Seeber following (16). Yet, as films became longer and visually more sophisticated, the production of sound with records was no longer possible. By 1914, the "Tonfilm" had become a defunct option. Other experiments to incorporate sound were "Dirigentenfilme," with a live conductor and musicians accompanying the film and singers following the images. Oftentimes the image of a conductor would be incorporated into the beginning of the film.
5. Michaela Krützen, "'Esperanto für den Tonfilm': Die Produktion der Sprachversionen für den Tonfilm," *Positionen deutscher Filmgeschichte: 100 Jahre Kinematographie: Strukturen, Diskurse, Kontexte* (Munich: Diskurs Film, 1996), 124.

6. Von Sternberg recounts his first experience with sound film when filmmakers experimented with crude forms of synchronization: "As a child I had seen and heard my first talking picture, in which Caruso made motions with his face to synchronize with a phonograph recording from *I Pagliacci*. It was ineffective not only because his voice did not seem to issue from him, but because I felt no need both to see and hear it" (Josef von Sternberg, *Fun in a Chinese Laundry*, New York: MacMillan Co., 1965, 218). This may explain the tribute von Sternberg pays to Leoncavallo's 1892 opera *I Pagliacci* (in German, *Der Bajazzo*) when Lola admonishes Rath for acting like the jealous Bajazzo every time she has a bit of fun. Chapter 1 touches on the complex intertextual allusion to the opera that resonates both with Rath's jealous attack of Lola and the sophisticated representation of the fragile boundaries between life and stage. In the opera's prologue, the character Tonio, a member of a traveling show, assures the audience that they will be witnessing a true story. The stage becomes the site of an adulterous love triangle played out twice; the second time ends with the "actual" death both of the wife of Canio and her lover at the hand of her husband.
7. Krützen, "'Esperanto für den Tonfilm': Die Produktion der Sprachversionen für den Tonfilm," 124. See also Charles O'Brien and Rudolf Arnheim, "Tonfilm-Verwirrung," *Kritiken und Aufsätze zum Film*, edited by Helmut H. Diederichs (Frankfurt: Fischer, 1979), 61–64. French filmmaker René Claire, a staunch opponent of sound film, declared in 1929 the Tower of Babel as the symbol of the talkies, an image many critics borrowed, including sound enthusiast Ernst Hugo Correll, Ufa's director of production after 1928.
8. Wolfgang Jacobsen, *Erich Pommer: Ein Produzent macht Filmgeschichte* (Berlin: Argon, 1989), 90.
9. See Viktor Rotthaler, "Die Musikalisierung des Kinos: Die Komponisten der Pommer-Produktion," *MusikSpektakelFilm: Musiktheater und Tanzkultur im deutschen Film, 1922–1937*, edited by Hans-Michael Bock, Wolfgang Jacobsen, and Jörg Schöning (Munich: Edition Text + Kritik, 1998), 123–35.
10. The USA was not importing silent films after 1929. See Mühl-Benninghaus, 116–17.
11. Asta Nielsen, "Tod der Filmkunst," *Vossische Zeitung* 403 (August 26, 1928) (my translation). See also *Asta Nielsen: Die schweigende Muse*, translated by H. Georg Kemlein (Munich: Hanser, 1977); Rudolf Arnheim, *Film als Kunst* (Frankfurt: Suhrkamp, 2002), 189–260.
12. Herbert Ihering, *Von Reinhardt bis Brecht: Vier Jahrzehnte Theater und Film, 1924–1929*, vol. 3 (Berlin: Aufbau Verlag, 1959). ("Von einem Sprechfilm kann erst dann die Rede sein, wenn die Bewegung, der Kontrast und der Wechsel des stummen Films auch im gesprochenen möglich sind. Einschnitte wirken, als Akzent, nicht als Dehnung. Lange Dialogpartien—schlimm. Schlimmer als im Theater!"). See also, Herbert Ihering, "Der akustische Film. *Alhambra*," *Berliner Börse-Courier* 439 (September 19, 1922), 54.
13. For a comprehensive discussion of the industrial beginnings of sound, see Klaus Kreimeier, *Die Ufa Story: Geschichte eines Filmkonzerns* (Munich: Hanser Verlag, 1992).
14. In order to avoid duplicating the image, filmmaker Walter Ruttmann, like the Russian filmmakers Eisenstein, Pudovkin, and Aleksandrov, proposed using a counterpoint technique. Ruttmann claims, "Man versuche sich klarzumachen, dass Tonfilm seiner Gestaltungsmethode nach nichts anderes sein kann als Kontrapunkt" (One tries to understand that the structure of a sound film can be nothing else but contrapunctual).
15. Many musicians were being phased out by 1928 with more technologically sophisticated speakers and the use of records for sound. See Mühl-Benninghaus's comprehensive study of the development of sound in *Das Ringen um den Tonfilm: Strategien der Elektro- und der Filmindustrie in der 20er und 30er Jahren* (52).
16. See von Sternberg's autobiography *Fun in a Chinese Laundry* for anecdotes describing Jannings's narcissistic, jealous behavior both on and off stage.
17. "Emil Jannings: German and the International Sound Film," *Der Film* 11 (1929), 17. In contrast, von Sternberg is quoted as saying that he avoids stage actors because "tradition hampers them," and they "forget to act like human beings," in Philip Scheuer, "Big Scenes Tabooed," *Los Angeles Times* (November 30, 1930), B9.

18. "Emil Jannings: German and the International Sound Film," 17.
19. Thomas Saunders, *Hollywood in Berlin: American Cinema and Weimar Germany* (Berkeley: University of California Press, 1994), 225.
20. Michaela Krützen "'Esperanto für den Tonfilm': Die Produktion der Sprachversionen für den Tonfilm," 121.
21. Saunders, 233. He notes: "Beginning in 1930 the quota system was indirectly tightened by legal redefinition of a 'German' film. Previously, a feature film had been classified German so long as it was made in Germany in no less than fourteen studio days and was at least 1500 meters long. Effective 1 July 1930 the production company had to be German; the script writer, composer, director and majority of personnel in each production area had to be German speaking residents; all studio work and, if feasible, all outdoor scenes had to be shot in Germany. In 1932 these stipulations were considerably sharpened; the producer and seventy-five percent of all production personnel had to be German, and, most importantly, a German was redefined as a legal citizen of the Reich" (234).
22. Krützen reports that the cost of filming two versions was relatively high: "Inklusiv der Sprachversion kostete *Der blaue Engel* über 2,3 Millionen RM. ... Das *Universal Filmlexikon*, das 1932 genau Buch über die Sprachfähigkeiten der Darsteller führt ... gilt bei Albers, der kaum Englisch und Französisch spricht, allein Deutsch an" (Including the different language versions, *The Blue Angel* cost over 2.3 million marks ... The Universal Film Lexicon, which listed the language capabilities of actors, shows Albers, who hardly speaks English or French, as speaking only German). Michaela Krützen, *Hans Albers: Eine deutsche Karriere* (Weinheim: Beltz Quadriga, 1995), 83.
23. Wilhelm Thiele directed *Die drei von der Tankstelle* (1930) in both German and English, hiring French actors for the French version, with the exception of Lillian Harvey, who played both German and French versions.
24. "German Dialog in N.Y.," *Foreign Film News* (December 10, 1930), 7. See Michaela Krützen, *Hans Albers*, 146–47.
25. In her biography of *Hans Albers: Eine deutsche Karriere*, Michaela Krützen writes that von Sternberg spoke every English sentence for the German actors; a few roles were synchronized retrospectively. "Hans Albers' text was reduced to a few sentences, and not without cause: In the English version of *Bombs on Montecarlo* (1931), which Hans Albers starred in, American critics claimed that he was incomprehensible" (84–85).
26. With the introduction of sound, a number of German actors went to England to improve their English language skills. See "Tonfilmateliers in Neubabelsberg," *Die Filmwoche* 30 (1929), 707–8. The article also describes the haste with which the German studios built soundproof rooms.
27. Quoted in the introduction of Peter Baxter, ed., *Sternberg* (London: British Film Institute, 1980), 2–3.
28. "New UFA Talkie Praised in Berlin," *New York Times* (April 2, 1930), 36.
29. Ihering, *Von Reinhardt bis Brecht*, 3 (my translation). ("Zum erstenmal kommt eine Frauenstimme im Tonfilm mit Timbre, Klangfarbe, Ausdruck heraus.")
30. Saunders, 230. For a discussion of the many considerations that had to go into building a soundproof studio, see "Tonfilmateliers in Neubabelsberg," *Filmwoche* 30 (1920), 707–8.
31. Sternberg, 138. See also, Wolfgang Jacobsen, *Babelsberg: 1912 Ein Filmstudio 1992* (Berlin: Stiftung Deutsche Kinemathek und Argon, 1992), 145–65.
32. Sternberg contends that sound, "is different than the continuity of the visual pattern ... There was no way to jump or transfer sound after the film was completed, as is done in the dubbing process" (Sternberg, *Fun in a Chinese Laundry*, 138).
33. Ibid., 321.
34. *Filmkurier*, 80 (February 4, 1930), quoted in Jacobsen, *Erich Pommer*, 98 (my translation) ("Tonfilm erfordert von Anfang bis Schluss stärkste Aufmerksamkeit des Ohres, wenn ein paar Dialogstellen unverständlich bleiben, findet man sich schwer wieder zurecht. Es erweist sich, dass die vorausschauend bei besonders guten Stellen des Films eingesetzten

"Beifallspausen", in denen der Film stumm weiterlauft, zu klein sind. Das Klatschen donnert in die nachste Szenen über und wird wegen der Notwendigkeit des Zuhörens gewaltsam abgewürgt.")

35. In *Fun in a Chinese Laundry*, von Sternberg claims that Dietrich came without music and without an accompanist, so that Hollaender played for her (236). Yet, it was Peter Kreuder that played, and according to Volker Kühn (www.gema.de/presse/news/n171/kreuder.shtml), he and Dietrich had practiced their routine.

36. Friedrich Hollaender, *Reichsfilmblatt* (1930) (my translation). ("Der Regisseur, von Sternberg, hatte den Wunsch geäussert, meine Komposition vor Beginn seiner Atelierarbeit kennenzulernen. Starke Befruchtung des eigenen Schaffens erwartete er von der Musik. Schon mit dem Schlager: 'Ich bin von Kopf bis Fuss auf Liebe eingestellt' war die Charakterrrolle von Marlene Dietrich, der verführerischen Varietésängerin Lola Lola, so scharf umrissen, dass durch dieses Chanson eine klare Grundlinie für die Handlung gewonnen war. Dieses Chanson schuff sofort die Atmosphäre, nach der der Stoff gebieterisch verlangte. Hollaender goes on to describe "die Fülle der dramatischen Gegensätze, die sich im Verlauf der Handlung entwickeln.")

37. Kurt Pinthus, *Das Tagebuch*, 11 (1930) (my translation). ("Dieser bisher kostspieligste Tonfilm der Ufa-Produktion (Erich Pommers) ist zweifellos von allen bisher in Deutschland gefertigt der künstlerisch wertvollste und zukunftsträchtigste.") Also in Wolfgang Jacobsen, *Erich Pommer*, 98–100.

38. Kurt Pinthus, *Das Tagebuch*, 11 (1930) (my translation). ("Noch nie bisher sah man so deutlich, wie der Tonfilm sich zu eigener Gattung entwickeln kann, in manchem durch Kombinierung oder Kontrastierung der Mittel von Theater und Film über Theater und Film hinaus.")

39. Herbert Ihering, "The Blue Angel and the American Tragedy," *Sternberg*, edited by Peter Baxter (London: British Film Institute, 1980) 25.

40. Sabine Hake, *The Cinema's Third Machine: Writing on Film in Germany 1907–1933* (Lincoln: University of Nebraska Press, 1993), 84.

41. Siegfried Kracauer, *From Caligari to Hitler* (Princeton, NJ: Princeton University Press, 1947), 219. Bronfen reads the clown as: "Er führt die Selbstreflektion als Moment der Trennung und der Distanz ein, und er tut dies bezeichnenderweise genau in jenem Moment, in dem der Held der Handlung, Prof. Rath, sich anschickt, seine kritische Vernunft aufzugeben und mit dem libidinösen Gehalt des Theaterraums, der für ihn an der figure der Lola festgemacht wird, zu verschmelzen" (He introduces self-reflection as a moment of separation and distance, and does this significantly just at the moment in which the hero to the plot, Professor Rath, decides to forsake critical reasoning, and meld with the libidinal contents of the theater space that Lola embodies). (Bronfen, "Vertreibung aus dem vertrauten Heim: *Der blaue Engel* (Josef von Sternberg)." *Heimweh: Illusionsspiel in Hollywood*. Berlin: Verlag Volk & Welt, 1999, 126).

Judith Mayne argues in "Marlene Dietrich, *The Blue Angel*, and Female Performance": "Lola wants as much to be bourgeois as Rath wants her to fall in love with him. Both of these 'desires' are repressed. Consider the scene when Rath sits in the loge—the symmetry of gazes—he looks, she emanates desirability—more centered. But the symmetry is disturbed a bit by other women performers on stage and the shot of the clown who, in Kracauer's words, is 'the silent witness'". The clown along with the female statue "strain" the scene and "traces of the carnivalesque atmosphere remain ... but they have been repressed and marginalized." (36) What is more, his gaze "disturbs" and displays the illusion of the relationship between Lola and Rath. It alludes to the folly of their union.

42. Elena Boland, "UFA Film Wins Plaudits," *Los Angeles Times* (April 6, 1930), B9. "I think that the speech and the music are so stylized that after hearing them, one could go to another of my pictures, close his eyes and know from the sound that I had directed it."

43. Caryl Flinn, *Strains of Utopia: Gender, Nostalgia, and Hollywood Film Music* (Princeton, NJ: Princeton University Press, 1992), 25.

44. Sternberg, *Fun in a Chinese Laundry*, 219.

45. S.S. Prawer, *The Blue Angel* (London: British Film Institute, 2002), 40.
46. Ibid.
47. Flinn, 26. Flinn discusses how the Wagnerian use of leitmotiv, "helped music to produce meaning in two ways, first by anticipating them and second by retrospectively constructing them. The assumption here is that when the leitmotiv is first heard, the auditor experiences a vague emotional response that is only more fully understood later when the leitmotiv is repeated and readily associated with an object or theme."
48. "Dance, Western." (2006). In *Encyclopaedia Britannica*. Retrieved October 25, 2006, from Encyclopaedia Britannica Online: http://search.eb.com/eb/article-22125
49. Ibid., 20.
50. See Nicolas Vazsonyi, "Hegemony through Harmony: German Identity, Music, and the Enlightenment around 1800," edited by Nora Alter and Lutz Koepnick (New York: Berghahn Books, 2004). Vazsonyi shows how intricately linked are notions of German national identity to music, particularly that which is considered "serious" music. Analyzing Morrow's research on the understanding of instrumental music as early as 1760, Vazsonyi writes: "Morrow's study shows that around 1760 German critics began to extol instrumental music for its intellectual, 'serious' and truly 'German' properties. They now declared it to be a 'manly' idiom …"(34).
51. Even though the film did well at the box office, von Sternberg claims, "not a single person noticed my attempt to put sound into its proper relation to the image. … The one exception was a fellow director, the scholarly and sensitive Ludwig Berger, who sent a telegram, which read: 'Saw your *Thunderbolt* and congratulate you with all my heart. It is the first rounded out and artistically elaborated sound film. Bravo'" (*Fun in a Chinese Laundry*, 219–20). Berger, a German director, directed *Day and Night* (1932), which Sabine Hake praises for its sound innovation in "Provocations of the Disembodied Voice: Song and the Transition to Sound in Berger's *Day and Night*," *Peripheral Visions: The Hidden Stages of Weimar Cinema*, edited by Kenneth S. Calhoon (Detroit: Wayne State University Press, 2001), 55–72.
52. A similar motif of exclusive love and loyalty appears in the folksong, "Ach wie ist's möglich denn." The speaker is rendered helpless here, which foreshadows Rath's own position. Melody by Friedrich Silcher, 1827; Wilhelmine von Chezy, 1812:

| Ach wie ist's möglich denn, | Oh, how is it possible |
| Daß ich dich lassen kann. | That I can leave you. |
| Hab' dich von Herzen lieb. | I love you with all of my heart. |
| Das glaube mir. | Believe me. |
| Du hast die Seele mein, | You have taken |
| So ganz genommen ein. | My whole soul |
| Da ich kein' And're lieb', | So that I cannot love another |
| Als dich allein. | Only you. |

53. Kathryn Kalinak, "The Language of Music: A Brief Analysis of *Vertigo*," *Movie Music: The Film Reader*, edited by Kay Dickinson (London: Routledge, 2003), 20.
54. Despite his popularity, Schubert notably refused to write for the commercial market. The smaller compositions, which were performed in private homes and excluded from public concert venues, in addition to being romantic, are viewed as an expression of Germany's Biedermeier period, which was typified by a withdrawal into the private realm.
55. Wilhelm Müller and Franz Schubert, "Die schöne Müllerin," *Die Winterreise: Textausgabe* (Stuttgart: Philipp Reclam, 2001).
56. The first stanza reads: "Üb' immer Treu und Redlichkeit / Bis an dein kühles Grab, / Und weiche keinen Finger breit / Von Gottes Wegen ab."
57. Luise Discherl and Gunther Nickel, "Loise flöhen meine Lieda," *Der blaue Engel. Die Drehbuchentwürfe*, edited by Luise Dirscherl and Gunther Nickel (St. Igbert: Röhrig Universitätsverlag, 2000), 38. ("Hat man im 19. Jahrhundert, als Höltys Gedicht gern in Stammbüchern und Poesiealben geschrieben wurde, die Ironie nicht bemerkt, die es durch die Unterlegung mit Mozart's Musik erfuhr?")

58. S.S. Prawer, 44.
59. Werner Sudendorf, "Chronik zur Entstehung des Films," *Der blaue Engel: Die Drehbuchentwürfe*, edited by Luise Dirscherl and Gunther Nickel (St. Ingbert: Röhrig Universitätsverlag, 2000), 51–70. "Auf Wunsch des Ufa-Vorstandes sollen nachträglich Änderungen ausgeführt werden; so sollen 'verschiedene Geräusche, die man natürlicherweise hören müßte, auch hörbar sein'; auch soll der Tod des Professor Unrat deutlicher werden (Ufa-Vorstandsprotokolle, February 19 and April 2, 1930). April 7: Nach der Vorführung der englischen Fassung sollen Schnitte angebracht und Szenen nachsynchronisiert werden. –Die Ufa bezeichnet in einer Presseerklärung den Film als erfolgreichsten bislang in deutschen Kinotheatern gezeigten Tonfilm. April 12: Die Schlußszene des *Blauen Engels* wird nachträglich mit Musik versehen." (At first completely silent, the music in this scene was added at the behest of the Ufa board of directors. The chronology of changes after the film's premiere are as follows: April 2: the Ufa board of directors requested the following changes be made: the "various sounds that one naturally must hear should be heard; the death of the professor also should be made clearer.' April 7: after the screening of the English-language version the film should be edited and scenes synchronized after the fact. The Ufa claimed in a press release that the film is the most successful sound film to date shown in German movie theaters. April 12: music will be added to the last scene of *The Blue Angel*.)
60. Rebecca Comay, "Adorno's Siren Song," *New German Critique* 81 (Fall 2000), 27.
61. Elizabeth Bronfen, "Vertreibung aus dem Vertrauten Heim: Der blaue Engel (Josef von Sternberg)," *Heimweh: Illusionsspiel in Hollywood* (Berlin: Verlag Volk & Welt, 1999), 97–142.
62. Kaja Silverman, *The Acoustic Mirror* (Bloomington: Indiana University Press, 1988), 41.
63. All of the songs in both German and English versions of *The Blue Angel* are published in the April 4, 2000, *Newsletter of the Marlene Dietrich Collection* by the Filmmuseum Berlin-Deutsche Kinemathek, see www.marlenedietrich.org
64. Marcel Oms, "Josef von Sternberg," in Baxter, *Sternberg*, 67.
65. Quoted in Claudia Gorbman, *Unheard Melodies: Narrative Film Music* (London: British Film Institute, 1987), 80.
66. Joanna Pitman, *On Blondes* (London: Bloomsbury, 2003), 9.
67. Von Sling, "Warum werden Blondinen bevorzugt?" in *Uhu: Das Monats-Magazin*, (January 1928).
68. Comay, 23. Comay argues that the Sirens, sexually ambiguous creatures, actually threatened "the sexual identity of those who listened" (23). Does the same happen to Rath (after all, Lola is sexually androgynous, decked out in a top hat at the end)? Comay continues: "Odysseus strapped to the mast in solitary delectation would be the bourgeois as modern concertgoer, ... ."
69. See Dietrich's song "Illusionen," in which she sings about the sale of illusions. See Richard Mentele, *Auf Liebe eingestellt: Marlene Dietrich's schöne Kunst* (Bensheim: Bollmann, 1993), 120.
70. Volker Kühn, *Spötterdämmerung: Vom langen Sterben des grossen kleinen Friedrich Hollaender* (Berlin: Parthas, 1996): "Das neue Chanson ist eine Sache der Suggestion, ist die Bezwingung der Masse" (36). Hollaender claimed in "Cabaret," *The Weimar Republic Sourcebook*, edited by Anton Kaes, Martin Jay, and Edward Dimenberg (Berkeley: University of California Press, 1994): "Cabaret that fails to take pleasure in the attack, that lacks the taste for battle, is not fit to live. It is the traditional battlefield on which the only proper weapons—sharp words and loaded music—are capable of beating into retreat those cast of iron. ... Music as seductress—it always succeeds whenever it has magic in its gut: as a hymn in church, as a military march before the campaign, as an indictment from the podium" (57).
71. Electrola was reluctant at first to produce the film hits. Viktor Rotthaler writes: "So kommt es, dass von der ersten 'Kopf bis Fuss' Fassung nur 200 Exemplare ins Electrola-Musikhaus am Ku'damm gelangen. Innerhalb von nur zwei Tagen ist die Platte noch vor

dem Start des Films ausverkauft. Die Originalmatrizen sind zerstört worden, und so muss das Lied noch einmal aufgenommen werden" (As a result, only 200 copies of the first "Falling in Love again" version made it to the Electrola-Musikhaus on the Kudamm. The record was sold out two days before the film premiered. The original recording was destroyed and the song had to be recorded again.) Rotthaler, 124.
72. Patrick O'Connor, *The Amazing Blonde Woman: Dietrich's Own Style* (London: Bloomsbury, 1991), 21.
73. Lotte Eisner, *The Haunted Screen* (Berkeley: University of California Press, 1972), 314.
74. Peter Jelavich, *Berlin Cabaret* (Cambridge, MA: Harvard University Press, 1993), 5.
75. Prawer, 49.
76. H.H. Stuckenschmidt, "So wird heute gesungen: Choräle aus dem Schlamm, eine Feststellung," *Uhu: Das Monats-Magazin* (June 1930), 44 (my translation). ("Bürgerliche Solidität der Wunschtraum aller dieser Chansonetten, der latente Refrain ihrer Lieder. Höchst moralische Begriffe wie Liebe, Sehnsucht, Heimat und Heirat bildeten das Grundmaterial, aus dem auch die laszivisten Texte konstruiert waren.")
77. Ibid., 47 (my translation). ("Vor ihm <der Unterton> versagen alle ästhetischen und moralischen Massstäbe. Der Begriff des 'Schönen' ist endgültig abgeschafft, verdrängt durch die fraglos kultische Betonung und Verherrlichung des Sexus. Ob wir diesen Gesang bejahen oder verneinen ist Privatsache. Aber ausweichen können und dürfen wir ihm nicht. Denn er entspricht durchaus der Zeit, in der wir leben.")
78. Theodor Adorno, "On Popular Music," *Cultural Theory and Popular Culture: A Reader*, edited by John Storey (Athens: University of Georgia Press, 1998), 197.
79. Adolf Heinzlmeier, *Marlene: Die Biographie* (Hamburg: Europa Verlag, 2000), 117. She began her second career in 1953 with a benefit concert for Cerebral Palsy in Madison Square Garden in New York and then landed in Las Vegas to the tune of $30,000 a week.
80. Ibid.
81. *The Blue Angel* was the last feature film that Parufamet exported to the United States. See Mühl-Benninghaus, 180.
82. The advertisement appears in Christian Ferber, ed., Uhu: Das Monats-Magazin (Berlin: Ullstein Verlag, 1979), 33.
83. Dietrich's address book is published by Transit in Berlin, and compiled and edited by Christine Fischer-Defoy.

*Chapter 5*

# THE ACTUALITY OF *THE BLUE ANGEL*: DIETRICH, GERMANY, AND MASS CULTURE

> Heimat—One of the most beautiful words in the German language
> **Marlene Dietrich,** *Marlene Dietrich's ABC*
>
> Mother, have you forgiven me
> Mother, are you still thinking about it,
> Mother, have you forgiven what I have done to you,
> Homeland, have you forgiven me,
> Homeland, are you still thinking about it
> Homeland, have you forgiven what I have done to you
> Fortune took me away from here
> Away from my homeland and my house
> I left with all the others, and did not return home
> Mother, can you still love me,
> Mother, give me your hand
> I am still your child, a stranger in a strange Land
> Mother, I want to return to my homeland
> Mother, the world is so large
> Mother, I want to return to my homeland, take me into your lap.[1]
> **Text: F. Walicki, J. Grau, Marlene Dietrich; Music: C. Niemen**

On May 16, 1992, Marlene Dietrich's last wish—to be buried next to her mother in Friedenau, Berlin, the city of her birth in 1901—was fulfilled.[2] Her mother's daughter, and Germany's daughter, had finally come home. In many ways, Dietrich symbolized the prodigal daughter, replacing the long-standing return of biblical sons to the familial nest after venturing out, a theme that was replayed in a number of street film melodramas during the Weimar Republic. It was "the return of the Blue Angel" ("die Heimkehr des blauen Engels"),[3] as Hellmuth Karasek noted in the German weekly magazine *Der Spiegel*. But it actually was more than just a return; it was a comeback in the Hollywood sense of rising to stardom for a second time, even posthumously. Yet, as with any comeback, it drew varied responses. While her fans lined the streets and threw flowers at her funeral and tended her grave, those who viewed her as a fallen angel openly scorned the "Berlinerin," who avoided traveling to Germany under Hitler, abandoned her homeland, and refused Joseph Goebbels's invitation to become Ufa's leading female star.[4] What added to her critics' resentment of her was that she traded in her German citizenship in 1939 for American citizenship. This step, according to her daughter, Maria Riva, made the "Americanization of Lola complete."

Moreover, Dietrich returned at the end of the war wearing the victor's uniform.[5] The *Tageszeitung* criticized the negative commentary of Dietrich's posthumous return. "Evelyn Künneke was allowed to tell the BZ (Berliner Zeitung) that she does not like it when someone betrays their homeland."[6] Evoking the title of Margarete and Alexander Mitscherlich's 1967 book *The Inability to Mourn*, the *Spiegel* magazine presented the mixed reception as yet another example of Germany's difficult relationship to its past; the attitude expressed in Künneke's widely quoted statement was further evidence that "the German sense of justice did not set in the shameful inability to partake in the funeral rite."[7] Given Dietrich's ambivalent reception, few guests of any notoriety attended the funeral, and the Berlin senate ended up canceling the honorary gala planned in the Deutsches Theater. Ulrich Roloff-Momin, Senator for Culture in Berlin, in summary called hers "a German fate, that still stirs the emotions."[8] In many ways, Dietrich's posthumous reception was only a continuation of her postwar relationship to Germany.

Indeed, Dietrich had long been in the crossfire of working through Germany's past and its politics. This chapter thus explores Dietrich's reception in Germany as the "Blue Angel" after her death. I will argue that her image has been used in various ways to establish a new national identity, particularly since German unification—an identity that throughout the twentieth century has been identified with crisis. As Roloff-Momin observed, "Her burial in Berlin would be understood world wide as a sign that the despotic fascist regime and the unnatural division of the city of her birth have been overcome."[9] An advertisement that appeared as a centerfold in the *Spiegel Reporter* indirectly supports his claim. It juxtaposes Dietrich, in black and white, with the caption "what remains," and Chancellor Angela Merkel, in color, "the iron girl" and "figure of integration" with the caption "what is to come," and bears out directly Dietrich's role in the project of national healing (see Figure 5.1). At the same time, it alludes to the role that mass culture has come to play in shaping cultural and national identities.[10]

It is telling, that on the occasion of Dietrich's one-hundredth anniversary, the government attempted to remedy its initial lukewarm welcome and addressed the complicated relationship between Dietrich and Germany since World War II. In 2002, ten years after her death, the movie legend finally was made an honorary citizen of Berlin. "This honor

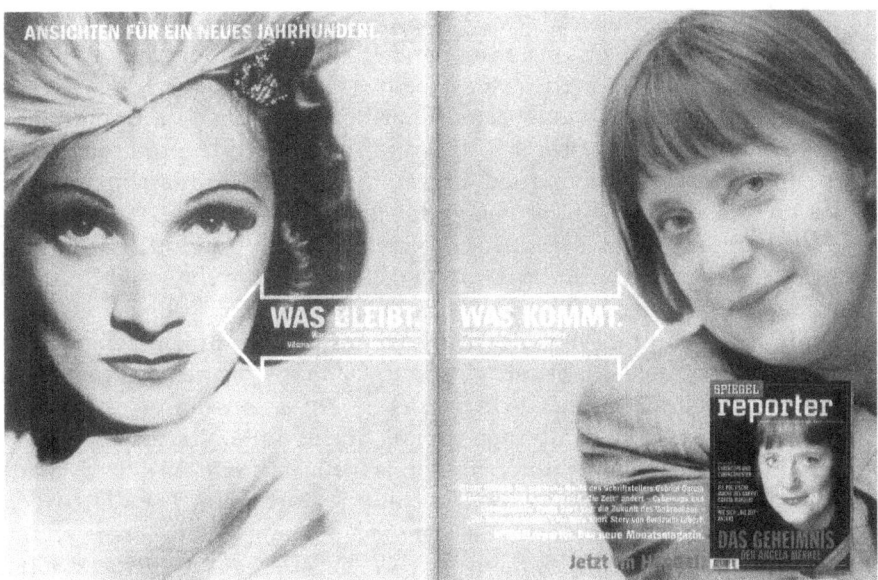

**Figure 5.1** Advertisement for *Spiegel Reporter*, March 2000. Source: *Spiegel Reporter.*

comes late," Mayor Klaus Wowereit admitted upon presenting the certificate of citizenship to Dietrich's grandson David Riva, "some may even say perhaps too late."[11] Wreaths from former Social Democratic President Johannes Rau and from the city of Berlin were laid ceremoniously at Dietrich's grave. The mayor's chief of staff, Andre Schmitz, evocatively asked forgiveness for the hostile reception Dietrich received in Germany in 1960, when picketers called her a traitor and demanded that she "go home" to the United States. In honor of Dietrich, Schmitz noted that she "was far ahead of many of her contemporaries." Johannes Rau stressed her commitment to "democracy and freedom" during the Nazi regime, while former Chancellor Gerhard Schroeder celebrated her memory as "Germany's first international star."[12]

Compared to her reception in the 1960s, a time still deeply mired in the painful memories of World War II, her posthumous commemoration marked a shift in attitude. Significantly, this shift belongs to the larger context of Germany reinventing itself and seizing the opportunity to project itself onto the image of its most prominent, internationally recognized cultural icon. Stated differently, the new republic eagerly drew and continues to draw on Dietrich's symbolic value as Germany's "first international star" to give a reunified Germany its facelift. Berlin's officials exploited Dietrich's image and her German films to lend glamour to the city, and a cosmopolitan, international flair. In effect, her image, as a surface that meaning can be projected upon, makes its utilization easy because of its simultaneous emptiness and dense scripting. The image can be evoked to remember and revive Berlin's golden 1920s, as well as to pay tribute to an anti-fascist tradition and create a national heroine. The inscription on Dietrich's gravestone reads, "Hier stehe ich an den Marken meiner Tage" ("Here I stand at the mark of my days")—a quote taken from Theodor Körner, a prominent German author who fought during the Franco-Prussian war and earned himself the title of "German boy hero."[13] It is a final declaration of her loyalty to Germany.

Thus, among other symbols chosen to give the nation its identity, Dietrich's image has been appropriated too to define the newly unified Germany and, more specifically, its capital, Berlin.[14] The "Blue Angel" has not only returned home, she has also been resurrected to lend cohesion to the newly "imagined community" and to facilitate the reestablishment of Berlin as Germany's capital, which was chosen after unification, instead of Bonn, the former West German capital. The evocation of *The Blue Angel* in this context is no coincidence, since it is the last film that Dietrich made in Berlin and the film that turned her into a global star. Thus Dietrich's image provides an interesting link between contemporary Germany and the Weimar Republic, when Berlin was considered the quintessential modern European city, the place of the most radical experimentation in the visual and performing arts, in mass entertainment and theater, in literature and architecture, in politics and notions of gender behavior and sexual liberation. The Weimar Republic, more specifically Berlin, was viewed as the laboratory of modernity and associated with a time that tested the fixtures of stale, authoritarian cultural norms and turned bourgeois assumptions on their heads. Political and social upheaval, the dramatic growth of an urban population, technological advancements, and cultural innovation turned it into a dynamic metropolis and one of the most interesting cities in Europe during the 1920s.

Dietrich's image is all the more attractive for contemporary Berlin, a *Kulturstadt* (city of culture), because of her association with theater, cabaret, and film. Moreover, Dietrich embodied the modern woman of the Weimar Republic in habit and appearance, in her aloof sex appeal and androgyny. Her image, therefore, evokes nostalgia for the excitement, glamour, and adventure of the roaring twenties, a sense of nostalgia that as Svetlana Boym writes "is retrospective as much as it is prospective." In this context, Boym's understanding of nostalgia is helpful. She states: "fantasies of the past determined by needs of the present have a direct impact on realities of the future." More fitting in the context of Dietrich is Boym's understanding of nostalgia as "a romance with one's fantasy."[15] Dietrich is an object of cultural politics; she is an expression of nostalgia for the glamour and edginess of the 1920s that a once divided Germany can turn to for its common legacy after forty-five years of separation. Her allegiance to her "Germanness," specifically to Berlin, make the exploitation of her image for national interests and for Germany's own culture industry all the more seamless.

Even though Dietrich was buried in Berlin, she was hardly laid to rest. A debate about naming a street to honor Germany's enigmatic star began with her return. To this day, the owner of the Blue Angel restaurant in Schöneberg collects signatures to have either a street or park in her old neighborhood in the vicinity of Leberstrasse 53 bear her name.[16] Finally, in 2002, the Marlene-Dietrich-Platz was designated, as part of the larger Potsdamer Platz, the new center of Berlin, thereby (inadvertently) locating the diva at the heart of the capital of the new Germany, the city that Zafer Şenocak describes as having been awoken by a kiss in 1989.[17] A plaque on the square reads: "Berlin's international star of film and chansons. Commitment to freedom and democracy for Berlin and Germany." In a further gesture to reclaim its star, Berlin acquired many of Dietrich's personal effects. Her daughter, Maria Riva, sold a collection of memorabilia to the Filmmuseum in the Potsdamer Platz, which has an ongoing Dietrich exhibit. No longer just a suitcase in Berlin, the theme of a popular song Dietrich included in her repertoire, the collection contained 600 suitcases and boxes that the cultural senator Roloff-Momin purchased for $5 million in 1993, with an enormous inventory of more than 16,000 photographs of Dietrich. In a publication for the Berlin Filmmuseum regarding the purchase of the collection, Werner Sudendorf writes: "We have few personalities who we can be proud of because of their political stance. The connection of cultural and political history will become tangible through Marlene Dietrich and the Marlene Dietrich Collection in an unambiguous and extraordinary way."[18]

**Figure 5.2** Advertisement for a Marlene Dietrich Exhibition in the department store KaDeWE, 2005. Source: Author's collection.

Of significance also is her commemoration in 2005 at Berlin's upscale department store Kaufhaus des Westens (KaDeWe), where Dietrich's clothes along with other memorabilia were displayed during the Berlin Film Festival that same year (see Figure 5.2).

Dietrich was known for her impeccable attire, and her allure, which owed as much to her exquisite sartorial choices (the clothes she designed with Travis Banton for films were famous) as her physical beauty. Each exterior showcase displayed a phase of her life, represented by either a film or a historical event and thus fusing her real-life and screen personae, the true sign of a star. Like many stories of Dietrich, the series of showcases—like miniature shrines—also begins with *The Blue Angel*, represented by the premiere poster and a photograph of von Sternberg setting up a scene with Emil Jannings and Dietrich, who is standing coyly behind a cloth partition with both men's gazes fixated on her (see Figure 5.3). Another showcase displays military boots and a helmet, as props, and a picture of Dietrich as a USO entertainer, a member of a civilian group that sent actors and celebrities during World War II to the front to boost the morale of American troops. Given her ambivalent reception in the 1960s, this showcase could be read as a gesture toward reconciliation and proof of a changed Germany.[19] At the same time, the KaDeWe displays point to her creation as an economic enterprise as well as to the complex relationship among cinema, mass culture, and modern consumerism. Besides staging or presenting "snapshots" of Dietrich's biography, these display cases, on a more

**Figure 5.3** Still taken on the set of *The Blue Angel*; Marlene Dietrich with Emil Jannings and Josef von Sternberg. Source: *Deutsche Kinemathek*.

theoretical level, serve as sites of spectatorial pleasure and consumer fetishism, much like the movie screen. While the star's image and body are "vehicles" that encourage consumption, they also are spectacles. They serve as sites of desire, self-reflection, and identification. More significant, these display cases define Dietrich's image as an intricate part of the Berlin cityscape and presume identification with the larger public consciousness. The display windows reflect back to the viewer Germany's history and draw the spectator into the narrative tableaux. Indeed, Dietrich's biography is profoundly enmeshed in a century of German history either through her film persona or her own life experiences, beginning with her childhood in Berlin and schooling in Weimar, and her adventurous exploits in 1920s Berlin subculture, and then later leading to her Hollywood career, her stand against fascism, her political engagement during World War II, and then afterward in her efforts to aid her hometown.

Since German unification, tributes to Dietrich, Berlin's poster child, have been ongoing. Volker Kühn's adaptation of Pam Gems's play *Marlene*, which included many of Dietrich's musical standards played to a full house, ran for years at the Renaissance Theater in Berlin after its premiere in 1998.[20] The play features the star *acutely aware* of the impact of images on audiences and of the fans' desire to emulate their stars and engage in fictional romances with them. In this play, the setting is Paris in the 1970s, and Marlene (played by Judy Winter) is backstage preparing for her performance (in the German adaptation the *dramatis loci* is Dietrich's famous 1960 concert in Berlin).[21] Allusions to Dietrich's biography are accompanied by the songs she performed throughout her career, like the one in the epigraph. In her portrait of the diva, Gems highlights Dietrich's obsessive attention to detail, her neurotic cleanliness (she disinfected the bathrooms in all of her dressing rooms and scrubbed the floors), her sexual generosity, her rivalry with Garbo, her moodiness, her erratic and demanding nature, her addictions, and her perseverance as the Prussian "Junker's daughter," and her *Selbstinszenierung* (self-staging).

Most important, Dietrich's cynicism and profound understanding of performance are showcased. In fact, she openly speaks of herself as a vehicle of deception and illusion: "Glamour! It's in your heads, sweethearts, not ours. We are making it for you!"[22] She exists as an image that will last forever because of the love affair of the camera with its subject. Understanding the power of the illusion, Gems's Dietrich carefully choreographs the details of her appearance from the time she steps onto the stage until she leaves it. After her performance, she commands her assistant Vivian to hand her the flowers she purchased for herself, and meticulously plans her exit. She will sign a few autographs, be driven to her hotel while perched on top of the car; once she arrives at the hotel, she will receive photographers and press, and then be whisked off to her suite. Mention is made of the fans that bring her mementos like offerings to a goddess. She seeks their adoration, but much more, she needs their money.

The play ends with a complex, soul-searching soliloquy, in which Dietrich takes stock of her relationship to Germany and German history in answer to the question, "And what are you, Marie Magdalene—Marlene?"[23] She contemplates questions of responsibility and guilt for the atrocities Germany committed during World War II. The staccato delivery reveals an attempt to speak the unspeakable, her inner torment, and sheer incomprehension: "Genocide. My own country. My people. The people of my flesh—of my mind—my uncles, my cousins—my forebears. All implicated. We did not know! Don't believe it. We knew."[24] She reflects on her return in the 1960s, when people spat on her in her own home town and nonetheless affirms that she is German and belongs there. The provocative portrayal of Dietrich as star, as illusion, and as historical figure serves as a mirror again for confronting the German past. The performance ends with her singing her signature song, "Falling in Love Again," which in the context of the Berlin performance appears to be both a tribute to *The Blue Angel*, which secured her stardom, and an intimate declaration of love for her country of origin.

In many ways, Dietrich made her symbolic repatriation quite easy since she steadfastly regarded herself as a "Berlinerin," as the title of her autobiography resolutely pronounces: *Ich bin, Gott sei Dank, Berlinerin* (Thank God, I am a Berliner). Time after time in biographies of Dietrich, her modus operandi is deciphered as German. Her self-discipline, her compulsive perfectionism, and her endurance are all attributed to her Prussian upbringing, as are her love of cooking sauerbraten and sauerkraut, along with her devotion to German literature, particularly Rilke and Goethe, and to German songs both classical and popular.[25] In fact, her repertoire throughout her career consisted of many songs in German, in part to counter the association of Germany with Nazism, as well as to serve as a symbolic sign of loyalty to her homeland, particularly Berlin. In an effort to disassociate German culture from Nazism and draw attention to her place of birth, Dietrich would sing in German even when it was not popular. For instance, in a radio broadcast in New York in the late 1940s, Dietrich sang "Falling in Love Again" in German. When she toured Israel in 1960 and 1966, she was told not to sing in German, but sang nine songs in her native language anyway. Hillel Tryster writes, "Her attitude and her commitment during the Second World War gave her an aura of moral accountability in Israel, which was appreciated as much as her allure as an artist."[26]

Even Dietrich's captivating androgyny and promiscuous sexuality were attributed to her coming of age during the Weimar Republic. Moreover, Dietrich was a strong advocate for Berlin in various phases of its political history. For instance, she used her influence to promote Berlin during the Berlin Blockade and secured funds for the restoration of the Hansa Viertel by having money channeled through the Marshall Fund.[27] Perhaps most telling is an excerpt from Dietrich's letters that appeared in the documentary *Marlene Dietrich: Her Own Song*, a cinematic biography that her grandson, David Riva, made. In the voice-over that accompanies an image of Dietrich knitting on the beach in southern France after becoming an American citizen, she muses: "Changing your nationality is not an easy step ... In my heart, I am still German. German in my soul, wherever that soul may be."[28] In the film, attention is paid to finding a German-accented voice to represent Dietrich in order to emphasize both authenticity and the characterization of the marked "otherness" throughout her life. This "otherness" was particularly exploited in her Hollywood films, as film scholar Marcia Landy observes: "The question of national identity plays a central, though subtle role among the many ways in which the Dietrich star persona was constructed. Dietrich's Germanness has always been part of her star signature."[29] She plays a German in *The Blonde Venus, Dishonored, The Scarlet Empress, A Foreign Affair, Witness for the Prosecution,* and *Judgment at Nuremburg*; in many other films she is cast as "foreign." Both her local and international identities accordingly appeal in different ways to different markets.

For Germany, Dietrich's image primarily recalls Berlin's golden 1920s and serves to bridge past and present. It also establishes an interesting link to the United States and the prospect of an imaginary mutual identity or filial relationship between the two countries, albeit an ambivalent and conflicted one. Since the 1920s, the topic of Americanization has preoccupied Germany, with reactions to Americanism, long associated with modernity and technological innovation, ranging from blaming it for corrupting authentic German culture and for its enactment of cultural imperialism to celebrating America as a democratic model. If we recall the project of the New German cinema to establish a repertoire of images different from Hollywood's in order to allow Germans to reflect on their own cultural and political context as well as to counter what was seen as American cultural hegemony, we encounter the ambivalence in Germany that fluctuated between a fascination for and a loathing of Hollywood productions. In 1993, the swell of support for quotas as outlined in the GATT (General Agreement on Tariffs and Trade) to protect the German film industry against the dominance of Hollywood imports reveals the ongoing anxiety over the Americanization of European culture.

In a speech on the first anniversary of German unification, filmmaker Wim Wenders lamented the cultural vacuum in Germany that American films all too eagerly fill.[30] Judging from his remarks, Germany seems locked in an Oedipal struggle with America, a topic that looms large in the German imagination. Michael Ermarth claims that the United States "continues to call forth visceral responses across the spectrum of German opinion." Describing the time after the fall of the Berlin Wall, he provocatively asserts, "The Germans are discovering themselves all over again and finding that they are Americans."[31]

Given this context, what role does Dietrich, both German and

American, play in the very tense choreography of preserving national uniqueness, while being drawn to the "other"? Admittedly, fastening a shared identity on an icon of mass culture is fraught with difficulties. Diverging attitudes toward popular culture in Germany, and toward the United States, are intermingled with contempt for mass culture (an attitude Dietrich ironically shared), and a fascination with it. In reclaiming Dietrich, it is conceivable that Germany receives recognition as an equal partner in American cultural history, and in its most powerful resource, cinema. Through Dietrich, Germany even gains international recognition as a contributor to the culture industry. Thus, as an icon of entertainment and as a citizen of the United States, Dietrich straddles two continents and Germany, through her, participates in Hollywood's fame.[32]

In Germany as elsewhere, popular culture has taken on a major role in shaping national identity in ways that literature did before the twentieth century. Thus, the tension between German national identity and mass culture staged in *The Blue Angel*, and discussed in Chapter 1, appears less antagonistic in present-day Germany. It can be said that *The Blue Angel* anticipated the significance of mass culture in defining various national subjectivities. Dietrich, in short, embodies the merger of mass culture and national identity today as much as she did then in her performance as the cabaret singer Lola Lola. By national identity, I mean the multiple discourses that surface to define a nation, however porous the boundaries of the nation have become.

Employing Dietrich's image to promote the new Germany's political and cultural agendas is not new. Dietrich's persona as well as her filmic image have always been enmeshed in and appropriated for a variety of complex political and cultural negotiations.[33] In fact, the re-release of *The Blue Angel* in 1953 was used to prove that fascism in Germany had been defeated and that the power of democratic thinking had prevailed. After being banned for seventeen years, the film played in all major German cities and, according to its press release, participated in "a victory march <Siegeszug> over the screens of German movie theaters."[34] Advertised as a monument of Germany's cinematic heyday, when "the collaboration of great intellects made German cinema world renowned,"[35] the announcement of the screening lends the film a meta-narrative function that is linked closely to Dietrich's persona and her historical positioning. If, as Gertrud Koch has noted, "the coincidence of her departure for Hollywood with the rise of National Socialism turned her portrayal of Lola ... into an image iconic of both memory and leaving," then the re-release was a way to revitalize her return.[36]

Recent studies on Dietrich have focused on her star value during the 1930s, and particularly on her German reception during this period, and on how her image was used to promote Nazi ideology and to create a unified *Weltanschauung*. Erica Carter's intriguing study shows that pre-World War II German critics spoke of Dietrich as the embodiment of an essentialized

German identity, whose "boundless beauty" allowed her to transcend spatial boundaries. Carter writes that images of Dietrich that resonated best with Nazi concepts of stardom and cinema may be seen in the enthusiastic reviews in Germany of Frank Borzage's *Desire* (1936), one of Dietrich's favorite films, in which she plays a jewel thief in Spain. Pre-World War II reviews, Carter notes, show how "Dietrich's image was 'managed' through the rescripting of her personal life as a story of return to home and father/mother Germany: that returned Dietrich also to a symbolic place as an icon not of Hollywood, but of German nation."[37] The *Mitteldeutsche Nationalzeitung*, for instance, fantasized about her return to represent the German "soul" and turned her into an ideal in very much the same way that she is transformed into a sublime statue in Rouben Mamoulian's 1933 Hollywood film *Song of Songs*: "We are convinced that an actress like Marlene Dietrich, with her wealth of foreign experience, would be an extraordinary gain for the German film industry. What a precious task for a German director to transform Dietrich the vamp into Mrs. Dietrich. By no means a Gretchen with braids and pudgy red cheeks, but a woman, whose inner strength can give expression to her German spirit."[38]

Yet, as we know, Dietrich did not return home, despite her many trips to Europe while the Nazis were in power. To fill the gap left by Dietrich's absence during the Third Reich, Ufa created a Dietrich-copy. Swedish-born Zarah Leander, a Dietrich stand-in with a husky singing voice and masculine edge to her mannerisms, became Ufa's leading female star. Dietrich refused to cross the border into Germany until after the war, and then entered Germany as an entertainer for the USO. She returned again briefly in the 1960s, to a highly charged and mixed reception.

While reviews of Dietrich's films and Dietrich's image were used in support of Nazi ideals before her demonstrative rejection of the regime, postwar Hollywood filmmakers capitalized differently on her "Germanness." In *A Not So Foreign Affair*, Andrea Slane maps a trajectory that begins with Lola in *The Blue Angel* and that ends with her playing a Nazi, a role she reluctantly accepted, in Billy Wilder's *A Foreign Affair* (1948) and *Witness for the Prosecution* (1957), and Stanley Kramer's *Judgment at Nuremberg* (1961).[39] Slane's paraphrasing of Austrian émigré Billy Wilder's choice to cast her in *A Foreign Affair* astutely sums up Dietrich's representation in postwar Hollywood films. He "had reportedly chosen Dietrich specifically as a pre-Hitler icon in order to inflect postwar Berlin with both the triumph over Nazism and the sadness over the destruction of the city and its pre-Nazi life."[40]

*A Foreign Affair* ties into *The Blue Angel* in its representation of a cabaret singer in postwar Berlin, with Friedrich Hollaender as her musical accompanist in such songs as "The Ruins of Berlin" and "Black Market." Moreover, the "Blue Angel" poster outside the "Lorelei" nightclub, which occupation forces illicitly visit, acknowledges the failed potential of the edgy culture of the Weimar Republic and leaves open the direction of the next performance. The film also posits a complexly loaded image of Germanness in its representation of Erika von Schlutow. She is a composite of folklore and history: she is the siren of the Rhine that Heinrich Heine adulates in his poem *Die Lorelei*, whose beauty and song cause men to shipwreck, and a Valkyrie of Wagner's *The Ring of the Nibelungen*, and a postwar German performer who fraternizes with Nazis and Americans (a figure that is reminiscent of the infamous German actress/director Leni Riefenstahl). Both Slane's and Carter's research exemplifies the ways in which the image of Dietrich surpasses her function within the fictions that cast her. Indeed, as a star, she exists as a composite of her films, of her public persona, of her reception; as an icon of popular culture, she remains a powerful signifier in a larger arena of discourses. Even in her Hollywood films, Dietrich participates in German history.

Keeping in mind Dietrich's hybrid German/American identity and her role as a representative of mass culture, it is interesting to turn to a group of recent films that, as Lutz Koepnick observes, use and reclaim a tradition of German popular culture as a productive site of contemporary national identity. In contrast to the highly contested place of mass culture in definitions of Germanness during the Weimar Republic, mass culture today, as I mentioned earlier, plays a major role in the formation and conceptualization of national identity. In other words, the *Bildungsbürger* now goes to the movies for cultural edification. Koepnick borrows the term "heritage films," which was coined to describe a body of British films, to understand the emergence of a cluster of German films after unification, that premiere popular culture and its past. Among those that Koepnick lists is Joseph Vilsmaier's 2000 film *Marlene*.[41]

Based on Marlene Dietrich's life, this mainstream biopic, starring Katja Flint in the role of Dietrich, participates in the pervasive repatriation of Dietrich in post-Wall Germany and in returning Dietrich to her rightful home, in ways that eerily resonate with the 1930s reviews that Carter discusses. Drawing as much criticism and/or admiration as its fictional star, the film disappointed expectations of a box office hit, despite its steep budget of 5 million Marks.[42]

In order to entice prospective audiences, the film trailer employs strategies familiar to tabloids in its promise of a behind-the-scene look at the film diva's life. It promises to penetrate the surface of the silver screen image to reveal Dietrich's true identity, if not "authentic identity," through a glimpse into her private life, a realm that the historical Dietrich vigilantly shielded from the curious, consuming public eye.[43] Similarly, Brigitte Häring's review of the film piques interest by asking: "Who actually was the person Marlene Dietrich, how did the greatest film diva live, when she was not a diva but rather a mother, a wife, a housewife or a mere person?"[44] This preoccupation with the intimate spheres of Dietrich's life has but one purpose in Vilsmaier's film and that is to secure Dietrich's "Germanness," to represent her loyalty, and reveal her profound emotional attachment to the place of her birth, all of which she must forfeit in pursuit of fame—a line the von Sternberg character prophetically recites in the film. Her homesickness (*Heimweh*) is sharply reflected in her vacuous life in the United States, where she pops pills and drinks in order to anesthetize herself against her loss. Thus, the story of her life in the United States is largely dismissed in *Marlene*. Instead, the film centers both visual and emotional energy on her encounters with Europe.

To reveal the so-called person behind the film idol, Vilsmaier, a self-proclaimed director of *Heimat* films, resorts to a mixture of melodrama, epic, and romance. He titillates his audience with Dietrich's libertinage; he capitalizes on her affairs, her indiscretions, and on her addictions. More important, he sidesteps her various roles as wife and mother, and instead fulfills Dietrich's alleged dream of a great love, which indeed drives the melodrama. In *Marlene*, the Dietrich character meets the fictional Carl Seidlitz (played by Heino Ferch) on the streets of Berlin during the production of *The Blue Angel*, and she continues to meet with him surreptitiously from 1929 until his death in 1945. One such meeting takes place in Salzburg, Austria, where Marlene is vacationing with her family and Tamara (the historical life companion of Dietrich's husband Rudolf Siebert; she posed as a nanny to avoid disrupting the public image of Dietrich and her family). Significantly, her meeting with Carl takes place after Marlene leaves the famous Lanz shop, dressed in a dirndl and accompanied by her husband and daughter both in folkloric attire, thus aligning Marlene with traditions of Heimat. But first, a local girl asks Marlene for her autograph; two pictures signifying the two poles of Dietrich's existence are pasted in her notebook, one of an angel encircled in flowers, and the other of the glamorous Marlene as Berlin's exotic modern woman and Hollywood transplant, with a cigarette propped in her mouth in a pose from her role in *Blonde Venus*. Carl calls to Marlene from behind a gate, where she runs to join him. Declaring their love for each other, the gate symbolically locks in their secret.

Marlene and Carl continue their rendezvous in the Alps, the Salzkammergut in Austria, where they hike up a path wearing day backpacks and knickerbockers, surrounded by idyllic pastoral scenes; the vastness and beauty of the landscape powerfully reflects the magnitude of their love and longing. At an alpine hut, a gramophone plays one of Dietrich's songs and they dance. It is in this scene that the couple comes to accept the terms of their separation, since each one is bound to their duty. Later on, during her tour as a USO entertainer for American soldiers at the front, Marlene risks her life to meet Carl secretly in an abandoned house in the Ardennes in France. Seidlitz, her eternal love interest, is portrayed as an officer and gentleman who, despite Marlene's urging, never leaves Germany. To emphasize his commitment and his loyalty to Germany, Carl is represented as one of the officers who attempted to assassinate Hitler in 1945. He is featured as a hero who has risked his life to stop the murderous regime. His rootedness stands in sharp contrast to her nomadic lifestyle. He represents Heimat.

Throughout the film, the center of Vilsmaier's—that is, Marlene's—emotional gravity remains German-identified. It centers on Carl, who is a standard-bearer for a German identity based on passion, conviction, and ethical choices that require personal sacrifice. In his presence, the Marlene character does not have to pretend; she can be authentic. In other words, it is in this relationship that the "real" Marlene emerges, the person that the film promises to deliver. In the language of the film, Carl stands in for a Germany that Dietrich can love, a Germany that she never wanted to leave and for which she longed.

An additional scene further establishes Dietrich's intense attachment to Germany and should be mentioned in this context. A wounded German soldier, a prisoner of war, who is dying in an American front-line hospital, recognizes Marlene. In contrast to the wounded Americans who are lying on cots, and whose quarters are filled with jazz music and high spirits, the adjacent German prisoners of war, a row of bloody, mutilated bodies (similar to representations in paintings by Otto Dix or Georg Grosz), are lying on hay and have been left to die. The image arouses a sense of horror and sadness. When Marlene enters the room, a wounded German soldier familiarly calls out "Marlene," and announces that he too is a Berliner. Holding his hand, Marlene sympathetically smiles and states, "maybe we'll get along again one day" ("vielleicht werden wir uns eines Tages wieder vertragen"). She asks why he participated in such a senseless war, to which he responds that he was never asked. In revisioning the image of the German soldier as victim rather than perpetrator, he is aligned with Dietrich. Like her, he was caught in the maelstrom of history. Moreover, their allegiance can not only be measured by the uniforms they wear. Marlene closes his eyes—she is the last person he sees. A wisp of music from Wagner's opera *Die Meistersänger*, in which the characters Eva and Walter fall in love after "exchanging tender glances," underscores their encounter and lends pathos to the already overdetermined melodrama, while displacing the secret love onto the "nationalized" body of the dying soldier. This scene serves to soften the image of Dietrich as a traitor who sang for "her boys," that is, American soldiers. It is no coincidence that Vilsmaier relies on melodrama to bring Dietrich home; it is the genre of intensified emotion, of sentimentality that serves to open up the audience to an acceptance of a deeper understanding of Dietrich—one that Hollywood could never deliver.[45] To that end, Vilsmaier embellishes Dietrich's life.[46]

While based in part on Maria Riva's biography of her mother, the director rescripts Dietrich's persona in an effort to bring her home. Thus, it is only at the end of the film, when the credits roll and after a brief explanation of what happened to the key historical figures in Dietrich's biography, that the audience learns of Vilsmaier's artistic intervention. In the fadeout, the audience learns that "the name Carl Seidlitz does not appear in her journal. Who her great love was remains a secret." Thus the melodrama that yearns for closure remains open, and Dietrich's mystery is sustained. Yet, her image has been transformed.

*Marlene* begins with documentary footage of Dietrich's 1975 performance of "Ich bin von Kopf bis Fuss" in Carnegie Hall—her signature song from *The Blue Angel*, which brings to mind her seduction of the unsuspecting spectator and her calling as pure object of desire. As Judith Mayne has written, "If *The Blue Angel* has a special place in the mythology of Marlene Dietrich, it is in part because the film articulates a narrative and visual structure which would be associated with Dietrich for virtually all of her career."[47] Even on "foreign territory," that is, in Carnegie Hall, her German "Blue Angel" identity fills the screen preceded by celebratory fireworks over the New York skyline. Vilsmaier's opening fanfare cuts from Dietrich singing onstage to the making of *The Blue Angel* and then to the streets of Berlin, where Marlene meets Carl, and thereby turns the film into a memory piece driven by desire. At the end, the film circles back to that same night in Carnegie Hall, but this time, Dietrich breaks off her *Blue Angel* tribute to sing Pete Seeger's war protest song, "Where have all the flowers gone" / "Sag mir wo die Blumen sind" in German. In the documentary footage of this performance, the historical Dietrich pays tribute to the memory of someone special, as well as to others, who have fallen in war.

The film's trajectory thus begins with *The Blue Angel* and ends with a song that acknowledges loss and the passage of time. This parting song, and with it the sense of loss articulated, projects the loss of homeland as her true love, which is revealed as the film's and her true secret. That is to say, *Marlene* recuperates Dietrich, the traitor, and makes her pleasingly consumable again, as a figure of identification and adoration. The "real and private" Dietrich is closely aligned with Germany, embodied in the fictional love Carl. Thus, the film allows its spectators to forgive Marlene her treason, but more importantly, it pardons her for abandoning her place of origin and for withholding her image for Germans to dream on. As the film emphasizes, she loved her Heimat, which figures as a "truer" Germany, untainted by Nazism. Furthermore, the film calls for claiming Dietrich as a popular icon and illustrates how mass culture becomes a significant player in scripting national identity—a role that *The Blue Angel* anticipates. Vilsmaier uses Dietrich, the legend, in order to redeem her and recuperate German national identity. Her image, a well-tended illusion, is used to restore a sense of national cohesion to a post-unified Germany. She is a manifestation of a Germany that can be admired and adored and that is both national and international.

Vilsmaier is not the first to call Dietrich home. Her image has been evoked in a number of films in various incarnations, but most commonly in her portrayal of Lola. Rainer Werner Fassbinder's film *Lola* (1981), starring Barbara Sukowa, belongs to his BRD Trilogy, which includes *The Marriage* of *Maria Braun* and *Veronika Voss*, and pays tribute to *The Blue Angel* in its title character and milieu, and seduction of an upstanding citizen. Fassbinder's film features Lola as a 1950s cabaret singer and prostitute who performs for the corrupt elite during the economic miracle. Lola is the personal whore of the cabaret owner, the developer and adulterer Schuckert (Mario Adorf), who has fathered her child. The unsuspecting bourgeois here is von Bohm (Armin Müller-Stahl), the city's new building superintendent, who falls in love and later marries Lola, compromising his principles. Fassbinder's *Lola* is a critique of the 1950s economic miracle with Lola, an allegory for Germany, entangled in a *ménage à trois* with capitalism preying on Prussian values of honor and uprightness and with the sexualized female body as seductive, deceptive interlocutor.

By the same token, in *Lili Marleen* (1980), Fassbinder relates the story of the title song and the career of Lale Anderson (played by Hanna Schygulla, often referred to as an incarnation of Dietrich), whose first recording of "Lili Marlene" moved German troops to cease fire during its broadcast in Belgrade in 1941. Fassbinder's interest in the power of mass culture, and particularly in the Third Reich's finely tuned manipulation of mass entertainment and spectacle to move audiences and with them a nation, are made obvious here.[48] Even though the film showcases Anderson, Dietrich's image haunts the film's periphery. Not only does the title call to mind Dietrich's own name, but the song also became a part of her repertoire after 1943. She sang it in English and in French, thus popularizing it for the American, British, and French soldiers for whom she performed. The song is so closely associated with Dietrich that in Stanley Kramer's *Judgment at Nuremberg* the Dietrich character, the wife of a general who is being tried for war crimes, hears the song coming from a nearby bar. The Dietrich character tells the American presiding judge (played by Spencer Tracy), who is walking down the street with her, "I wish you could understand German. The words are very beautiful, very sad, much sadder than in the English version. The German soldier knows that he is going to lose his girl."[49] On her abbreviated tour through Germany in 1960, Dietrich performed *Lili Marleen* at the Titania-Palast in Berlin.

In Tom Tykwer's 1999 *Run Lola Run*, the name Lola also evokes *The Blue Angel*, and represents a seductively dynamic Lola, who, like her namesake, strains convention both in terms of narrative and gendered assumptions. Even Wim Wenders's 1987 *Wings of Desire*, which features two angels who accompany a storyteller in search of the lost Potsdamer Platz and who watch German history as it unfolds, bears the "ghost" of *The Blue Angel* in its title and in the downward trajectory of one angel, who gives up the omniscient eternal sphere for the world of the senses and sensations. It is interesting to note that Wenders claimed to experience his "Germanness" only in Berlin, since it is the only place in Germany in which history lives.[50] A more direct evocation of Dietrich's signature film is E. Kutlug Ataman's 1999 film *Lola and Billy the Kid*, which enlists the name Lola to feature cross-dressing, performance, camp, ambiguous sexual identity, and the encounter with the sexualized other. The title character, a male transvestite named Lola, is feminized by his male lover, who cannot accept his homosexuality and who goes by the name of Billy the Kid, a play on the Western cowboy and outlaw, the archetype of the strong masculine hero.

Unlike Ataman's Lola, who is murdered in the film, and whose ambiguous sexuality deeply threatens his lover's sense of masculinity, von Sternberg's Lola never loses her provocative power or life. On the contrary, Dietrich's cross-dressing did not function to hide illicit desire, but to excite and add to her mystery and allure. It placed her outside conventional gender definitions and provided her with the power of the desiring/desired object—an icon for everyone. Marjorie Garber adds, "Dietrich's reputation, Dietrich's image, is built on this structure of cross-gender representation,"[51] which explains her appeal for both male and female audiences that both Marjorie Garber and Judith Mayne discuss. In her own way, Dietrich reconciled and challenged dichotomies, broke taboos, violated categories, and projected a sense of freedom, lawlessness, and independence—qualities and expressions of femininity that are accepted and capitalized on at specific historical times. A pioneer in many ways, Dietrich can be counted among those who first expanded the repertoire of femininity, certainly through her behavior and even her androgynous attire, especially when donning a suit, that freed women from restrictive clothing and allowed them to pursue careers and leisure activities previously unavailable to them: trousers, smoking jacket, top hat, and monocle. Dietrich's daring attire may have been accepted in Berlin, but it was still too risqué for a Puritan United States. When she made her debut on American shores in New York on April 9, 1930, after leaving Berlin on the night of *The Blue Angel* premiere, she was warned against wearing trousers. Intent on creating a star, her Paramount public relations strategists wrapped her in a mink coat.

As her immensely varied reception shows, Dietrich's image is easily exploited because of her elusiveness, her transitoriness, and the complexity of her representation. Erich Maria Remarque, one of Dietrich's many lovers, best describes the openness of Dietrich's face and captures her allure in a character he modeled after her in his novel *Arch of Triumph*. He writes, "the bold, light face that did not ask but was there just waiting … It was like a beautiful house that waited for carpets and paintings. It harbored all possibilities—it could be a palace or a whorehouse. It depended on the person that filled it."[52] Because of Dietrich's indeterminacy, her malleability, and her multivalent identities, and because of her ambiguous gender and sexual identity, Dietrich escapes specificity and invites projections rooted in various registers of desire, be they national or sexual. Marjorie Garber notes, "Her presence—or even her evocation—has itself become a sign of the provocative destabilization of gender that is the very signature of the erotic."[53] Her image remains a projection screen, that is, an imaginary space open for multiple contradictory desires and agendas. The surplus of photographs and film close-ups that have immortalized her still provide plenty of venues for contemplation and dreaming. She was made for the camera, as numerous scenes of Dietrich's face reflected in mirrors show.

In many ways, her comparison to Garbo's enigmatic allure is not falsely placed. Roland Barthes describes Garbo's face as perfect, evoking "ecstasy." She is an ephemeral essence and even "an Idea." Her images often seem dreamy; she resides at a distance and casts her image to be looked at, rarely meeting the eye of the camera directly.[54] Like Garbo, Dietrich's surface sexual charisma invites and entreats fantasy; her image is open for erotic contemplation, which allows her to remain seductive for all viewers.[55] In contrast to Garbo, however, Dietrich's face longs for proximity; she dares the viewer to trespass and delight in her, on her own terms. Her ocular mastery, the foregrounding of the power of her gaze as an erotic medium that disregards social conventions, fixes the spectator much like in *The Blue Angel*, when Lola turns her spotlight on Rath. Both present and absent, she was and remains a figment of the imagination, as well as a product of the camera and lighting that she fastidiously controlled.

A contemporary virtual exhibition on Dietrich at the State Museum in Hagen, Germany, sums up the significance of a star and addresses Dietrich specifically: "A star is a public figure, the personification of desires and fears of a nation, he <sic> is the prototype of his time. His task is to produce an image, which catches fire from physical operational readiness and nevertheless remains immaterial."[56] Capitalizing on Dietrich's aura (in various media), the exhibit invites its spectators to play out their desires and fantasies, which the image serves to ignite. The image, however, is intangible, which perhaps makes it more irresistible. It is the site of desire heightened by its absence. In his discussion of film stars, Richard Dyer notes, "Audiences cannot make media images mean anything they want to, but they can select from the complexity of the image the meanings and feelings, the variations, inflections and contradictions, that work for them."[57] Given Dietrich's multiple identities, the image gains in complexity and becomes multiply accessible.

Since German unification in 1989, Dietrich has became a vehicle for recovering a liberal, energetic image of the roaring 1920s that the new Germany sought for its identity. The old Ufa studio, which East Germany turned into the DEFA studio, could now premiere its lost traditions and reclaim its old stars. Mass culture had become a much-exploited means to represent nations, and Germany was no exception. Dietrich became Germany's best advertisement, as renewed interest in her Weimar films attests, with her image used to project the vitality of a newly reunified nation. Thus Dietrich's image has become a significant vehicle, in the advertiser's sense of the word, to promote Germany. The Goethe Institute, a government-sponsored agency founded after World War II to promote German culture internationally, has ongoing events celebrating the international star, using her as a marketing device to sell Germany.[58] As recently as 2005, members of the Goethe Institute in Boston celebrated Dietrich's style by turning the institute into a 1930s Berlin with a "Blue Angel" ball and a Dietrich look-alike contest.[59] Dietrich's image is equally helpful in advertising the new Germany "at home." Her image serves to draw tourists to the Potsdamer Platz, and recharge a space that was once the hub of Germany, if not Europe. Her image functions as a mirror into which the new Berlin casts a glance to remember its golden years and to capitalize on the image of the trendsetter that she was and the legend that she remains. Her daughter, Maria Riva, insightfully distinguishes between star and legend when she describes Dietrich's meticulous sculpting of her image for von Sternberg's *The Devil Is a Woman*: "There are people who know something is missing even in apparent perfection, and then there are those who realize it only after they are shown what it was. My mother was one of the former—most performers belong to the latter. It may be one of the subtle differences between Legend and Star."[60] The embellishment of her image was her art; it still draws audiences like "moths to a light," not so much to her films, but to the mystique and aura that she cultivated.

Dietrich's mythic status, therefore, is the vehicle for a much larger genre than those represented in her films—it is deployed to give life to the myth of Berlin, as well as the new Germany.[61] This myth, as Hans Joachim Hoffmann submits, is created in retrospect and is based on Berlin's desire to project itself as a significant metropolis. Thus Berlin draws from its past, particularly its interwar period, its golden years, to recreate the city as a magnetic space indebted to the arts and the vast array of cultural arenas. A brochure put out by the office of tourism exemplifies the strategies developed to market the capital, with Dietrich's name mentioned along with Berlin's other creative celebrities.[62] At the same time, Dietrich-tourism is promoted in guidebooks that mark the various places she frequented in Berlin. Much like Lola's image in the advertisement that succeeded in luring Rath into The Blue Angel nightclub, Dietrich's renown serves as a magnet to bring foreign tourists as well as Germany's own inhabitants back to a city whose existence, at least in the western part of the city before unification, was uncertain. With figures like Dietrich, the city can reclaim its former urbanity and worldliness.

The author Zafer Şenocak claims that Berlin has long existed as an anomaly, which explains the awkwardness of its new status: "Now that we have a true capital we do not know what to do with it."[63] Berlin remains a space that is filled with the traces of its tumultuous history, leaving no space without controversy.[64] Given Dietrich's relationship to her homeland and its history, it seems fitting that the legend returns. Her defiance of conventions and her contentiousness defines Berlin's uniqueness; besides, her personal history is profoundly enmeshed in its history.

The reinvention of a German national identity that includes integrating both East and West has received much attention lately, with the new national "feeling" visible in a variety of cultural products ranging from popular music to art and cinema. Yet, despite efforts like those of Vilsmaier and others to repatriate Dietrich, she cannot be contained. She retains her status as an inimitable diva whose image is contradictory and ambiguous. Dietrich's excesses expanded not only notions of gender but national affiliations as well. Her coffin was draped with the German, American, and French flags. Marlene, cosmopolitan, cross-dresser, and femme fatale, the embodiment of glamour and self-invention, a figure of independence, individual empowerment, and subversion, is someone for everyone. Her image continues to captivate audiences through her static sensuality and bravado, her coolness and her passion, her forthrightness and mystery. As Francine du Plessix Gray writes, "She blended the personae of bisexual adventuress, devoted grandmother, and down-to-earth hausfrau ... I doubt whether any woman in public life has projected, well into her 70s, more varied, more ambivalent images of human sexuality."[65] Because of her "openness," Dietrich provides an imaginary space for multiple and often contested desires, needs, and gains. She becomes a figure that Germany can invest in with significant returns by marketing her origins as that place that initially defined her. German mass culture thus fine-tunes its subject and enlists her to provide access to the past and future that it simultaneously longs to become. The plethora of biographies, the countless photographs and their reproductions, the ongoing exhibitions, the numerous websites that establish a global community among her fans, the Marlene Dietrich newsletter and Marlene Dietrich Collection that the Stiftung Deutsche Kinemathek oversees, in addition to her many impersonators and spin-offs, attest to the continued fascination with Dietrich and the various personas she performs.[66] The release of *The Blue Angel* on DVD in 2001, in both its German and English versions, with an interview and a clip of Dietrich's audition, is further evidence of the film's continued popularity. Her image in *The Blue Angel* both resists time and evokes historical specificity. Above all, the image retains its iconic status and invites the viewer to dream. Judging from Dietrich's contemporary "presence" in Berlin, it seems that Germany has forgiven its Blue Angel. She has been accepted back into the nation's heart and conquered it.

## Notes

1. The original text that was written for the German adaptation of Pam Gems's play *Marlene* is: Mutter, hast du mir vergeben / Mutter, denkst du noch daran / Mutter, hast du mir vergeben, was ich dir angetan / Heimat, hast du mir vergeben / Heimat, denkst du noch daran / Heimat, hast du mir vergeben, was ich dir angetan / Das Glück lockte mich fort von hier / Fort von Heimat und Haus / Ich ging mit all den andern und kam nie mehr

nach Haus / Mutter, kannst du mich noch lieben / Mutter, gib mir deine Hand / Bin dein Kind doch geblieben, fremd in fremdem Land / Mutter, ich will in die Heimat / Mutter, die Welt ist so groß / Mutter, ich will in die Heimat, nimm mich in deinen Schoß.
2. According to Dietrich's grandson, David Riva, the decision to bury Dietrich's mother in Friedenau was arbitrary since she did not live in that Berlin neighborhood. Upon her mother's death, Dietrich contacted an American general and requested that he oversee the burial. Owing to the laws against fraternization, he smuggled the body out by night and drove around looking for a burial place in bombed-out Berlin. David Riva recounted the story upon the screening of his film *Her Own Song* in Tucson (2004). Also see, *Der Künstler Friedhof in Friedenau* (Berlin: Edition Friedenauer Brücke, 2006).
3. Hellmuth Karasek, "Filmhimmel ohne blauen Engel," *Der Spiegel* (May 11, 1992).
4. Elfriede Jelinek, "Das zweite Gesicht," in *Adieu Marlene: Nachruf aus Deutschland*, edited by Fred Ostrowski (Berlin: Mariposa Verlag, 1992), 16. In a eulogy to Dietrich, Austrian author Elfriede Jelinek writes: "Diesem gierigen Griff der Nazis nach allem, was es gibt, diesen Ansprüchen auf die ganze Welt, die die Goebbels und Hitlers auf nichts als Natur (Rasse, Blut, Boden) gegründet hatten, ihnen hat sich die Dietrich als Wirklichkeit ein für allemal entrissen." ("Dietrich, as a reality, freed herself once and for all from the greedy clutches of the Nazis, who grasped for everything that exists, whose claims on the whole world for Goebbels and Hitler were based on nothing but nature (race, blood, soil).")
5. Maria Riva, *Marlene Dietrich By Her Daughter* (New York: Knopf, 1993), 495.
6. Jörn Kabisch, "Eine Nummer zu groß für Berlin," *Der Tagesspiegel* (December 27, 2001): ("Evelyn Künneke durfte in der BZ erzählen, sie möge es nicht, wenn jemand sein Vaterland verleumde.") See also, Cornelia Köster, "Marlene—Heim ins Reich," *Freitag* (April 16, 1993); Daniela Pogade, "Späte Ehrung—wieder ohne Senat," *Berliner Zeitung* (November 24, 1994); Günter Görtz, "Verspätete Hommage an Marlene Dietrich," *Neues Deutschland* (October 5, 1992).
7. Hellmuth Karasek, "Der ungeliebte Engel: Der Jahrhundertstar Marlene Dietrich—von der lasziven Kindfrau zur weltweit angehimmelten, in ihrer Heimat oft geschmähten Göttin der Filmgeschichte," *Der Spiegel* 25 (June 19, 2000): http://www.spiegel.de/spiegel/0,1518,82400,00.html ("in der blamablen Unfähigkeit zu Trauerfeiern ... ging deutscher Sinn furs Recht nicht unter").
8. Landespressedienst Berlin, *Aktuelles der Woche* (May 21, 1991). See also "Kein Adieu für Marlene Dietrich," *Süddeutsche Zeitung* 113 (May 16, 1992); Nikolas Busse, "Trauriger Abschied für Marlene Dietrich," *Berliner Zeitung* 113 (May 15, 1992).
9. Mathias Frankensein and Nikolas Buss, "Maximilian Schell spricht den letzten Gruss," *Berliner Zeitung* (May 16, 1992): "Ihre Beisetzung in Berlin wäre ein weltweit verstandenes Zeichen, dass faschistische Gewaltherrschaft und die widernatürliche Teilung ihrer Heimstadt überwunden seien" (my translation). See Marion Dressler, "Späte Geste am Grab der Diva," *Berliner Zeitung* (December 28, 2001).
10. *Spiegel Reporter* (March 2000), 4. The Vilsmaier film is reviewed in this edition, which explains the concrete motivation for the juxtaposition of Dietrich and Merkel.
11. "Germany Makes Posthumous Amends," *New York Times* (May 17, 2002).
12. Ibid. See also, Steffi Kammerer, "Die fünfte Frau: Berlin schliesst Frieden mit Marlene Dietrich," *Süddeutsche Zeitung* (May 16, 2002).
13. Theodor Körner, a nineteenth-century playwright, volunteered for military service during the Franco-Prussian war (1813) despite his promising career and his cultural engagement.
14. See Brian Ladd's discussion of the highly contested "Neue Wache" and the replica of Käthe Kollwitz's *Pieta* as a symbol of mourning the victims of war in *Ghosts of Berlin: Confronting German History in the Urban Landscape* (Chicago: University of Chicago Press, 1997).
15. Svetlana Boym, *The Future of Nostalgia* (New York: Basic Books, 2001) xvi and xiii respectively.
16. See Ulrike Wiebrecht, *Blauer Engel aus Berlin: Marlene Dietrich* (Berlin-Brandenburg: be bra verlag, 2001), 143–49. See also, Ute Frings, "Für Emigranten ist auf Berliner

Strassenschildern kein Platz," *Stuttgarter Zeitung* (November 30, 1996); Daniela Treuenfels, "Debatte um Marlene-Ehrung zieht sich in die Länge," *Berliner Zeitung* (March 9, 1997); Kai Ritzmann, "Gedänkstätte für die Dietrich: Brauner plant Marlene-Memorial," *Berliner Morgenpost* (July 27, 1997); "Unterschriften für die Diva," *Berliner Zeitung* (October 20, 2004).
17. Zafer Şenocak, "The Capital of the Fragment," *New German Critique* 88 (Winter 2003), 141.
18. Lothar Schwab and Elisabeth Moortgat, eds., *Deutsche Kinemathek: Das Filmmuseum* (Berlin: Stiftung Deutsche Kinemathek, 1994), 88. See also, Moritz Rinke, "Ein Tag mit Marlene," *Tagesspiegel* (December 31, 1994).
19. The fact that this "snapshot" of Dietrich's work as an entertainer for U.S. troops is not regularly vandalized, as her grave was for years, attests to the changing historical climate. The highly charged reception of her German tour in 1960 demonstrated that Germany was not ready to accept her back into its fold. She was greeted with tomatoes and eggs and, for example, with "eine Mischung aus Bosheit, falsch verstandener Vaterlandsliebe und sogar Antisemitismus ... 'Der jüdische Snob und der intellektuelle Mob werden sich vor Begeisterung über Ihren Auftritt kringeln ... In die Kloake mit ihnen und ihren geschäftstüchtigen Smocks. Vaterlandsverräterin!' wütet ein anonymer Briefschreiber" (with a mixture of meanness, misunderstood patriotism and even anti-Semitism ... An anonymous letter writer raged, 'The Jewish snob and the intellectual mob will crackle with enthusiasm for your performance ... In the sewer with you and your entrepreneurial Smocks.'"). See Hermann Kreutzer and Manuela Runge, eds., *Ein Koffer in Berlin: Marlene Dietrich—Geschichten von Politik und Liebe* (Berlin: Aufbau Taschenbuch, 2001), 141–42.
20. Christian Schröder, "Weiss nicht, zu wem ich gehöre: (Wieder)-Geburt einer Diva," *Tagesspiegel* (June 30, 1998).
21. Judy Winter, "Mein Leben mit Marlene," *Berliner Morgenpost* (December 27, 2001).
22. Pam Gems, *Marlene* (London: Oberon Books, 1998), 28.
23. Gems, 51.
24. Gems, 53.
25. Apropos being in the kitchen, Maria Riva relates an anecdote about Dietrich's contribution with other stars to the war effort in the United States: "The European contingent preferred the kitchen detail. Hedy Lamarr made hundreds of sandwiches. Dietrich scrubbed pots in clinging dress and attractive snood, up to her elbows in dirty dishwater—it drove Bette Davis crazy. I once heard that wonderful four-octave voice of hers declare: 'If I find those dames back there one more time ... I'll brain them! What is it with those hausfraus? Show them a kitchen and they're off? Like a horse to water! I need glamour out *here* for the boys—not in there with the pots!'" (Riva, 525).
26. Hillel Tryster, "Der blaue und weisse Engel: Marlene Dietrich in Israel 1960 und 1966," *Marlene Dietrich*, edited by Werner Sudendorf and Hans-Peter Reichmann (Berlin: Deutsche Kinemathek, 1995), 80.
27. Kreutzer and Runge, eds., 124. Dietrich's grandson, David Riva, told the story of her Israel performance at a showing of *Her Own Song* in Tucson, Arizona, in the spring of 2004.
28. David Riva, dir., *Marlene Dietrich: Her Own Song*, 2001.
29. Quoted in Andrea Slane, *A Not So Foreign Affair: Fascism, Sexuality, and the Cultural Rhetoric of American Democracy* (Durham, NC and London: Duke University Press, 2001), 222.
30. See Wim Wenders, "Reden über Deutschland," *The Act of Seeing: Essays und Gespräche* (Frankfurt am Main: Verlag der Autoren, 1993). Wenders, a longtime contributor to the New German Cinema, was among the more vociferous advocates for a home-grown cinema. His road movies, particularly those made during the 1970s and 1980s, often featured protagonists equipped with cameras or some other means of recording experience, on a journey toward self-knowledge in the sense of a *Bildungsroman*.
31. Michael Ermarth, "German Unification as Self-Inflicted Americanization: Critical Views on the Course of Contemporary German Development," *Here, There and Everywhere: The Foreign Politics of American Popular Culture*, edited by Reinhold Wagenleitner and Elaine Tyler May (Hanover, NH: University Press of New England, 2000), 253.

32. On the occasion of the 2006 Berlin Film Festival and the many acclaimed entries from Germany, an article in *Der Spiegel* magazine celebrates Germany's relationship with Hollywood, as well as revealing a sense of inferiority to the United States: "Germany, so it seems, is once again accepted in Hollywood as a film nation. ... Even German directors are sought again in Hollywood like they haven't been in a long time." *Der Spiegel* (February 2, 2006).
33. See the interview of Hellmuth Karasek and Helmut Sorge with Marlene Dietrich, "'Logik macht das Leben leichter': Marlene Dietrich über Berlin, Hollywood, Paris und ihr Leben," *Der Spiegel* 25 (June 19, 1991): http://www.spiegel.de/spiegel/0,1518,269335,00.html
34. "Klassischer Film-Ewig Jung: Anmerkungen zur Wiederaufführung des Filmes *Der blaue Engel*," *Super-Verleih*, 1953.
35. "Klassischer Film-Ewig Jung."
36. Gertrud Koch, "Exorcised: Marlene Dietrich and German Nationalism," *Women and Film: A Sight and Sound Reader*, edited by Pam Cook and Philip Dodd (London: Scarlet Press, 1993), 10–15.
37. Erica Carter, "Marlene Dietrich—the Prodigal Daughter," *The German Cinema Book*, edited by Tim Bergfelder et al. (London: British Film Institute, 2002), 75.
38. Quoted in Helga Bemmann, *Marlene Dietrich: Im Frack zum Ruhm: Ein Porträt* (Leipzig: Kiepenheuer, 2000), 99. ("Wir glauben fest daran, dass eine Schauspielerin wie Marlene Dietrich mit ihrer reichen ausländischen Erfahrung für Deutschlands Filmschaffen einen unschätzbaren Gewinn darstellen wird. Welch schätzenswerte Aufgabe könnte es für einen der besten deutschen Regisseure sein, aus dem Vamp Dietrich die Frau Dietrich widerzugestalten. Beileibe nicht ein Gretchen mit Hangezöpfen und dicken roten Backen, aber doch eine Frau, die aus inneren Kräften ihr deutsches Wesen zu gestalten vermag.")
39. Taking her cue from Kracauer's reading of Lola as a protofascist (and showing how other representations of the fascination with Nazism are conflated with representations of illicit sexuality and camp à la Visconti's *The Damned*), Slane argues that Dietrich's "Germanness/Lolaness" allowed her to play with an ambiguous identity that took on "a double rhetorical function she continued to play for the rest of her career" (240). See also, Geoffrey Wagner, "Revaluation: *The Blue Angel*," *Sight and Sound* 21.1 (August–September 1951), 42.
40. Slane, 232.
41. Lutz Koepnick, "Amerika gibt's überhaupt nicht: Notes on the German Heritage Films," *German Pop Culture: How "American" Is It?*, edited by Agnes Müller (Ann Arbor: University of Michigan Press, 2004), 191-208. See also Eric Rentschler, "An Icon between the Fronts: Vilsmaier's Recast *Marlene*," *Dietrich Icon*, edited by Gerd Gemünden and Mary R. Desjardines (Durham, N.C.: Duke University Press, 2007), 328-46.
42. See, for example, Merten Worthmann, "Heim ins Reich: Joseph Vilsmaiers Filmbiografie "Marlene" feiert das Deutschtum der Diva," *Die Zeit* (November 2000); Thomas Klingenmaier, "Jenseits von Marlene Dietrich," *Stuttgarter Zeitung* (March 12, 2006) addresses Dietrich's overwhelming presence—it has overshadowed other stars of early German cinema like Renate Müller and Lilian Harvey.
43. See Andrea Weiss, "'A Queer Feeling When I Look At You': Hollywood Stars and Lesbian Spectatorship in the 1930s," *Stardom: Industry of Desire*, edited by Christine Gledhill (London: Routledge, 1991), 283–99. With a similar ambition to tell all but for a different purpose, Weiss quotes a tabloid that claims to unveil Dietrich's secrets and to tell "the untold story of Marlene Dietrich," listing her female lovers. Dietrich's androgyny, which was deemed gossip in the 1950s tabloid, has since become commonplace and even a powerful part of her allure.
44. Brigitte Häring, "*Marlene*: Leben zwischen Mythos und Legende," http://www.mybasel.ch/freizeit_kino_archiv.cfm?printer
45. It is interesting to note that Dietrich was considered "box office poison" in the late 1930s, along with Katherine Hepburn, Greta Garbo, Joan Crawford, and Bette Davis—all strong women who no longer spoke to the time. Dietrich experienced a comeback with George Marshall's 1939 *Destry Rides Again*, venturing into a completely new genre for her, the Western.

46. See Heinz Wagner's synopsis of the opera, in *Das grosse Handbuch der Oper* (Hamburg: Florian Noetzel Verlag, 199), 761.
47. Judith Mayne, "Marlene Dietrich, *The Blue Angel*, and Female Performance," *Seduction and Theory: Readings of Gender, Representation and Rhetoric*, edited by Diane Hunter (Champagne-Urbana: University of Illinois Press, 1989), 41.
48. Caryl Flinn eloquently discusses Fassbinder's attention to the song, which "was so full of meanings that it became virtually meaningless." She argues against critics who accused Fassbinder and Raben of fetishizing the song. Instead, Flinn claims "that they were exaggerating its fetishistic function to the point of exhaustion, consigning it to empty, vicious repetition." *The New German Cinema: Music, History, and the Matter of Style* (Berkeley: University of California Press, 2004), 51.
49. Christian Peters, *Lili Marleen: Ein Schlager macht Geschichte* (Bonn: Haus der Geschichte, 2001).
50. See Wim Wenders, "An Attempted Description of an Indescribable Film," *The Logic of Images: Essays and Conversations* (London: Faber and Faber, 1991), 74.
51. Marjorie Garber, "From Dietrich to Madonna: Cross-gender Icons," *Women in Film: A Sight and Sound Reader*, edited by Pam Cook and Philip Dodd (London: Scarlet Press, 1993), 17.
52. Quoted in Merten Worthmann, "Heim ins Reich: Joseph Vilsmaiers Filmbiografie *Marlene* feiert das Deutschtum der Diva," *Die Zeit* (November 2000). Erich Maria Remarque, *L'Arc de Triomphe*, "das kühne, helle Gesicht, das nicht fragte, das nur da war und wartete ... Es war wie ein schönes leeres Haus, das auf Teppiche und Bilder wartete. Alle Möglichkeitenwaren in ihm—es konnte ein Palast und eine Hurenbude werden. Es kam auf den an, der es füllte."
53. Garber, 16. Garber reminds us of the tribute to Lola in The Kinks' song of the 1970s: "Girls will be boys and boys will be girls / It's a mixed-up world / it's a shook-up world—except for Lola."
54. Roland Barthes, "The Face of Garbo," *Mythologies* (New York: Hill and Wang, 1972), 56–57.
55. A wonderful commentary on the relationship between Dietrich and Garbo is found in the 1991 film *Meeting of Two Queens*. Using footage from various Dietrich and Garbo films, Chilean filmmaker Cecila Barriga splices together footage to suggest a love relationship between the two silver screen divas, Queen Christina and Scarlet Empress. The fourteen-minute short film enacts a proximity that they never shared in actual life. It is said that Garbo refused to meet with Dietrich, who then seduced Garbo's lovers, among them Mercedes de Acosta and John Gilbert—a mediated proximity that the film oversteps.
56. The excerpt is taken from the Marlene Dietrich exhibition that ran at the Historical Museum in Hagen at the following address: http://www.historisches-centrum.de/ausstellung/marlene/marl1.htm
57. Richard Dyer, *Heavenly Bodies: Film Stars and Society* (New York: St. Martin's Press, 1986), 5.
58. "Marlenes 100. Geburtstag soll Touristen nach Berlin locken," *Berliner Zeitung* (September 22, 1999).
59. See www.archives.here-now.org/topics/_arts/al_020214.asp
60. Riva, 323.
61. The February 29, 2000 edition of the *Spiegel Reporter* features a picture of Chancellor Angela Merkel on the front cover with the caption: "The Secrets of Angela Merkel." A synopsis of the accompanying article reads: "Whoever wants to get to know the secrets of Angela Merkel, whoever wants to grasp why a woman from the East can become a symbol of integration for a truly western party has to accompany her from one crisis committee meeting to another and to go there where she comes from." ("Wer das Geheimnis der Angela Merkel ergründen will, wer begreifen will, warum eine Frau aus dem Osten zur Integrationsfigur einer erzwestlichen Partei werden kann, muss mit ihr von Krisensitzung zu Krisensitzung ziehen und dorthin gehen, wo sie herkommt.") The advertisement for this issue of the *Spiegel Reporter* features a picture of Merkel on one side of the page with an arrow pointing to her and the text "what is to come," and an image of Marlene Dietrich on the other page, with the text "what remains."

62. In this context, see the use of the culture of the Weimar Republic as a marketing strategy that Berlin's office of tourism employs: Berlin Tourismus Marketing GmbH / Presse- und Öffentlichkeitsarbeit, http://www.berlin-tourist-information.de Berlin, January 2004.
63. In his essay on Berlin, in *Atlas of a Tropical Germany: Essays on Politics and Culture, 1990–1998*, edited by Leslie Adelson (Lincoln: University of Nebraska, 2000), Zafer Şenocak claims, "German dreams and nightmares lie close together. There is an urge to present oneself as open to the world, cosmopolitan, but there is also a defensive response to the metropolis and its monstrous-seeming physiognomy. Small-town folk do not turn into big-city people overnight" (144).
64. See Ladd, *Ghosts of Berlin*.
65. Francine du Plessix Gray, *Vogue Magazine*, (March 2003), 608.
66. My thanks go to Silke Ronneburg at the Deutsche Kinemathek for showing me the compilation film of Dietrich citations. The list is quite extensive. It includes a Betty Boop and Madonna performance, a scene from Mel Brooks's *Blazing Saddles*, an Armani advertisement, Meret Becker singing in Wortmann's film *Kleine Haie*, a scene from Batman, and, of course, *La Cage aux Folles* directed by Edouard Molinaro.

# FADE OUT: THE CREDITS

*Produced by:* Erich-Pommer-Produktion der Universum-Film AG (Ufa). *Directed by:* Josef von Sternberg; *Written by:* Robert Liebmann, Karl Vollmoeller, Carl Zuckmayer; *Adapted from:* Heinrich Mann's *Professor Unrat*; Cinematography: Günther Rittau, Hans Schneeberger; *Set Design:* Otto Hunte, Emil Hasler; *Music:* Friedrich Hollaender; *Lyrics:* Friedrich Hollaender, Robert Liebmann, Richard Rillo; *Location Manager:* Viktor Eisenbach; *Costumes:* Tihamer Varady, Karl Ludwig Holub; *Editor and Assistant:* Sam Winston; *Sound:* Fritz Thiery, Herbert Kiehl; *Photography:* Karl Bayer, Laszlo Willinger

As in many early films, whose casts and crews were relatively small compared to today, *The Blue Angel*'s credits roll at the start of the film. Yet, owing to the dramatic turns each biography took either immediately following the premiere of *The Blue Angel* or a few years after Hitler's rise to power in 1933, I include them here at the end. The personal biographies of the cast, producer, scriptwriters, composers, and crew, as far as they can be tracked, represent the many different and unforeseen directions taken by the lives of those who were involved in Germany's thriving film industry. Some of those paths led to stardom or a precarious existence in exile, while others led to an experience of unparalleled tragedy. In his study of *The Blue Angel*, S.S. Prawer offers a cursory look at the lives of some of the most prominent contributors to the film.[1] Using his work as a point of departure, this appendix provides a more comprehensive look at the biographies of those who contributed to making this classic Weimar film, and its star.

Indeed, *The Blue Angel* stands at the crossroads of German film history in more ways than one. It is evidence of the interrelationship of culture and politics, and, more specially, the deeply entrenched affiliation between film and German political and cultural history. The timing of the film, as discussed previously, coincided with economically and politically difficult years of the Weimar Republic. Reviews of the adaptation of Heinrich Mann's novel that sprang up from various political quarters—which arguably helped political foes to reinforce their platforms—reflect the political (and discursive) climate of the time. Shortly after the Nazis came to power in 1933, *The Blue Angel* was withdrawn from circulation and placed into the "poison cabinet" with the explanation that the film insults German national dignity. At the time, the Ministry of Culture and Propaganda headed by Joseph Goebbels controlled Germany's film production, using it as a tool for the Nazis' political agenda, in addition to keeping the masses entertained.

Thus as the credits roll, we are called upon to take stock of the various directions that German film history took. What stands out most when reading the various biographies is how concentrated Berlin's cultural scene was during the Weimar Republic, and how interconnected were the professional lives of the key figures in *The Blue Angel*. These extraordinarily talented personalities met on Berlin stages, in plays and in cabarets, as well as on various film sets, and contributed significantly to the vibrant cultural energy and innovation associated with the interwar period. Since Dietrich's biography is mentioned throughout the book, it would be redundant to review it here. Just one last remark, Dietrich cannot be counted among the 1,500 German exiles who were forced out of Germany's film industry in 1933, either because of their Jewish background or because of their refusal to conform to the blood-and-soil ideology of the Third Reich.[2] On Dietrich's heels followed a number of renowned artists who fled Germany—Billy Wilder, Fritz Lang, Max Reinhardt, Joe May, Curt Siodmak, Robert Siodmak, and Fritzi Massary, to name a few—and who made Hollywood their home, some more successfully than others. Other friends of Dietrich's like Richard Tauber and Elisabeth Bergner went to London. Dietrich helped many of them with their transition and worked with some later on.

The following list is not comprehensive since information often is unavailable.

The credits begin with the producer of *The Blue Angel*, **Erich Pommer**, who spent time in Hollywood before being forced into exile in 1933, as a German Jew. As one of Germany's most accomplished producers, he was responsible for many of the films made during the interwar years that achieved both national and international recognition. His film career began in 1907, when the Berlin division of the Léon Gaumont Cinematography and Film Company employed Pommer at the age of eighteen to sell film, in addition to acting, working as a projectionist, editing the Gaumont-Newsreels, and helping to design film posters for press releases. In 1910, Pommer took over the Gaumont branch in Vienna, which called for traveling throughout the Austro-Hungarian Empire, until he joined the French company Éclair in Vienna, for whom he produced his first film in 1913. While serving in the German army soon after in 1915, Pommer established his own Decla studios. Equipped with a good business sense and with confidence in cinema's artistic potential, Pommer became one of the first to promote the internationalization of German cinema, thus bringing German productions out of isolation. He was known as someone who supported his directors, who encouraged innovation and who believed in the financial viability of art films: "I thus come to the main demands of film." He stated, "It should contain everything. It should fulfill the needs of the most demanding spectator as much as entertain the least demanding spectator through its clear, suspenseful plot. That one artistically works on such a film goes without saying. But art in this instance is not the end in itself, but rather an aid."[3] Through the merger of Germany's three largest film studios (Decla, Ufa, and Meester), and with Pommer at the helm, Germany's film industry (Ufa) blossomed.

In 1924, Pommer and Lang traveled to New York for the premiere of *The Nibelungen*, and continued on to Hollywood, where they visited American studios and met with film producer Samuel Goldwyn. The visit confirmed Pommer's belief in a potential market for German films abroad. Yet, he was forced to leave Ufa in 1926 because of the disputed *Metropolis* budget and returned to the United States, where he produced three films for Paramount—the first one being *Hotel Imperial*, with the Swedish director Mauritz Stiller and film star Pola Negri. Disillusioned with Hollywood's restrictive working conditions, and at the urging of Ludwig Klitzsch, General Director of Ufa, Pommer returned to Berlin in 1927 to establish the Pommer Production Company under the umbrella of Ufa. In 1929, he played a key role in preparing German studios for the conversion to sound; his first film, *Melodie des Herzens* (Melody of the Heart) joined *The Blue Angel* and later *Die drei von der Tankstelle* (The Three from the Gas Station) in attaining international success.

Pommer fled to France in 1933 after the termination of his Ufa contract.[4] There he worked for Fox-Europa and produced Fritz Lang's 1934 film *Liliom*. With the closure of Fox's European division, owing to the failing gold standard, Pommer moved his next project, *Music in the Air*, to Hollywood in 1934, and then returned to Europe to settle in London where he worked with Alexander Korda, and founded Mayflower, his own production company with Charles Laughton. A failing economy forced his return to the United States, where he worked until his poor health effected the termination of his contract with Paramount.

Despite his poor health, Pommer dreamt of remaking *The Cabinet of Dr. Caligari* and *The Blue Angel*. In 1940, he even bought the rights to remake *The Blue Angel* from Heinrich Mann for one dollar, but lacked the financial backing needed within the stipulated time frame. In 1950, Darryl Zanuck expressed interest in remaking *The Blue Angel* with Pommer, but the plan never reached fruition. In this version, Pommer imagined the story set in 1946, in southern France, depicting a love affair between a French soldier and an American singer.[5]

After World War II, Pommer assisted the American military in rehabilitating the German film industry. He started to produce films in Germany again, enlisting actors and screenwriters, with whom he worked during the Weimar Republic. Pommer died in 1966 in Los Angeles, California.

## Screenwriters

**Carl Zuckmayer**, acclaimed author and playwright, left Germany to live in the United States in 1939, after his plays were banned and his German citizenship revoked. Zuckmayer returned to Europe from Vermont to live in Switzerland in 1958. He collaborated on the script for *The Blue Angel*, but is best known for his plays *Der Hauptmann von Koepnick* (1931, The Captain from Koepnick), and *Des Teufels General* (1946, The Devil's General), which was filmed in 1955. He died in Switzerland in 1977. **Robert Liebmann** left Germany in 1933 for France. He wrote the script for Hans Albers's 1932 film *Der Sieger* (The Victor), as well as the lyrics for the title song of the play *Hoppla, jetzt komme ich* (Hoppla, I'm coming). In 1934, Liebmann worked with Billy Wilder in Hollywood on the screenplay of Joe May's *Music in the Air*, which Pommer produced, and *Lumières des Paris* (1937, Lights of Paris).[6] **Karl Vollmöller**, known as both author and screenwriter, left Germany and worked with von Sternberg in Hollywood on *The Shanghai Gesture* (1941). In 1911, he wrote the screenplay *The Miracle*, which was performed on Broadway in the 1920s. He is the author of the novel *Schmutziges Geld* (Dirty money), which was adapted in 1928 for film and directed by Richard Eichberg. Vollmöller died in Los Angeles in 1948.

## Actors

### *Emil Jannings ... Professor Immanuel Rath*

**Emil Jannings** became one of Ufa's most celebrated actors. Born Theodor Friedrich Emil Janenz on July 23, 1884, Jannings lived as a German citizen in Rorschach, Switzerland, before moving to Leipzig and then Görlitz. His mother was a Volga German and his father an American factory owner, who traveled much and who eventually left his wife with their four children. In his memoir, *Mein Leben*, Jannings describes his difficulties with school and the pursuit of his rather short-lived career as a merchant marine at the age of fifteen, which he abandoned to become an actor. His first performance in Görlitz led to other stage performances in the provinces, where, in addition to learning his trade, he learned to supplement his meager earnings by "Zettlen" (selling tickets and simultaneously begging for food). His nomadic existence took him to Burgstein, Spremberg, and Glogau, before receiving his first major role in 1915, in Max Reinhardt's Deutsches Theater, where he and Werner Krauss became close friends.[7]

In *Mein Leben*, published posthumously in 1951, Jannings predominantly outlines the development of his prolific career. Among the characters that most fascinated him, he recalls Judge Adam in Heinrich von Kleist's play *Der zerbrochene Krug* (*The Broken Jug*), who Jannings portrayed on various stages throughout Germany, as well as in film. Ironically, his initial attitude toward film was lackluster at best: "I never went to the movies and thought that the whole thing was pure show until I realized with growing envy that this peculiar profession was earning a number of my colleagues a pretty penny."[8] His entrée into film was Louis Ralph's 1914 *Passionels Tagebuch*, followed by *Im Schützengraben* and *Arme Eva*, all made in the same year. Other films soon followed such as Lubitsch's 1918 *Die Augen der Mumie Ma* with Pola Negri, and 1919 *Madam Dubarry*, which afforded him international recognition. In 1922, he established, with Paul Davidson, the Emil Jannings Film Corporation, which folded after one year.[9] After World War I, Jannings starred in some of Germany's most significant silent films, most notably in Friedrich Murnau's *The Last Laugh*, *Tartuffe*, and *Faust*, and Ewald André Dupont's *Varieté*. Because of his extraordinary success in Germany, Paramount recruited Jannings in 1926, as it did many prominent German actors and directors. Based on his performance in Viktor Fleming's 1927 *The Way of the Flesh* and Josef von Sternberg's 1928 *The Last Command*, Jannings received one of the first Oscars for best actor.

Despite his desire to remain in the United States, Jannings soon understood the threat that the introduction of sound posed to his career. Since his English was neither fluent enough for audiences to understand, nor for him to portray characters in all of their complexity, Jannings half-heartedly returned to Germany in May of 1929. He settled in Austria (Wolfgangsee), and months later began work on *The Blue Angel*.

Tellingly, Jannings hardly mentions *The Blue Angel* in his memoir except to credit himself with taking von Sternberg to see Kaiser's play, *Two Bow Ties*, and with recommending Dietrich for the part of Lola. In his own memoir, von Sternberg remembers going against his own vow never to make another film with Jannings because of the difficulties he had with the actor during the filming of *The Last Command*. While making *The Blue Angel*, von Sternberg constantly had to placate Jannings, an extreme narcissist, who periodically launched into jealous fits over von Sternberg's relationship to Dietrich. Dietrich recalls the crew waiting hours for Jannings to appear on the set. Moreover, Jannings advised her to ignore von Sternberg's suggestions, if she aspired to becoming a star.[10] His jealousy of her was so great that he nearly strangled Dietrich in the scene in which Rath attacks Lola.

After making *The Blue Angel*, Jannings continued his theater and film career in Germany.[11] It was not until the Third Reich that Jannings' career made a comeback. He received numerous awards from the government in recognition of his talent. Jannings starred in films such as *Der alte und der junge König* (Hans Steinhoff, 1935), in which he played Friedrich Wilhelm I, the King of Prussia, *The Broken Jug* (Gustav Ucicky, 1937), *Robert Koch* (Hans Steinhoff, 1939), and the anti-British propaganda film and one of the most expensive films produced during the Third Reich, *Ohm Kröger*

(Hans Steinhoff, 1941). In 1938, Joseph Goebbels awarded him the "Adlerschild," and in 1944, conferred Jannings the title of "State Artist," in honor of his talent and enthusiastic support of the regime.[12]

Like many German actors who remained in Germany during the Nazi period, Jannings was denazified after 1945, but remained a persona non grata in the international film community because of his support of the regime. After the war, he converted from Protestantism to Catholicism, became an Austrian citizen, and withdrew to his farm in Austria, where he died of cancer in 1950.[13]

## Kurt Gerron ... Kiepert, The Magician

One of the most vibrant figures in Berlin's cabaret and film scene, **Kurt Gerron** was deported to Auschwitz at the end of October 1944, and murdered. Born Gerson on May 11, 1897, in Berlin, he changed his name to Gerron in 1921, in order to avoid being associated with Berlin's large fashion center, Gerson. Gerron first studied medicine. With the outbreak of World War I, after being drafted and seriously wounded, Gerron returned to studying medicine until his recruitment as a physician. Realizing the futility of patching up his fellow soldiers only to send them back to the front, Gerron became a pacifist, and after the war participated in the Revolutionary Soldier Councils in 1919. Breaking off his medical studies because of his newly discovered interest in acting, Gerron first tested his abilities at an artist café and then accepted his first minor film role in *Spuk auf Schloss Kitay* in 1920. Because of an overactive thyroid, Gerron gained weight after the war, which stayed with him throughout his life and became his trademark. Between 1921 and 1922, he performed at Trude Hesterberg's Wilde Bühne and at Rosa Valetti's cabaret Grössenwahn. By the mid-1920s, Gerron was appearing on stages throughout Berlin and in a number of films. In 1925, he played a longshoreman in E.A. Dupont's film *Varieté*, and a pimp alongside Hans Albers in Richard Oswald's film *Halbseide*. To Gerron's chagrin, he was typecast in seedy roles, from which he never was able to break away. Among his most noteworthy roles was Tiger Brown in Bertolt Brecht's 1929 *Threepenny Opera* and the performance of the songs "Und der Haifisch, der hat Zähne" (Mac, the Knife) and "Soldaten wohnen auf den Kanonen." His performance in *Happy End* was Gerron's last performance in a play by Brecht, owing to a heated exchange between director and actor.

In *The Blue Angel*, Gerron delivers one of his finest film performances. As Ulrich Liebe writes, *The Blue Angel* "turns Kurt Gerron into a known entity; his performance will outlive him and secure him posterity."[14] After making *The Blue Angel*, Gerron continued to prove his versatility. During the day, he could be found on a film set performing the role of a lawyer in *Die drei von der Tankstelle*, and then in the evening playing the role of a film director in Fritz von Unruh's play *Phaea* at the Deutsches Theater.[15] His last films were Hanns Schwarz's 1931 *Bomben auf Monte Carlo*, E.A. Dupont's 1931 film *Salto Mortale*, and Joe May's 1932 *Zwei in einem Auto*, filmed for Pathé in Paris.

In addition to his film, theater, and cabaret performances—his Nelson-Revues were known as smash hits—Gerron became one of Ufa's most accomplished directors within five years of making his first film, *Der Liebe, Lust und Leid* (1926). His film career began with six cabaret shorts and flourished with such popular feature-length comedies as *Meine Frau, die Hochstaplerin* (1931). In 1933, Gerron directed one of his final films, *Heute kommt's drauf an*, starring Hans Albers who conducts the Weintraub Syncopators. While "the popular Gerron still seems to be safe at the premier of the film in March 1933, ... even though the *Völkische Beobachter* reported that the weak plot 'reflects the intellectual niveau of the director Kurt Gerson,'" his career in Germany would soon come to an abrupt end.[16] On April 1, 1933, Goebbels called for the expulsion of so-called "non-Germans" from Germany's film studios ("die Entjudung der Kulturberufe"), and four days later, Gerron was forced off the set while filming *Amor an der Leine*. He left without protest but in tears.[17] Hans Steinhoff, a devoted Nazi, finished the film.

In June of 1933, the Gerrons, like many German Jews, left for Paris, where Kurt Gerron performed in cabarets, and where, through old contacts, he was able to direct the film *Incognito* and co-direct *Une femme au volant*. However, as job opportunities in France became scarcer with the influx of German émigrés, French nationals, who saw their jobs threatened, pressured studios. Gerron, consequently, moved to Vienna, where he directed *Bretter, die die Welt bedeuten* with Tobis films. Because of the dwindling market for his films (since his films could not be exported to Germany), he again faced unemployment. Forced to leave Austria, Gerron moved to Holland, where he became fondly known as "Papa Gerron," directing films despite the linguistic barriers. Jealous of his success, the local talent put a nail in his film career. The Nelson-Revue, whose cast lived in Amsterdam in exile, provided Gerron with a last home and source of income. Jewish actors were permitted to perform for Jewish audiences only, once the Nazis occupied the Netherlands in 1941. In 1943, as the mass deportation of Jews began, Gerron and his wife Olly were transported to Westerbork, a camp close to the German–Dutch border, and then in 1944, to Theresienstadt. Here, Gerron established the cabaret Das Karussell, content to have an activity to pass the time.[18] It was here that Gerron directed the infamous propaganda film, *Der Führer schenkt den Juden eine Stadt* (Hitler gifts the Jews a city). It was used to assure the Red Cross and the international community that the conditions in Theresienstadt were humane.[19] Gerron had hoped that his cooperation would spare him and his wife their lives, but instead they were deported to Auschwitz soon after the completion of the film.

## Hans Albers ... Mazeppa, The Strongman

**Hans Albers** stayed in Germany throughout the Third Reich and became one of Germany's most popular actors during the 1930s and 1940s; his fans affectionately referred to him as "the blonde Hans." His career began in 1911. Like Jannings, Albers started as a "Volksschauspieler," playing on provincial stages in Schandau and Güstrow, before moving to the Thalia Theater in Hamburg, the city of his birth, where he continued to play minor roles. Military service interrupted his acting career, until he was wounded and released from service. In 1917, Albers decided to leave the provinces and try his luck in Berlin; however, theater audiences barely took any notice of the unknown actor. He attracted more attention as the companion of the famous opera singer Claire Dux. With her help, Albers landed a job at the Theater des Westens, and continued to play minor roles, which he depended on for his livelihood, like Dietrich and many other stage actors during the 1920s. In 1923, Albers left Dux and began his lifelong relationship with the actress Hansi Burg, whose father, Eugen Burg, was a well-known actor and theater director. Through Burg, Albers was able to establish himself as an actor in comedies and revues, where he was typecast as the petty criminal and elegant womanizer, playing to such famous female stars as Blandine Ebinger and Fritzi Massary. By the mid-1920s, Albers could be seen almost every evening on Berlin's most prominent stages.[20]

Although Albers appeared in over a hundred silent films, his success was launched with sound. The orthochromatic film stock that was used during the 1920s worked to his disadvantage, giving the blonde and light-blue-eyed Albers a washed-out look.[21] Capitalizing on his experiences in revues and musicals as an actor and singer, Albers reportedly brought a naturalness to sound film that silent film actors had not yet achieved. In his first major role in Carl Froelich's 1929 film *Die Nacht gehört uns*, Germany's first successful sound film, Albers, according to Kracauer, quickly became "Deutschlands Filmliebling Nr. 1" (Germany's number one film darling).[22] Von Sternberg cast him as Mazeppa in *The Blue Angel* after seeing Albers in the Kaiser play *Two Bow Ties*. From there, he went on to play the title role in Richard Eichberg's 1930 film *Der Greifer*, Carl Froelich's 1930 *Hans in allen Gassen*, and to star, for the first time, in the 1931 play, *Liliom*, which became an immediate hit because of Albers's new fame. The films that followed were all blockbusters, so that Albers soon became one of Germany's highest-paid actors. His extraordinary appeal stemmed from his representation as an everyman.[23] He was cast as a go-getter, as the name of the film *Der Draufgänger* implied, who stole the hearts of his audiences. He was also known among directors as someone who did not learn his lines and was dependent on "der Neger," a blackboard, on which his lines were written.[24]

In April of 1933, the dramatic political changes in Germany that took hold of Germany's film industry would affect Albers both professionally and personally. Among the many first victims of Goebbels's anti-Semitic plan to rid the film industry of Jews was Eugen Burg, Hansi Burg's father and Albers's close friend, who, despite his conversion to Protestantism, was forced to leave his film career. Burg died in 1944 in Theresienstadt. Albers's companion, the German Jewish actress Hansi Burg, left Germany, but the couple continued to see each other abroad. Pressured to end his relationship with Burg, Albers officially informed the Propaganda Ministry of their separation. Shortly thereafter, Burg married a Norwegian, Erich Blydt, but returned to Berlin to live with Albers until 1939. Since Albers chose to remain in Germany because of his career, he and Burg agreed to separate temporarily once war broke out. Burg fled to England through Switzerland and returned to Germany in 1946 to live with Albers.

Yet, even though Albers stayed in Germany, it was known that he was no friend of the regime. Actors who were allowed to remain in Germany were required to join the film ministry by July 14, 1933. Despite the number of warnings and threats, Albers stalled at becoming a member of the *Reichsfilmkammer* until January 10, 1934. He was tolerated because of his immense fame, which he exploited on every occasion. Also, in answer to the question of race and religion on a questionnaire, Michaela Krützen writes that Albers responded, "possibly Lutheran," in contrast to Willy Fritsch who answered "Arian Catholic."[25] Many tensions persisted in the relationship between Albers and the Nazi Party, especially early on, when the Nazi regime rigorously imposed its agenda on cultural production. For instance, accustomed to receiving top billing, Albers protested when his name appeared together with other actors' names in the credits, a policy the Nazis initially introduced to dismantle the star system and promote collectivity. Despite Albers's continued success, the Ufa reduced his salary, which led to a dispute with the head of the Reichsfachschaft Film. He was expelled briefly from the Reichsfilmkammer and the play *Liliom*, so closely associated with Albers's name, was banned. Furthermore, on returning home from location shots in Norway for *Peer Gynt*—one of Bavaria's most costly films—a travel ban was imposed on him. With the relaxation of the initial concept of the "collective propaganda film," Albers's travel ban was lifted and his salary raised. His successful career as an actor under the Third Reich continued with such popular films as *Sergeant Berry* (Selpin, 1938), *Wasser für Canoga* (Selpin, 1939), *Münchhausen* (von Baky, 1941), and *Die grosse Freiheit Nr. 7* (Käutner, 1943).

With the end of the war, Albers made a number of films with many of the same directors with whom he worked during the Third Reich, and who along with him were denazified. Because of his age and the emergence of a new generation of talent that appealed more to the time, it became increasingly difficult to maintain his star status. Albers died in 1960, at the age of sixty-nine, and was buried in Hamburg.

### Rosa Valetti ... Gusti Kiepert

**Rosa Valetti** left Germany in 1933, and performed in Vienna and Prague and then in Palestine, where she died in 1937. She was born Rosa Vallentin in 1878. Famed as a character actress on Berlin's stages, in cabaret, and in film, she founded the cabaret Grössenwahn in 1920 on the Kurfürstendamm, where she sang such provocative political songs as "Die rote Melodie," (lyrics by Kurt Tucholsky and music by Friedrich Hollaender) and "Berlin Simultan" (lyrics by Walter Mehring). In 1922, Valetti gave up cabaret to devote herself fully to acting. She appeared in Brecht's *Three Penny Opera* in 1929, as Frau Peachum, and in an array of minor roles in other Weimar films.

### Karl Huszar-Puffy ... Innkeeper

Born **Karoly Huszar** in Budapest, Hungary in 1884, Huszar was a former champion swimmer, stage actor, and musical comedy writer. In Germany, he appeared in Fritz Lang's *Der müde Tod* (1921) and *Dr. Mabuse, der Spieler* (1922), and, like many other European actors, Huszar decided to try his luck in Hollywood.[26] By 1924, he changed his name to Charles Puffy, and performed in such films as John McDermott's *The Love Thief* (1926) and Alexander Korda's *Yellow Lily* (1928). With the advent of sound, Huszar returned to Germany to play minor roles in a number of films, among them *Ich küsse Ihre Hand, Madam*, directed by Robert Land and starring Marlene Dietrich, in which he played Dickerchen. Von Sternberg describes him as a "rotund, jovial actor who often beat me at chess and who was among my most ardent admirers."[27] Huszar-Puffy left Germany in 1933, and died in Tokyo in 1942.

### Reinhold Bernt (Bienert) ...The clown

**Reinhold Bernt** remained in Germany during the Third Reich, playing minor roles in numerous films and writing screenplays. After studying acting, he founded, along with his older brother, the actor Gerhard Bienert, the politically progressive troupe "Gruppe junger Schauspieler" (group of young actors) which traveled abroad, before appearing in films and on stages in Berlin. In 1930, Bernt played in the Nelson-Revue, *Glück muss man haben*, directed by Kurt Gerron, and took on a number of minor roles in films. During the 1930s, Bernt turned to screenplay writing primarily for the Bavarian comedians Karl Valentin and Lisl Karstadt. In 1949, he signed on with DEFA (the East German Film Studio). Known as a leftist actor, Bernt performed in *Der Draufgänger*, starring Hans Albers, and later in in Staudte's *Rotation* (1949). He appeared on stages in minor roles in West Germany. He died by his own hand in 1981.[28]

### Carl Balhaus ... Pupil Ertzum

**Carl Balhaus** was born in 1906. He performed in a number of films throughout the 1920s and 1930s. After World War II, he worked in Munich as a director of radio plays and theater. From 1956 to 1962, Balhaus worked as a DEFA director and for television, and afterwards as a theater director in Leipzig. He died in 1968.[29]

### Robert Klein-Lörk ... Pupil Goldstaub

**Klein-Lörk** emigrated to the United States in 1933.

### Rolf Müller ... Pupil Angst

**Rolf Müller** was born in 1904. After 1933, he performed as a high school student in Carl Froelich's film *Traumulus* (1935), and in Robert Stemmle's *Der Raub der Sabinnerinnen* (1936). He died in 1988.

### Roland Varno ... Pupil Lohmann

**Roland Varno** was born in 1907 in Utrecht. Varno emigrated to the United States and played minor roles in films such as *My Name is Julia Ross* (1945).

### Ilse Fürstenberg ... Rath's Housekeeper

**Ilse Fürstenberg** remained in Germany during the Third Reich and continued to play minor roles in film. She was born Ilse Irmgard Funcke in Berlin on December 12, 1907, and attended the acting school at the Deutsches Theater in Berlin. She performed in Mannheim and Konstanz before returning to Berlin in 1928. After 1950, she performed at the Theater am Ku'damm and worked for Rias-SFB. She died in Basel, Switzerland in 1976.

### Eduard von Winterstein ... Headmaster

**Eduard von Winterstein** remained in Germany during the Third Reich. He began his acting career in 1889, performing in Idstein, Stralsund, and Gelsenkirchen with his sister and mother, Luise Dub. His first major roles were Egmont and Hamlet, in Annaberg. Two years later in 1895, he signed a three-year contract with the Schiller Theater in Berlin, where he met his second wife Hedwig Pauly. Tired of playing minor roles, Winterstein signed on with the Lessing Theater, where he played under the direction of Max Reinhardt. He continued to perform on Berlin's stages until after World War II.[30] Winterstein appeared in 150 films, beginning in 1911 and ending with the 1960 DEFA film, *Der schweigende Stern*. He received many awards for his work with DEFA. He died in 1961 in Berlin.

### Wilhelm Diegelmann ... Capitan

Born in 1861, **Wilhelm Diegelmann** began his career in 1913, with *Insel der Seligen*, which was followed by a number of film classics such as Lubitsch's *Prinz Sami* (1917) and *Anna Boleyn* (1920), Fritz Lang's *Der müde Tod* (1921), and Joe May's *Das indische Grabmal* and *Der Tiger von Eschnapur* (1921). Well known as a silent film actor, his transition into sound film was short-lived. He died in 1934 in Oberbayern.[31]

### Gerhard Bienert ... Policeman

**Gerhard Bienert** remained in Germany during the Third Reich. He attended the acting school of the Deutsches Theater, and founded with his brother "Gruppe junger Schauspieler" (group of young actors). During World War I, he became a lieutenant, and, after 1922, played on Berlin's stages (Reinhardt, Piscator, Barnowsky). After 1945, he performed at the Deutsches Theater and Theater am Schiffbauerdamm, worked for radio, and performed in many DEFA films until his death in 1986.

## Music

**Friedrich Hollaender** was born on October 18, 1896 to Victor and Rosa Hollaender, born Perl, while they were in London working for the Barnum Bailey Circus as composer and singer respectively. Hollaender's father was a composer and musical director for such varied venues as the Metropol Revue or the popular cabaret Überbrettl, or the Deutsches Theater in Berlin. Following in his parent's footsteps, Hollaender began his musical career in 1913, with two children's songs.[32] He spent World War I on the western front as the musical director of the Deutsches Theater, and then joined the postwar revolutionary forces in 1919, along with other authors and intellectuals. Resigning himself to the failure of the revolution, he turned to theater as a form of social change, and collaborated with a number of famous, like-minded Berlin intellectuals. In 1919, Hollaender composed music for Else Lasker-Schüler's play *Die Wupper*, directed by Max Reinhardt, who recruited Hollaender, along with a group of young authors, for his newly established cabaret, Schall und Rauch. Hollaender became the most ardent supporter of the new art form, writing countless texts and songs throughout the 1920s. In 1919, he met his first wife, the actress and cabaret performer Blandine Ebinger, whom he helped to stardom with the performance of the song "Johnny, wenn du Geburtstag hast." She performed it first at Rosa Valetti's Grössenwahn. The song gained popularity through Marlene Dietrich's performance in her 1930 film *Song of Songs*. In 1931, Hollaender founded his own Tingel Tangel, which became one of Berlin's most popular cabarets, and which provided an outlet for the multi-talented Hollaender who composed and wrote for such great performers as Kurt Gerron and the Nelson-Revue. His composition "Höchste Eisenbahn" (1932) poignantly anticipates the need for German Jews to flee Germany. For his revue *Es war einmal*, Hollaender invited musicians and authors (Eisler, Toller etc.) to rewrite well-known fairytales.

Alongside Hollaender's innovative cabaret compositions, the Ufa film studio commissioned Hollaender, often referred to as a "Hans in allen Gassen," to compose music for silent films and then later for sound films. In addition to the songs that he wrote for *The Blue Angel* ("Ich bin von Kopf bis Fuss auf Liebe eingestellt," "Nimm dich in acht vor blonden Frauen," and "Kinder, heut' abend, da suche ich mir was aus"), Hollaender scored music for eight other films in 1930. In 1932, he directed his own film, *Ich und die Kaiserin*, starring Conrad Veit and Lilian Harvey.

In 1933, Hollaender's career in Germany ended abruptly. The Nazis closed the Tingel Tangel, and shortly after the successful premiere of his film, they ransacked his apartment. The signs to leave were all too clear; Hollaender fled Germany to Paris with his second wife, Heidi Schoop, on the night the Reichstag burned. While in Paris, he met other displaced German Jews who awaited passage to elsewhere. After arranging a three-month probationary contract with Paramount, Hollaender, who changed his name to Frederick Hollander, was able to leave for the United States. Within a few months of his arrival, he wrote *Those Torn From the Earth*, a novel that depicts the life of exiled artists. Yet, despite his initial difficulties in Hollywood and the failed attempt to reestablish the Tingel Tangel, Hollaender went on to become a successful film composer. With the exception of Billy Wilder's film *A Foreign Affair*, he had to give up writing witty song lyrics.[33]

Hollaender returned to Germany in 1952, tired of Hollywood, but after visiting Dachau the horror so shocked him that he returned to the United States. Three years later, he moved to Munich where he wrote for the cabaret "Münchner 'kleine Freiheit.'" Realizing that times had changed, Hollaender retired from theater in 1961, devoting himself wholly to writing his memoir. He died in 1976 in Munich.

**Mischa Spoliansky** immigrated to England in 1933, where he continued his successful career "writing songs for at least 100 movies."[34] Spoliansky was born on December 28, 1898 in Bialystok, in the northeastern part of Poland. His father was the well-known opera singer, Pawlov Spoliansky. Mischa Spoliansky's childhood years are marked by his family's peripatetic lifestyle, moving from Warsaw, to Kalisz, to Vienna, to Dresden in an attempt to flee anti-Semitism, and then, more significantly, by his mother's death when Spoliansky was five years old. He began his formal training in piano, violin, and cello in Dresden and gave his first concert at the age of ten. Shortly thereafter, he lost his father.

In 1914, Spoliansky moved to Königsberg, and then, with the outbreak of World War I, to Berlin, where he continued studying music at the

Sternschen Konservatorium, and supported himself by playing the piano in various coffee houses. The Ufa Film and Theater orchestra included Spoliansky's early compositions in its repertoire, and through his work as the musical director of a Russian cabaret, Spoliansky met Friedrich Hollaender. In 1919, Hollaender invited Spoliansky to join the cabaret Schall und Rauch. Landing in Berlin's most vibrant cabaret scene, he composed music for the works of Kurt Tucholsky, Klabund, Joachim Ringelnatz, and accompanied cabaret performers like Rosa Valetti and Trude Hesterberg on piano.[35] In 1922, Spoliansky met Marcellus Schiffer and Margo Lion and collaborated with them on such cabaret hits as "Die Linie der Mode," performed at Hesterberg's Wilde Bühne, and other famous revue songs like, "Es liegt in der Luft" and "Wenn die beste Freundin mit der besten Freundin" (texts by Marcellus Schiffer), both of which Dietrich performed with Lion. Spoliansky also composed the music for the revue, *Two Bow Ties*, which resulted in von Sternberg recruiting him and "The Weintraub Syncopaters" for *The Blue Angel*. Spoliansky could play twenty-four instruments, sometimes two at a time.

After World War II, Spoliansky returned to Munich in hopes of continuing his career, yet without success. He contributed to two plays: Carl Zuckmayer's 1957 musical version of *Katharina Knie* (1928), with Hans Albers, and *Wie lernt man Liebe*, which premiered in 1967. He died on June 28, 1985 in London.

**Fritz Thiery** continued to work in Germany during the Third Reich. He was born in Mannheim on December 19, 1899. He studied engineering, worked for Siemens until 1929, and then became a sound expert ("Tonphotograph") for Ufa and assisted in building Ufa's Babelsberg-Atelier. From 1939 to1940, he supervised the Trick Film department at Babelsberg, and then directed production until 1945. After the war, he worked as a trustee for Bavaria Filmkunst and together with Erich Pommer worked to rehabilitate Germany's film industry.

## Cinematography

Director of Photography **Günther Rittau** worked as cameraman and director throughout the Third Reich. He was born in 1893 in Königshütte. He became involved in filmmaking in 1919, after studying science, medicine, architecture, and art at the Technical Institute in Berlin, specializing in photochemical processing. After his military duty, he worked in the department of cultural films (Kulturfilm) for Decla and Ufa, where he developed his skills as a cameraman. He was the cameraman for many silent films, developing special effects for films such as Fritz Lang's *Nibelungen* (with Carl Hoffmann) and *Metropolis* (with Karl Freund), Joe May's 1928 *Heimkehr* and 1929 *Asphalt*, as well as sound films such as *Melodie des Herzens* (1929), *Die drei von der Tankstelle* (1929), and

Karl Hartl's 1932 film *F.P. 1 antwortet nicht*. After World War II, he founded his own production company Stella-Film. Rittau's last feature-length film was *Die fidelen Detektive* in 1957. He died in 1971 in Munich.

**Hans Schneeberger** continued his work as cameraman on minor films throughout the Third Reich. He was born in 1895 in Brandberg/Zillertal, Austria and attended the Technical University in Munich, where he studied architecture and photography (Kameraausbildung) with Arnold Fanck. He was the cameraman for films such as G.W. Pabst and Arnold Fanck's 1929 *Die weisse Hölle vom Piz Palü*, Leni Riefenstahl's 1932 *The Blue Light*, and Fanck's 1933 *S.O.S. Eisberg*. In 1954, he was awarded the German Film Prize.[36]

## Set Design

**Otto Hunte** remained in Germany during the Third Reich and worked on numerous films. He was born in 1881 in Hamburg, where he studied at the College of Applied Arts. Between 1904 and 1913 he worked as a set designer for theaters in Berlin, and, after World War I, began working as a set designer and architect for Ufa. He worked on the set for Fritz Lang's *Nibelungen*, *Metropolis*, and *Spionen*, and became one of Germany's most renowned set designers. His career seamlessly continued throughout the Third Reich, crafting sets for thirty films, one of them the 1940 anti-Semitic Nazi propaganda film *Jud Süss*. In 1946, he worked on the set of *The Murderers Among Us* directed by Wolfgang Staudte, and then retired from the film industry in 1947. He died in Potsdam-Babelsberg in 1960.

**Emil Hasler** attended the Art Academy in Berlin and worked on stage sets until 1919, when he began working as a set designer in film ateliers. He collaborated on films such as Ernst Lubitsch's film *Die Bergkatze* (1921) and Ewald André Dupont's film *Varieté* (1925). He continued to work freelance throughout the Third Reich, during which time he contributed to 150 films, including *Münchhausen* (1943). After World War II, he worked for DEFA until 1959, and then during the 1960s for West German television.[37]

## Notes

1. S.S. Prawer, *The Blue Angel* (London: British Film Institute, 2002), 20.
2. See issue on "Film and Exile," in *New German Critique* 89, edited by Gerd Gemünden and Anton Kaes (Spring/Summer 2003); Lutz Koepnick, *The Dark Mirror: German Cinema between Hitler and Hollywood* (Berkeley: University of California Press, 2002); Thomas Elsaesser, "Ethnicity, Authenticity, and Exile: A Counterfeit Trade? German Filmmakers and Hollywood," *Home, Exile, Homeland: Film, Media, and the Politics of Place*, edited by Hamid Naficy (London and New York: Routledge, 1999), 97–124.
3. Wolfgang Jacobsen, *Erich Pommer: Ein Produzent macht Filmgeschichte* (Berlin: Argon, 1989), 56–57. ("So komme ich denn zur Hauptforderung des Films. Er soll alles enthalten.

Er soll den Anspruchsvollen befriedigen können wie auch den Anspruchslosen durch eine klare, spannende Handlung unterhalten. Dass man auch künstlerisch an einem solchen Film arbeitet, ist selbstverständlich. Aber die Kunst ist hier nicht Selbstzweck, sondern Hilfswerkzeug.)

4. Rainer Rother, ed., *Die UFA, 1917–1945: Das deutsche Bilderimperium* (Berlin: Stiftung Deutsche Kinemathek, 1993). When Ludwig Klitzsch invited Pommer to join the NSDAP (National Socialist German Worker's Party) on condition that he convert to Christianity, Pommer pointedly asked Klitzsch how his party could reconcile that a so-called second-class citizen could make first-rate films in the party's name.
5. See Jacobsen, 140.
6. See www.filmportal.de
7. See www.filmportal.de
8. Emil Jannings, *Mein Leben*, written by C.C. Bergius (Munich: Wilhelm Goldman, 1951), 109. ("Ich besuchte keine Kinos und hielt das Ganze für eine ausgesprochene Schaubudenangelegenheit, bis ich mit waschsendem Neid sah, dass einige Kollegen schönes Geld mit diesem sonderbaren Gewerbe verdienten.")
9. See www.filmportal.de. Also, Herbert Ihering, *Emil Jannings: Baumeister seines Lebens und seiner Filme* (Heidelberg: Verlagsanstalt Hüthig, 1941).
10. See Marlene Dietrich, *Ich bin Gott sein Dank, Berlinerin*, translated by Nicola Volland (Berlin: Ullstein, 2000), 81.
11. Joseph Wulf, ed., *Theater und Film im Dritten Reich: Eine Dokumentation* (Gütersloh: Sigbert Mohn Verlag, 1964), 331.
12. Michaela Krützen, *Hans Albers: Eine deutsche Karriere* (Weinheim: Beltz, 1995), 247: "künstlerischen Vorstandes der *Tobis*, trug das Komturkreuz der italienischen Krone, wurde 1939 mit der Goethemedaille und 1944 mit dem Kriegsverdienstkreuz geehrt. Den "Nationalpreis für Film und Buch" nahm er am 1. Mai 1937 entgegen, und seit 1941 trug er den 'Ehrenring des deutschen Films'."
13. http://www.filmportal.de CineGraph—Lexikon zum deutschsprachigen Film, edition text+kritik (Munich: Richard Boorberg Verlag 1984).
14. Ulrich Liebe, *Verehrt, Verfolgt, Vergessen: Schauspieler als Naziopfer* (Weinheim: Beltz, 2005), 41.
15. Liebe, 42.
16. Krützen, 149.
17. Liebe, 50.
18. Ilona Ziok, dir. *Kurt Gerrons Karussell* (1999).
19. Malcolm Clarke and Stuart Sender, dirs. *Prisoner of Paradise* (2003).
20. See www.filmportal.de
21. Krützen, 75.
22. Quoted in Krützen, 80.
23. Krützen, 133.
24. Krützen, 86.
25. Krützen, 148.
26. Hans J. Wollstein, "Charles Puffy," *New York Times* (October 16, 2006), 1. There are different accounts of Puffy's death. In the catalogue of a Marlene Dietrich exhibition, it states that he fled Budapest in 1941 through Russia and Japan in an attempt to reach Hollywood. He was interned with his wife in Vladivostock and died of dysentery in a gulag in Kazakhstan. See Werner Sudendorf and Hans Peter Reichmann, eds., *Marlene Dietrich*, Exhibition Catalog (Berlin: Kunst und Ausstellungshalle der Bundesrepublik Deutschland and Stiftung Deutsche Kinemathek, 1995).
27. Josef von Sternberg, *Fun in a Chinese Laundry* (New York: Macmillan, 1965), 43.
28. See *Glenzdorfs Internationales Filmlexikon: Biographisches Handbuch für das gesamte Filmwesen* (Bad Minder: Prominent-Filmverlag, 1961).
29. See Werner Sudendorf and Hans-Peter Reichmann, eds., *Marlene Dietrich*, 42.

30. Michaela Krützen writes that the Nazis kept a list of actors who were married to Jews and who were allowed to remain in the RFF. Winterstein's name appears among them. 154.
31. See http://www.cyranos.ch/smdieg-d.htm
32. See Friedrich Hollaender, *'und sonst gar nichts! Das Friedrich Hollaender Chanson-Buch*, edited by Volker Kuhn (Hannover: Fackelträger, 1996). Friedrich Hollaender, *Von Kopf bis Fuß. Revue meines Lebens* (Berlin: Aufbau, 2001).
33. Ibid.
34. *Cabaret Berlin: Revue, Kabarett und Film Music Between the Wars*, edited by Lori Münz (Hamburg: Edel Classics, 2005), 117.
35. Ibid. Also see, Jörg Süssenbach and Klaus Sander, directors, *Bis ans Ende der Welt*, ARTE.
36. See Sudendorf and Reichmann.
37. See the Marlene Dietrich Collection newsletter for an interview with Emil Hasler on his experiences on the set of *The Blue Angel: Newsletter 2* (March 15, 2000): www.marlenedietrich.org/pdf/News02.pdf

# BIBLIOGRAPHY

Abrams, Lynn. "From Control to Commercialization: the Triumph of Mass Entertainment in Germany 1900–25" *German History* 8.3 (1990), 278–93.
Adorno, Theodor. "On Popular Music." *Cultural Theory and Popular Culture: A Reader.* Edited by John Storey. Athens: University of Georgia Press, 1998, 197–209.
Arnheim, Rudolf. "Tonfilm-Verwirrung." *Kritiken und Aufsätze zum Film.* Edited by Helmut H. Diederichs. Frankfurt: Fischer, 1979, 61–64.
———. *Film als Kunst.* Frankfurt: Suhrkamp, 2002.
Bach, Steven. *Marlene Dietrich: Life and Legend.* New York: Morrow, 1992.
Baer, Volker. "Die Heimkehr der Marlene Dietrich." *Film-dienst* 20 (September 28, 1993), 34–35.
Balász, Béla. *Der Geist des Films.* Frankfurt am Main: Suhrkamp, 2001. (First published in 1930.)
———. *Theory of Film: Character and Growth of a New Art.* New York: Dover, 1970.
Baxter, Peter. *Sternberg.* London: British Film Institute, 1980.
———. "On the Naked Thighs of Miss Dietrich." *Movies and Methods II.* Edited by Bill Nichols. Berkeley: University of California Press, 1985, 557–64.
Bell-Metereau, Rebecca. *Hollywood Androgyny.* New York: Columbia University Press, 1993.
Bemmann, Helga. *Marlene Dietrich: Im Frack zum Ruhm: Ein Porträt.* Leipzig: Kiepenheuer, 2000.
Benjamin, Walter. "The Work of Art in the Age of Mechanical Reproduction." *Illuminations.* Translated by Harry Zohn. New York: Schocken Books, 1968.
Bollenbeck, Georg. "German Kultur, the Bildungsbürgertum, and Its Susceptibility to National Socialism." *German Quarterly* 73.1 (Winter 2000), 67–83.
Bourdieu, Pierre. "Distinction and The Aristocracy of Culture." *Cultural Theory and Popular Culture.* Edited and Introduced by John Storey. Athens: University of Georgia Press, 1998.
Boym, Svetlana. *The Future of Nostalgia.* New York: Basic Books, 2001.
Bronfen, Elisabeth. "Vertreibung aus dem vertrauten Heim: *Der blaue Engel* (Josef von Sternberg)." *Heimweh: Illusionsspiel in Hollywood.* Berlin: Verlag Volk & Welt, 1999, 97–142.
———. "Seductive Departures of Marlene Dietrich: Exile and Stardom in the *Blue Angel.*" *New German Critique* 89 (Spring/Summer 2003), 9–32.
Buck-Morss, Susan. "Dream World of Mass Culture: Walter Benjamin's Theory of Modernity and the Dialectics of Seeing." *Modernity and the Hegemony of Vision.* Cambridge, MA: MIT, 1991.
Carter, Erica. "Marlene Dietrich – The Prodigal Daughter." *The German Cinema Book.* Edited by Tim Bergfelder et al. London: British Film Institute, 2002, 71–80.
———. *Dietrich's Ghosts: The Sublime and the Beautiful in Third Reich Film.* London: British Film Institute, 2004.
Claus, Horst. "Varieté – Operette – Film: Berührungspunkte und Konkurrenzkampf aus der Sicht des Fachblattes 'Der Artist.'" *Musik Spektakel Film: Musiktheater und Tanzkultur im deutschen Film, 1922–1937.* Frankfurt am Main: Edition Text + Kritik, 1998, 67–84.
Coates, Paul. *Film at the Intersection of High and Mass Culture.* New York: Cambridge University Press, 1994.
Conor, Liz. *The Spectacular Modern Woman: Feminine Visibility in the 1920s.* Bloomington: Indiana University Press, 2004.

Constable, Catherine. *Thinking in Images: Film Theory, Feminist Philosophy and Marlene Dietrich*. London: British Film Institute, 2005.
Corrigan, Timothy. *Film and Literature: An Introduction and Reader*. Englewood Cliffs, NJ: Prentice-Hall, 1999.
Danius, Sara. *The Senses of Modernism: Technology, Perception, and Aesthetics*. Ithaca and London: Cornell University Press, 2002.
Davidson, David. "From Virgin to Dynamo: 'The Amoral Woman' in European Cinema." *Cinema Journal* 21.1 (Fall 1981), 31–58.
Desjardins, Mary. "Meeting Two Queens. Feminist Film-making, Identity Politics, and the Melodramatic Fantasy." *Film Quarterly* 3 (Spring 1995), 26–33.
Deleuze, Gilles. *Cinema 1: The Movement–Image*. Translated by Hugh Tomlinson and Barbara Habberjam. Minneapolis: University of Minnesota Press, 1986.
Dietrich, Marlene. *Marlene Dietrich: Ich bin, Gott sei Dank, Berlinerin*. Translated by Nicola Volland. Berlin: Ullstein Verlag, 2000.
———. *Marlene Dietrich's ABC*. Garden City, N.Y.: Doubleday, 1961.
Dirscherl, Luise, Gunther Nickel, and Werner Sudendorf, eds. *Der blaue Engel. Die Drehbuchentwürfe*. St. Ingbert: Röhrig Universitätsverlag, 2000.
Doane, Mary Ann. "The Erotic Barter: *Pandora's Box*." *The Films of G.W. Pabst: An Extraterritorial Cinema*. Edited by Eric Rentschler. New Brunswick, NJ: Rutgers University Press, 1990.
Döblin, Alfred. "Das Theater der kleinen Leute." *Prolog vor dem Film: Nachdenken über ein neues Medium, 1909–1914*. Edited by Jörg Schweinitz. Leipzig: Reclam, 1992, 153–55.
Donovan, Siobhán, and Robin Elliott. *Music and Literature in German Romanticism*. Rochester, NY: Camden House, 2004.
Dyer, Richard. *Heavenly Bodies: Film Stars and Society*. New York: St. Martin's Press, 1986.
Eisler, Hanns. *Composing for the Films*. New York: Oxford University Press, 1947.
Eisner, H. Lotte. *The Haunted Screen*. Berkeley: University of California Press, 1972.
Ermarth, Michael. "German Unification as Self-Inflicted Americanization." *"Here, There and Everywhere:" The Foreign Politics of American Popular Culture*. Edited by Reinhold Wagenleitner and Elaine Tyler May. Hanover, NH and London: University of New England Press, 2000, 251–70.
Firda, Richard. "Literary Origins: Sternberg's Film *The Blue Angel*." *Literature/Film Quarterly* 7 (1979), 126–36.
Flinn, Caryl. *Strains of Utopia: Gender, Nostalgia, and Hollywood Film Music*. Princeton, NJ: Princeton University Press, 1992.
Frame, Lynne. "Gretchen, Girl, Garçonne: Weimar Science and Popular Culture in Search of the Ideal New Woman." *Women in the Metropolis: Gender and Modernity in Weimar Culture*. Edited by Katharina von Ankum. Berkeley: University of California Press, 1997, 12–40.
Frevert, Ute. *Women in German History: From Bourgeois Emancipation to Sexual Liberation*. New York: Berg, 1984.
Garber, Marjorie. "From Dietrich to Madonna: Cross-Gender Icons." *Women and Film: Sight and Sound: Reader*. Edited by Pam Cook and Philip Dodd. London: Scarlet Press, 1993, 16–20.
Garncarz, Joseph. "Made in Germany: Multiple-Language Versions and the Early German Sound Cinema." *"Film Europe" and "Film America": Cinema, Commerce and Cultural Exchange, 1920–1939*. Edited by Andrew Higson and Richard Maltby. Exeter: University of Exeter, 1999, 249–73.
Geduld, Harry M. *Birth of the Talkies: From Edison to Jolson*. Bloomington: Indiana University Press, 1975.
Gems, Pam. *Marlene*. London: Oberon Books, 1998.
Gemünden, Gerd, and Mary R. Desjardins, eds. *Dietrich Icon*. Durham, NC: Duke University Press, 2007.
*Glenzdorfs Internationales Filmlexikon: Biographisches Handbuch für das gesamte Filmwesen*. Bad Minder: Prominent-Filmverlag, 1961.
Haemmerling, Konrad. *Sittengeschichte des Kinos*. Dresden: P. Aretz, 1929.

Hake, Sabine. *The Cinema's Third Machine: Writing on Film in Germany, 1907–1933*. Lincoln: University of Nebraska Press, 1993.

———. "Provocations of the Disembodied Voice: Song and the Transition to Sound in Berger's *Day and Night*. *Peripheral Visions: The Hidden Stages of Weimar Cinema*. Edited by Kenneth S. Calhoon. Detroit, MI: Wayne State University Press, 2001, 55–72.

Hansen, Miriam Bratu. "Benjamin, Cinema and Experience: 'The Blue Flower in the Land of Technology.'" *New German Critique* 40 (1987), 179–224.

———. "Mass Culture as Hieroglyphic Writing: Adorno, Derrida, Kracauer." *The Actuality of Adorno*. Edited by Max Pensky. Albany: State University of New York Press, 1997.

Heinzlmeier, Adolf. *Marlene: die Biographie*. Hamburg: Europa Verlag, 2000.

Hofmannsthal, Hugo. "The Substitute for Dreams." *German Essays on Film*. Edited by Richard W. McCormick and Alison Guenther-Pal. Translated by Lance W. Garmer. New York: Continuum, 2004, 52–56.

Hollaender, Friedrich. "Cabaret." *The Weimar Republic Sourcebook*. Edited by Anton Kaes, Martin Jay and Edward Dimenberg. Berkeley: University of California Press, 1994, 56–57.

———. *Von Kopf bis Fuss: Revue meines Lebens*. Edited by Volker Kühn. Berlin: Aufbau, 2001.

Ihering, Herbert. *Von Reinhardt bis Brecht: Vier Jahrzehnte Theater und Film, 1924–1929*. Vol. 3. Berlin: Aufbau Verlag, 1959.

Jacobsen, Wolfgang. *Erich Pommer: Ein Produzent macht Filmgeschichte*. Berlin: Argon, 1989.

Jacobsen, Wolfgang, Anton Kaes, and Hans Helmut Prinzler. *Geschichte des deutschen Films*. Stuttgart: Metzler, 1993.

Jannings, Emil. *Mein Leben*, written by C.C. Bergius. Munich: Wilhelm Goldman, 1951.

Jelavich, Peter. *Berlin Cabaret*. Cambridge, MA: Harvard University Press, 1993.

Jelinek, Elfriede. "Das zweite Gesicht." *Adieu Marlene: Nachruf aus Deutschland*. Edited by Fred Ostrowski. Berlin: Mariposa, 1992.

Kaes, Anton, ed. *Kino-Debatte: Texte zum Verhältnis von Literatur und Film, 1909–1929*. Munich: Deutscher Taschenbuchverlag, 1978.

———. ed. *Weimarer Republik: Manifeste und Dokumente zur deutschen Literatur, 1918–1933*. Stuttgart: Metzler, 1983.

———. "Weimarer Republik." *Geschichte des deutschen Films*. Edited by Wolfgang Jacobsen, Anton Kaes, and Hans Helmut Prinzler. Stuttgart: Metzler, 1993, 39–100.

Karasek, Hellmuth. "Filmhimmel ohne blauen Engel." *Der Spiegel* 20 (May 11, 1992).

———. "Der ungeliebte Engel." *Der Spiegel* 25 (June 29, 2000), 246.

Koch, Gertrud. "Between Two Worlds: Von Sternberg's *The Blue Angel* (1930)." *German Film and Literature*. Edited by Eric Rentschler. New York: Methuen, 1986, 60–71.

———. "Exorcised: Marlene Dietrich and German Nationalism." *Women and Film: A Sight and Sound Reader*. Edited by Pam Cook and Philip Dodd. Philadelphia, PA: Temple University Press, 1993, 10–165.

Kracauer, Siegfried. *From Caligari to Hitler*. Princeton, NJ: Princeton University Press, 1947.

———. "Internationaler Tonfilm?" *Der verbotene Blick: Beobachtungen, Analysen, Kritiken*. Leipzig: Reclam, 1992.

———. "Die kleinen Ladenmädchen gehen ins Kino." *Der verbotene Blick*. Leipzig: Reclam, 1992, 156–60.

———. *Theory of Film: The Redemption of Physical Reality*. Princeton, NJ: Princeton University Press, 1997.

Kreimeier, Klaus. *Die Ufa Story: Geschichte eines Filmkonzerns*. Munich: Carl Hanser, 1992.

Kreutzer, Hermann, and Manuela Runge, eds. *Ein Koffer in Berlin: Marlene Dietrich-Geschichten von Politik und Liebe*. Berlin: Aufbau Taschenbuch, 2001.

Krützen, Michaela. *Hans Albers: Eine deutsche Karriere*. Weinheim: Beltz Quadriga, 1995.

———. "'Esperanto für den Tonfilm': Die Produktion der Sprachversionen für den Tonfilm." *Positionen deutscher Filmgeschichte: 100 Jahre Kinematographie; Strukturen, Diskurse, Kontexte*. Munich: Diskurs Film, 1996, 119–54.

Kühn, Volker. *Spötterdämmerung: Vom langen Sterben des grossen kleinen Friedrich Hollaender*. Berlin: Parthas, 1996.

Ladd, Brian. *Ghosts of Berlin: Confronting German History in the Urban Landscape*. Chicago: University of Chicago Press, 1997.
Lemke, Karl *Heinrich Mann an seinem 75 Geburtstag*. Berlin: Aufbau Verlag, 1946.
Liebe, Ulrich. *Verehrt, Verfolgt, Vergessen: Schauspieler als Naziopfer*. Weinheim: Beltz, 2005.
Long, Christopher P. "Art's Fateful Hour: Benjamin, Heidegger, Art and Politics." *New German Critique* 83 (Spring/Summer 2001), 89–115.
Mann, Heinrich. *Professor Unrat*. Frankfurt am Main: Fischer, 1994 (originally 1905).
Mann, Heinrich, and Joseph von Sternberg. *The Blue Angel*. Translated and introduced by Stanley Hochman. New York: Frederick Ungar, 1979.
Mayne, Judith. "Marlene Dietrich, *The Blue Angel*, and Female Performance." *Seduction and Theory: Readings of Gender, Representation and Rhetoric*. Edited by Diane Hunter. Champagne-Urbana: University of Illinois Press, 1989, 28–46.
McCormick, Richard. *Gender and Sexuality in Weimar Modernity*. New York: Palgrave, 2001.
McCormick, Richard, and Alison Guenther-Pal, eds. *German Essays on Film*. New York: Continuum International Publishing, 2004.
Mentele, Richard. *Auf Liebe eingestellt: Marlene Dietrichs schöne Kunst*. Bensheim: Bollmann, 1993.
Mitchell, W.J. *What Do Pictures Want? The Lives and Loves of Images*. Chicago, IL: University of Chicago Press, 2005.
Moreck, Curt. *Führer durch das lasterhafte Berlin*. Leipzig: Verlag moderner Stadtführer, 1930.
Mühl-Benninghaus, W. *Das Ringen um den Tonfilm: Strategien der Elektro- und der Filmindustrie in den 20er und 30er Jahren*. Düsseldorf: Droste, 1999.
Nietzsche, Friedrich. "David Strauss – the Confessor and the Writer." *Untimely Meditations*. Edited by Daniel Breazeale. Translated by R.J. Hollingdale. London: Cambridge University Press, 2001.
O'Brien, Charles. *Cinema's Conversion to Sound: Technology and Film Style in France and the U.S.* Bloomington and Indianapolis: Indiana University Press, 2005.
Ossietzky, Carl von. "Der Film gegen Heinrich Mann." *Die Weltbühne* 26.18, (1930), 665–66.
Ostrowski, Fred. *Adieu Marlene. Nachruf aus Deutschland*. Berlin: Mariposa, 1992.
Paech, Joachim. *Literatur und Film*. Stuttgart: Metzler, 1997.
Petro, Patrice. *Aftershocks of the New: Feminism and Film History*. Brunswick, NJ: Rutgers University Press, 2002.
Pfannenschmidt, Christian, and Joseph Vilsmaier. *Marlene: Der Film*. Edited by Alfred Holighaus. Hamburg: Europa Verlag, 2000.
Pitman, Joanna. *On Blondes*. London: Bloomsbury, 2003.
Pommer, Erich. "The International Talking Film." *Universal Filmlexikon*. Edited by Frank Arnau. Berlin: Universal Filmlexikon, 1932, 13–16.
Prawer, S.S. *The Blue Angel (Der Blaue Engel)*. London: British Film Institute, 2002.
Rauch, Angelika. "The *Trauerspiel* of the Prostituted Body, or Woman as Allegory of Modernity." *Cultural Critique* (Fall 1988), 77–88.
Riva, David, dir. Documentary. *Marlene Dietrich: Her Own Song*. 2001.
Riva, David. *Marlene Dietrich Remembered*. Detroit, MI: Wayne State University Press, 2006.
Riva, Maria. *Marlene Dietrich: By Her Daughter*. New York: Alfred A. Knopf, 1993.
Rotthaler, Viktor. "Die Musikalisierung des Kinos: Die Komponisten der Pommer-Produktion." *Musik Spektakel Film: Musiktheater und Tanzkultur im deutschen Film, 1922–1937*. Edited by Hans-Michael Bock, Wolfgang Jacobsen, and Jörg Schöning. Munich: Edition Text + Kritik, 1998, 123–35.
Sanders-Brahms, Helma. *Marlene und Jo: Recherche einer Leidenschaft*. Berlin: Argon, 2000.
Sarris, Andrew. *The Films of Josef von Sternberg*. New York: Doubleday, 1966.
Saunders, Thomas J. *Hollywood in Berlin: American Cinema and Weimar Germany*. Berkeley: University of California Press, 1994.
Schebera, Jürgen. *Damals in Neubabelsberg: Studios, Stars und Kinopaläste im Berlin der zwanziger Jahre*. Leipzig: Edition Leipzig, 1990.
Schönbrunn, Walter. "Die Not des Literaturunterrichts in der grossstädtischen Schule." In *Weimarer Republik: Manifeste und Dokumente zur deutschen Literatur, 1918–1933*. Edited by Anton Kaes. Stuttgart: Metzler, 1983.

Schweinitz, Jörg. *Prolog vor dem Film: Nachdenken über ein neues Medium, 1909–1914.* Leipzig: Reclam, 1992.
Silverman, Kaja. *The Acoustic Mirror: The Female Voice in Psychoanalysis and Cinema.* Bloomington: Indiana University Press, 1988.
Slane, Andrea. *A Not So Foreign Affair: Fascism, Sexuality, and the Cultural Rhetoric of American Democracy.* Durham, NC: Duke University Press, 2001.
Soden, Kristine von, and Maruta Schmidt, eds. *Neue Frauen: Die zwanziger Jahre.* Berlin: Elefanten Press, 1988.
Spier, Ike. "Die sexuelle Gefahr im Kino." *Die neue Generation* 4. Edited by Helene Stöcker. (April 14, 1912), 192–98.
Spoto, Donald. *Falling in Love Again: Marlene Dietrich.* Boston, MA: Little Brown, 1985.
Staiger, Janet. *Perverse Spectators: The Practices of Film Reception.* New York: New York Press, 2000.
Sternberg, Josef von. *Fun in a Chinese Laundry.* New York: Macmillan, 1965.
———. "Introduction." *The Blue Angel: The Novel by Heinrich Mann, the Film by Josef von Sternberg.* New York: Frederick Ungar Publishing, 1979.
Storey, John. "The Culture and Civilization Tradition." *An Introduction to Cultural Theory and Popular Culture.* Athens: University of Georgia Press, 1998.
Stuckenschmidt, H.H. "So wird heute gesungen: Choräle aus dem Schlamm, eine Feststellung." *Uhu: Das Monats-Magazin* (June 1930), 44–47.
Studlar, Gaylyn. *In the Realm of Pleasure: von Sternberg, Dietrich and the Masochistic Aesthetic.* Urbana, IL: University of Illinois Press, 1988.
Sudendorf, Werner. "'Üb immer Treu und Redlichkeit': Zum *Blauen* Engel von Josef von Sternberg. *Mein Kopf und die Beine von Marlene Dietrich: Heinrich Mann Professor Unrat und Der blaue Engel.* Edited by Hans Wisskirchen. Lübeck: Kulturstiftung, 1996.
———. "'Deutsche sehe ich fast gar nicht mehr': Briefe von und an Marlene Dietrich." *Filmexil* 8 (November 1996), 5–44.
———. *Marlene Dietrich.* Munich: Deutscher Taschenbuch Verlag, 2001.
Süssenbach, Jörg, and Klaus Sander, dirs. Documentary. *Bis ans Ende der Welt: The Weintraub Syncopators* (2000).
Toles, George. "'This May Hurt a Little': The Art of Humiliation in Film." *Film Quarterly* 48 (Summer 1995), 2–14.
Tryster, Hillel. "Der blaue und weisse Engel: Marlene Dietrich in Israel 1960 und 1966." *Marlene Dietrich.* Edited by Werner Sudendorf und Hans-Peter Reichmann. Berlin: Deutsche Kinemathek, 1995, 80–87.
Uhlenbrok, Katja, ed. *Musik Spektakel Film: Musiktheater und Tanzkultur im deutschen Film, 1922–1937.* Munich: Edition Text + Kritik, 1998.
Vaerting, Mathilde. "Die heutige Rolle der Virginität im Seelenleben des jungen Mädchens." *Der Querschnitt* 12.4 (April 1932), 246–48.
Walker, Alexander. *Marlene Dietrich.* New York: Applause Books, 1999.
Ward, Janet. *Weimar Surfaces: Urban Visual Culture in 1920s Germany.* Berkeley, CA: University of California Press, 2001.
Wehnert, Stefanie, and Nathalie Bielfeldt, eds. *Mein Kopf und die Beine von Marlene Dietrich. Heinrich Manns 'Professor Unrat' und 'Der blaue Engel'.* Lübeck: Buddenbrookhaus, 1996.
Weinberg, Herman G. *Josef von Sternberg: A Critical Study.* New York: E.P. Dutton and Co., 1967.
Weiss, Andrea. "'A Queer Feeling When I Look At You:' Hollywood Stars and Lesbian Spectatorship in the 1930s." *Stardom: Industry of Desire.* Edited by Christine Gledhill. London and New York: Routledge, 1991, 283–99.
Weisstein, Ulrich. "Translations and Adaptations of Heinrich Mann's Novel in Two Media." *Film Journal* 1.3–4 (1972), 53–61.
Wiebrecht, Ulrike, ed. *"Marlene und Berlin: Sonderausgabe zum 100. Geburtstag." Vernissage: Die Zeitschrift zur Ausstellung* (2001).
Wiebrecht, Ulrike. *Blauer Engel aus Berlin: Marlene Dietrich.* Berlin-Brandenburg: be bra verlag, 2001.
Witkin, Robert W. *Adorno on Popular Culture.* London and New York: Routledge, 2003.
Witzig-Zalkind, Birgit. *Marlene Dietrich in Berlin: Wege und Orte.* Berlin: Edition Gauglitz, 2006.
Wood, Ean. *Dietrich: A Biography.* London: Sanctuary, 2002.

## Filmography of Dietrich's German Films

*Der kleine Napoleon* (The Little Napoleon, 1923)

*Der Mensch am Wege* (A Person by the Roadside, 1923)

*Der Sprung ins Leben* (The Leap into Life, 1924)

*Manon Lescaut* (1926)

*Kopf hoch, Charly!* (Heads up, Charly!, 1926)

*Eine Du Barry von Heute* (A Modern Day Du Barry, 1927)

*Madame wünscht keine Kinder* (Madame Doesn't Want Children, 1927)

*Der Juxbaron* (The Imaginary Baron, 1927)

*Sein grösster Bluff* (His Greatest Bluff, 1927)

*Café Electric* (Cafe Electric, Austrian 1927)

*Prinzessin Olala* (Princess Olala, 1928)

*Ich küsse Ihre Hand, Madame* (I kiss your Hand, Madam, 1929)

*Die Frau, nach der man sich sehnt* (The Woman Everyone Longs For, 1929)

*Das Schiff der verlorenen Menschen* (The Ship of Lost Souls, 1929)

*Gefahren der Brautzeit* (Dangers of the Engagement Period, 1929)[/ref]

# Index

"Ach, wie ist's möglich denn" (folksong), 122, 198
Adorno, Theodor, 19n, 29, 81n, 133
and Horkheimer, 27, 126
Albers, Hans, 44, 115, 136n, 170, 174–5, 180, 182n, 187n
Allen, Woody, 76–7
Amann, Betty, 3, 30
Americanization (of Germany), 7–8, 27, 142, 149
See also Americanism, 8, 29, 96, 149
Anderson, Benedict, 9
Anderson, Lale, 156
"Ännchen von Tharau" (folksong), 118, 121–22, 125
Anti-Semitism, 162n, 179
See Nazism
Arnheim, Rudolf, 49n
Arnim, Achim von, 122
*Asphalt*, 3, 30, 180
Atamann, E. Kutlug, 156–7
*Autorenfilm*, 12
See also *Filmdichter*, 26

Bacon, Lloyd, 114
Balász, Béla, 8, 19n, 23, 32, 49n, 74, 82n
Balhaus, Carl, 177
Barthes, Roland, 68, 158
Bassermann, Albert, 12
Bäumer, Gertrud, 94
Baxter, Peter, 21n, 61,63
Beckmann, Max, 40
Behne, Adolf, 11, 34, 36–7
Benjamin, Walter, 23, 31, 49n, 53–5, 61, 79n, 82n
Berlin
commemoration of Dietrich, 146
*Kulturstadt*, 144
See also Potsdamer Platz
Bernt, Reinhold, 118, 176
Bienert, Gerhard, 178

Bildungsbürger, 9, 14, 25, 28, 46, 77, 152
See also Bildungsbürgertum, 16–7, 28, 34, 48n, 54, 60
black ("Lenci") doll, 14, 67, 68, 81, 120, 121, 124
Blauer Engel restaurant, 145
*Blue Angel (Der blaue Engel)*
adaptation, 5, 26
German premier, 3, 12–3, 17, 24, 26, 51n, 115–16, 133, 139
remake, 82n, 150
reviews of, 24–5, 115–17
US premier, 4, 73
Bloch, Ernst, 121
*Blonde Venus*, 5, 55, 60, 108n, 149, 153
Borzage, Frank, 21n, 151
Bourdieu, Pierre, 35, 43, 57, 75
Boym, Svetlana, 144
Brecht, Bertolt, 12, 48n, 172, 176
Brentano, Clemens, 122
Brod, Max, 13, 96
Bronfen, Elisabeth, 6, 45, 62–3, 80n, 83n, 127, 137n
Brooks, Louise, 3, 19n, 69, 95

cabaret 83n, 129, 131–2, 139n
See Varieté
Carter, Erica, 81n, 150–52
clown, 41, 118–19, 137n
Corrigan, Timothy, 14, 48n

da Acosta, Mercedes, 164n
deception, and modernity, 60, 74–5
and performance, 16, 44, 131, 147
sound, 127
Deleuze, Gilles, 77–8
*Desire*, 151
Desjardins, Mary, 6
*Des Knaben Wunderhorn*, 123
*Destry Rides Again*, 45n, 163n
*Devil is a Woman*, 53–5, 159

*Diary of a Lost Girl* (*Tagebuch eines verlorenen Mädchens*), 3
*Die Frau, nach der man sich sehnt* (The woman for whom everyone longs), 3, 13–4, 20n, 190
Diegelmann, Wilhelm, 178
*Die Nacht gehört uns* (The Night Belongs to Us), 115, 174
"Die schöne Müllerin," 121, 124
Dietrich, Marlene (Maria Magdalena Dietrich-Siebert)
  acting style, 24, 32, 49n, 80n, 96–8
  in advertisements, 79n, 133
  "Berlinerin," 142, 148
  cross-dresser, 5, 91, 160
  as cultural icon, 16, 29, 144, 147, 150, 158–9
  fashion, 78, 80n, 92, 106, 146, 157
  *flaneur*, 100
  German American identity, 152
  legs, 26, 30, 61–2
  return to Germany (1960), 146, 151, 162n
  sexual ambiguity 30, 91–2, 96, 106, 160
  US citizenship, 142
  USO career, 133, 146, 151, 153
  Weimar's modern woman, 86–7, 144, 157
  *See also Ich bin, Gott sei Dank, Berlinerin*
Dirscherl, Luise, 6, 125
*Dishonored*, 5, 149
Dmytryk, Edward, 82n
Doane, Mary Ann, 59, 70, 109n
Döblin, Alfred, 33, 95
Dupont, André Ewald, 1, 171–3, 181
Dyer, Richard, 158

Eisner, Lotte, 55, 131–2
"Es liegt in der Luft" (song), 97
Expressionism, 30, 44, 96, 198

Fassbinder, Rainer Werner, 21n, 154, 156, 164
*Faust*, 1
  *See also* Gretchen 39, 89–90, 151
Femme fatal, 88
  Dietrich's image as, 5, 10, 55
fetishization of Dietrich, 5, 16
  consumerism 147
  and distance, 55, 61–4, 75
  leg fetish, 61, 73, 129
  and masochism, 64, 68, 77
Firda, Richard, 5
Fleisser, Marieluise, 108n
Flinn, Caryl, 119, 138n, 164n
Ford, Henry, 96

*Foreign Affair*, 149, 151, 179
Frankfurt School 17
Froelich, Carl, 9, 115, 174, 177
"Frühling kommt, der Sperling piept" (Spring has come, the sparrow sings) (song), 132
Fürstenberg, Ilse, 177

Garber, Marjorie, 96, 108n, 157, 164n
Garbo, Greta, 14, 147, 158, 163n, 164n
Gems, Pam, 147
Gemünden, Gerd, 6
gender and mass culture, 32–3, 35, 70, 81n, 85–6
  lexicon of, 90–1
  roles, 8, 29, 87
  *See also* modern woman
Germany
  Americanization, 7–8, 149–50
  Dietrich's posthumous reception, 142–4, 159–60
  German unification, 142, 144, 147, 149, 152, 158–9
  Germanness, 11, 24, 28–30, 123, 144, 149, 151–2, 156
  "Land of Poets and Philosophers," 9
  national identity, 7–9, 15–16, 25–6, 35, 40, 112, 123, 142, 149–60
  *See* Goethe-Institute
Gerron, Kurt, 38, 41, 172–3, 176, 179
Gilbert, John, 164n
Goebbels, Joseph, 142, 161n, 168, 172, 173, 175
Goethe Institute, 158–9
Goethe, Johann Wolfgang von, 39, 43, 78, 148
Grosz, Georg, 40, 95, 100, 154
Grune, Karl, 30

Haas, Willy, 111–12
Hake, Sabine, 34, 119, 138n
*Hamlet*, 40, 58
Hansen, Miriam, 27, 60, 81
Hasler, Emil, 40, 181, 183n
Heine, Heinrich, 128, 152
Hemingway, Ernest, 111, 134
Hermann, Elsa, 88, 107n, 108n
Hesterberg, Trude, 172, 180
Hirschfeld, Magnus, 102
Höch, Hannah, 61, 80n, 89
Hofmannsthal, Hugo, 12, 53, 77
Hollaender, Friedrich, 38, 117, 120, 123, 125–6, 129, 132, 137n, 139n, 167, 176, 178–9

Hölty, Ludwig Christoph Heinrich, 40, 120, 122, 125, 138n
Hugenberg, Alfred, 25–6
Hunte, Otto, 30, 40, 72–3, 116, 181
Huszar-Puffy, Karl (Charles Puffy), 21n, 81n, 176, 182n

"Ich bin die fesche Lola" ("They call me naughty Lola") (song), 45, 132
*Ich bin, Gott sei Dank, Berlinerin*, 19, 148
*Ich küsse Ihre Hand, Madam* (I Kiss Your Hand, Madam), 3, 13–4, 20–21n, 190
Ihering, Herbert, 49, 96, 113, 116, 118
*In the Realm of Pleasure*, 4, 56

Jannings, Emil, 170–72
　acting style, 32, 32, 49n
　Oscar for best actor, 3, 23, 171
　as Rath portraying a failed Odysseus, 126, 128, 139n
　relationship to Dietrich, 171
　relationship to von Sternberg, 24
　sound technology, 114–15
Jelavich, Peter, 7, 75, 100, 131
Jelinek, Elfriede, 161n
*Joyless Street* (*Die freudlose Gasse*), 13
*Judgment at Nuremberg*, 149, 151, 156
*Jungfrau von Orléans*, 38

Kaes, Anton, 8, 88
Kaiser, Georg, 23, 171, 174
Karasek, Helmut, 141
Keun, Irmgard, 98–9, 109n
"Kinder, heut' abend da suche ich mir was aus, einen Mann, einen richtigen Mann" ("Children, this evening I gotta get a man, just a man, a real man" (song), 131, 179, 198
*Kino-Debatte* 15, 47n
Klein-Lörk, Robert, 177
Klitzsch, Ludwig, 24, 169, 182n
Koch, Gertrud, 6, 30, 150
Koepnick, Lutz, 152
Körner, Theodor, 144, 161n
Kracauer, Siegfried, 6, 25–9, 48n, 49, 61, 81n, 82, 86, 111, 119, 137, 163, 174
　"The Little Shop Girls Go to the Movies," 76–7
Kramer, Stanley, 151, 156
Krützen, Michaela, 136n, 175, 182n
Kühn, Volker, 147
*Kultur*, 7, 38, 45, 48n, 97

Landy, Marcy, 149

Lang, Fritz, 53, 61, 64, 79n, 88, 95, 113, 168–9, 176, 178, 180, 181
Lautrec, Toulouse, 23
Leander, Zarah, 151
legs of Marlene Dietrich, 5, 16
　fetishization of 61, 73, 129
　and modern woman 108n
Leoncavallo, Ruggero (*I Pagliacci/ Bajazzo*) (opera), 44, 135n
Lethen, Helmut, 97–8
Liebmann, Robert, 26, 36, 117, 126, 132
Liedtke, Harry, 13
*Lili Marleen*, 156
Lion, Margo, 97, 100, 180
*Lola* (Fassbinder), 155–6
*Lola and Billy the Kid*, 156
Lubitsch, Ernst, 4, 171, 178, 181

McCormick, Richard, 30, 73
Madonna, 165n
Mamoulian, Rouben, 46n, 151
Mann, Heinrich, 5, 9–11, 19n, 20n, 24–6, 47n, 48n, 82n, 133, 167, 169
　and premier of *The Blue Angel* 26
Mann, Thomas, 26, 35, 48n, 50n
Mannheim, Lucie, 117
*Marlene* (Gems play), 147–8
*Marlene* (Vilsmaier film), 152–5
*Marlene and Jo: Recherche einer Leidenschaft*, 6
*Marlene Dietrich Collection*, 139n, 145, 160, 183
*Marlene Dietrich: Her Own Song* (documentary), 148, 162n
*Marlene Dietrich Newsletter*, 160
Marshall Fund, 148
Marshall, George, 163n
masochism, 64, 69, 128; and fantasy, 68
　masochistic aesthetic, 63, 68, 74, 77, 86
　and Rath, 64, 79, 93, 130
　*See also* von Sternberg
May, Joe, 3, 30, 168, 180
Mayne, Judith, 6, 41, 62, 77, 83n, 137n, 155, 157
*Meeting of Two Queens*, 164n
"Meine beste Freundin" ("My Best Girlfriend"), (song) 100–101, 180
*Melodie des Herzens*, 115, 180
*Melodie der Welt*, 114
Merkel, Angela, 142, 164n
Messter, Oskar, 9, 134n
*Metropolis*, 13, 79n, 88, 113, 169, 180–81
Mitchell, W.J., 14, 18
Mitscherlich, Alexander and Margarete, (*The Inability to Mourn*), 142

Modern woman of the Weimar Republic, 89, 108–9n
  and cinema, 102
  employment, 86, 94–6
  marriage, 101–5, 110n
  specularization of, 65, 98, 198
  symbol of modernity, 96–7
  types 89–92, 107n
  *See also* Weimar Republic
*Morocco*, 4, 5, 46, 55, 73, 133
Mozart, Wolfgang Amadeus, 125, 138n
Müller, Rolf, 177
Mulvey, Laura, 61–3, 80n
Murnau, Friedrich, 1, 4, 13, 44, 171

National Socialism, 150
  Nazi, 94, 143, 148, 15052, 155, 161n, 163n, 167–8, 172, 173, 175, 179, 181, 183n
  Third Reich, 6, 25, 151, 156, 168
Negri, Pola, 171
New Objectivity (Neue Sachlichkeit), 32, 96, 102, 109n, 131, 198n
Nielsen, Asta, 113
"Nimm' dich in acht vor blonden Frauen" ("Beware of Blonde Women") (song), 90, 92, 128–30, 179

Pabst, G.W., 3, 13, 19n, 59, 69, 95, 109n, 181
*Pandora's Box (Die Büchse der Pandora)*, 3, 5
  (play), 13, 19n, 69, 95, 109n (film)
Paramount Studio, 56, 64, 169, 171, 179
  contract with Dietrich, 4–5, 23, 157
  delayed premier of *The Blue Angel* 46, 73
  remake of *The Blue Angel* 82n
Petro, Patrice, 6, 29, 32, 74, 98
Pinthus, Kurt, 24, 113, 117–18, 137n
Pommer, Erich 13, 24, 26, 30, 36, 113, 137n, 168–9, 180, 182n
Porten, Henny, 9, 30
Potsdamer Platz, 145, 156, 159
  *See* Marlene-Dietrich-Platz, 145
Prawer, S.S., 6, 26, 48n, 119–20, 125, 132, 167
*Professor Unrat* (Mann's novel), 5, 9–10, 24
*Purple Rose of Cairo*, 76

Rahn, Bruno, 30
*Rancho Notorious*, 53, 61
Rau, Johannes, 143
Remarque, Erich Maria, 157, 164n
Rentschler, Eric, 163n
Rialto Theater (US premier), 4
Rittau, Günther, 116, 180–81
Riva, David, 83n, 143, 149, 161n, 162n
Riva, Maria, 78, 80n, 92, 142, 145, 154, 159, 162n

Romanticism, 79n, 96, 122, 131
  role of artist, 12
  *See also* Romantics, 12, 123
Rops, Félicien, 10, 21n, 23
*Run Lola Run*, 156
Ruttmann, Walter, 114, 135n

Sagan, Leontine, 40
*Salvation Hunters*, 21
Sanders-Brahms, 30
Sarris, Andrew, 32, 63, 102
Saunders, Thomas, 35, 114, 116, 136n
Schell, Maximilian 1, 134
Schiffer, Marcellus, 97, 100, 180
Schiller, Friedrich, 29, 38, 48n
Schneeberger, Hans, 116, 181
Schroeder, Gerhard, 143
Schubert, Franz, 121, 124, 138n
Schygulla, Hannah, 156
Seeger, Pete, 155
Şenocak, Zafer, 145, 165n
sex appeal, 46n, 89–90, 107–8n, 144
sexuality and cinema, 102
  Dietrich's ambiguity 91–2, 96, 106, 163n
  lesbian, 100, 163n
  modern woman 101–2
*Shanghai Express*, 5, 55
Siebert, Rudolf, 153
*Singing Fool*, 114
Slane, Andrea, 6, 151–2, 163n
*Song of Songs*, 46n, 151, 178
sound technology, emergence of, 112–14
specularization, display window and identity, 37, 81n, 99, 147
  modern woman 65, 98, 198
Spoliansky, Mischa, 117, 179–80
Spoto, Donald, 1, 73
Staiger, Janet, 6
Stöcker, Helene, 101–2
Storey, John, 32
street film, 20n, 30, 40, 45, 60, 100, 141
Studlar, Gaylyn, 5, 15, 56, 63–4, 68–9, 71–2, 77
  *See In the Realm of Pleasure*, 5, 56
Sudendorf, Werner, 6, 139n, 145

Tatar, Maria, 11, 95
Tauber, Richard, 13, 168
Tergit, Gabriele, 91, 108n
*The Artificial Silk Girl*, 109n, 81, 85, 98
*The Cabinet of Dr. Caligari*, 13, 40–1, 73, 169
*The Last Command*, 3, 171
*The Last Laugh (Der letzte Mann)*, 1, 13, 44, 171
"The Magic Flute," 125, 132
*The Scarlet Empress*, 55, 149, 164n

*The Spirit of Film*, 74
*The Street* (*Die Strasse*), 30
*The Tragedy of a Prostitute* (*Dirnentragödie*), 30
Third Reich, 6, 25, 151, 156, 168
*Thunderbolt*, 24, 118, 138n
Toeplitz, Jerzy, 111
Tracy, Spencer, 156
*Two Bow Ties*, (*Zwei Krawatten*), 23, 46n, 171, 174, 180
Tykwer, Tom, 156

*Üb immer Treu und Redlichkeit*, 40, 120, 122, 125, 138n

Valetti, Rosa, 38, 172, 176, 178, 180
Varieté, 12, 76, 118, 137
*Varieté* (film), 3, 172, 181
Varno, Roland, 177
Versailles Treaty, 7
Vilsmaier, Joseph, 152–5, 161n
*Völkische Beobachter*, 25, 47n, 173
Vollmoeller, Karl, 36, 170
"Von Kopf bis Fuss auf Liebe eingestellt" ("Falling in Love Again") (song), 36n, 41, 45, 47, 65, 67, 77, 96, 117, 120, 127, 131, 140n, 148
von Ossietzsky, Carl, 25
von Sternberg, Josef
    adaptation of *Professor Unrat* 11, 24–5
    experience filming in Berlin, 12–13, 18, 116
    lighting, 77–8
    on masochism, 82–3n
    poetics of image and sound, 17–8, 21n, 31
    relationship to Dietrich, 4, 21n, 61, 80n
    relationship to Jannings, 23–4, 171
    relationship to Mann, 26
von Winterstein, Eduard, 177, 183n

Wagner, Richard, 31, 119–20, 138, 152, 154
Waldoff, Claire, 91, 131
Wedekind, Frank, 5, 11, 19n
Weimar Republic
    consumer culture, 56
    crisis of identity, 60, 112, 122
    cultural antagonisms, 7, 9, 11, 15, 18, 24, 29, 32, 85
    fledgling democracy, 7, 34
    redefinition of public sphere, 101
    sobriety 97–8
    *See also* New Objectivity; modern woman
Weintraub-Syncopators, 38, 173, 198
Wenders, Wim, 149, 156, 162n
Wilder, Billy, 151, 168, 170, 179
*Wings of Desire*, 156
Winston, Carl, 115
*Witness for the Prosecution*, 149, 151
Wollen, Peter, 74
Wowereit, Klaus, 143

*Zivilization* (Civilization), 7, 97
Zuckmayer, Carl, 25–6, 36–7, 170, 180
Zweig, Stefan, 87

www.ingramcontent.com/pod-product-compliance
Lightning Source LLC
Chambersburg PA
CBHW072002290426
44109CB00018B/2103